Circus World

Circus World

Roustabouts, Animals, and the Work of Putting on the Big Show

ANDREA RINGER

UNIVERSITY OF ILLINOIS PRESS
Urbana, Chicago, and Springfield

Publication of this book is supported in part by a grant from
the Florence Dunbar Fund

Library of Congress Cataloging-in-Publication Data Names:
Ringer, Andrea author.
Title: Circus world : roustabouts, animals, and the work of
putting on the big show / Andrea Ringer.
Description: Urbana : University of Illinois Press, [2024] |
Series: The working class in American history | Includes
bibliographical references and index.
Identifiers: LCCN 2023052280 (print) | LCCN 2023052281
(ebook) | ISBN 9780252045868 (cloth) | ISBN
9780252087967 (paperback) | ISBN 9780252056741
(ebook)
Subjects: LCSH: Circus—United States—History. | Circus
workers—United States—History. | Labor—United
States—History. | BISAC: PERFORMING ARTS / Circus |
HISTORY / Modern / 19th Century
Classification: LCC GV1803 .R56 2924 (print) | LCC
GV1803 (ebook) | DDC 791.30973—dc23/eng/20231204
LC record available at https://lccn.loc.gov/2023052280
LC ebook record available at https://lccn.loc.gov/2023052281

To Kennedy and Declan

Contents

Acknowledgments

This work was made possible by archivists, librarians, and kind academics around the world. Pete Shrake at the Circus World Museum pulled more folders than I could even count during my visit in 2014 and has continued to answer my seemingly random circus questions. I lucked out and ended up in the archives at the same moment as circus scholar Fred Dahlinger. He followed up and kindly offered advice, knowledge, and personal archives. Lisa Phillips, Susan Nance, and Cathy Brigden have provided some of the most insightful comments in and out of conference presentations. Arguably the most fun of this has been looking through images, and I'm grateful for the expertise of Mark Schmitt at the Milner Library Special Collections as I embarked on that leg of the journey. Thank you, too, to Susan O'Shea at the John and Mable Ringling Museum of Art for aiding in my research on infant animals.

I am especially indebted to faculty at the University of Memphis. W. Chris Johnson helped me ask the right questions as I began working on the story of Eph Thompson. Andrew Daily brought some of the most brilliant suggestions at the beginning of this research project. Susan O'Donovan offered spot-on critiques that made the work better. Her guidance reshaped much of my historical thinking and provided the earliest insight that this could be a labor history. Sarah Potter gave indispensable advice on this project and encouraged me to pursue my hunches when I thought labor unions might be an important piece of the puzzle. I owe the biggest thank-you to my mentor Aram Goudsouzian, for his constant guidance on this project.

Research trips, interdisciplinary work groups, conversations, and conference presentations shaped this work during my research and writing journey. I'm grateful to have found the Labor and Working-Class History

Association (LAWCHA) early on. The support at those conferences made this book the labor history that needed to be. Thank you to Rosemary Feurer for curating LaborOnline and allowing circus work to be part of the conversation. At the University of Memphis, the Department of History, the Graduate School, the College of Arts and Sciences, and the Marcus W. Orr Center for the Humanities (MOCH) Freeburg Fellow program provided financial support for many of my endeavors. I'm grateful for the insights of other MOCH fellows, especially Beverly Tsacoyianis. I also want to thank my colleagues at the University of Memphis, particularly Isabel Machado, Troy Halsell, and Rebekkah Mulholland, for sharing ideas, notes, travels, stories, complaints, celebrations, and drinks. As the project continued to take shape after I left Memphis, I was able to lean on brilliant folks there to help me with research. Mandy Campbell spent hours in the archive as I was writing the chapter on animal motherhood, and Meridian McDaniel was a lifesaver with a last-minute trip to check on a source in special collections.

The last five years at Tennessee State University (TSU) have been incredibly enriching, and I would probably still be sitting on the manuscript if not for the support I found there. A faculty writing workshop led by John Barfield at Research and Sponsored Programs helped me write my favorite chapter (it's chapter 2, if you're wondering). I'm glad to have the opportunity to work closely with TSU colleagues Learotha Williams Jr., Keisha A. Brown, and Andrew Patrick on so many projects. K. T. Ewing has been sending me random circus sources since grad school and has offered unrivaled support for all my circus- and noncircus-related work. Pre-COVID Friday writing sessions at Red Bicycle and countless Zoom calls since with Sekhmet Maat have resulted in my best writing. Additional administrative support from Adebayo Oyebade, Erik Schmeller, Joel Dark, and Samantha Morgan-Curtis helps make TSU a nurturing environment for faculty.

Several workshops and speaking engagements have had a profound impact on this work. My animal motherhood chapter took shape at the Animals and the Left workshop hosted by Troy Vettese at the Weatherhead Center at Harvard University. Comments by Lisa Jean Moore and Gabriel Rosenberg made the chapter significantly better. The Bucerius Young Scholars Forum at the University of California, Berkeley, made this book a deeper story about migration. John Beck organizes Our Daily Work/Our Daily Lives at Michigan State University and, along with Paul Mishler, offered incredible insight into several running threads in this book on immigration and trains. The research grant and presentation opportunity from the Research Society for American Periodicals shaped chapter 7 and helped me do a better job of integrating circus programs throughout the book. Finally, I stalled far too long on my article on labor organizing under the big top for *LABOR: Studies in Working-Class History*. Thank you to Leon Fink, Patrick Dixon, and the readers for helping me through that publication, which also gave me a final push on this book.

I've had a wonderful experience at the University of Illinois Press. I began conversations with James Engelhardt, who convinced me rather easily that this was the right place for the book. Alison Syring transitioned into the role of acquisitions editor seamlessly and has been a tireless advocate for my work. I'm also grateful to the readers of this manuscript, whose comments improved it tenfold. I owe a special thank-you to Jeremy Zallen and Will Jones for detailed and much-needed suggestions for the entire manuscript. I am so grateful that this book had Jessica Hinds-Bond's careful and thoughtful copyediting skills behind it.

Thank you to Daniel for being my thankless research assistant and copying entire boxes of archives with few complaints. That dedication page would have been all yours if not for the babies, Kennedy and Declan. They each came into this world at significant points in this book project (usually before a deadline) and have made everything about it more fun and unpredictable. Thank you to every family member—parents, grandparents, aunts, uncles, cousins, and especially my mom—who make the kids' lives so much more fun. And a special thank-you to my grandmother Marylee Sund, who helped make sure her grandkids could go to college and has never failed to ask me how my work is going.

Circus World

Introduction

The Circus World in the Golden Age

Curious New Yorkers gathered onto a Brooklyn pier to watch the Greatest Show on Earth. The largest circus in the world was loading onto the SS *Furnessia* for an opening two-week stand in London during its 1889 season. The ship, dubbed "Noah's Ark" by the press, had been making trips across the Atlantic for nearly a decade, carrying immigrants from Britain to the United States. Its impressive size made it a perfect fit to carry the circus. Crowds had gathered for several days to watch the animals get their meals inside the metal cages that lined Baltic Street. The cages were covered, but people waited for glimpses beneath the tarps. They marveled at the sight of carpenters hurriedly building more than one hundred pens for the horses below deck under newly installed electric lights on the pier. They saw zebras that filled the pier's storehouse. The wharf was filled with trapezes, ornate wagons, costumes, and even the stuffed remains of Jumbo the elephant. Crowds anticipated live elephants, a staple of the circus thanks to P. T. Barnum, but their arrival would be just hours before the ship left the dock. Sideshow performers, circus managers, animal trainers, and aerialists hurried around the pier, readying the ship for the long journey.[1]

No big top performances were given that day, and the public did not expect anyone to don an intricate costume. But the performance of readying the ship was enough to draw large crowds. For more than a decade—since circuses began loading their shows onto trains traversing the country and showing under gigantic canvas tents, called big tops—audiences had marveled at the ticketed shows. But they had also watched the unique performance of camels being unloaded from train cars, tents being pulled into place by elephants, young men hammering tent stakes into the ground, horses pulling wagons across the lots, and animal handlers rolling cages of lions and tigers into the menagerie tent. Newspapers deemed this the "gratis performance," and it became a fundamental part of circus day. Ticket sales soared in the nineteenth century as men, women, and children not only flooded the big top and sideshow tents to watch high-paid performers, but also lined the railroad tracks to watch underpaid workers ready the lot.[2] And now, at the docks—despite the fact that no US circus had ever undertaken a transatlantic journey—the meticulous planning that had defined the rail shows for decades meant that precise measurements were in place. It was "as if the show spent most of its time on the water."[3]

For the workers, circus life on the Atlantic looked like their life on land. They loaded the boat in the public eye, shared cramped quarters once they were aboard, and found their living and working quarters to be nearly the same space. The solidarity among the new shipmates and the mobility of their workplace also resembled their regular place of employment. The close-knit bond among circus workers was necessary to keep such an intricate workplace running smoothly.[4]

Nearly a decade after this 1889 voyage, in 1897, the Brooklyn pier witnessed an almost identical scene. The Greatest Show on Earth, now solely under the direction of James A. Bailey following Barnum's death, prepared to make a second London debut. This time, the show committed to a five-year tour throughout Europe and departed with a substantially larger crew. New Yorkers gathered on the streets to watch the manual labor required to load the SS *Massachusetts* with camels, horses, elephants, zebras, and hyenas. As the circus pulled away into the Hudson River, the sideshow band stayed on the top deck and played the familiar tune "Mr. Johnson, Turn Me Loose," recalling for viewers the mix of entertainment and labor that had defined circus days.[5]

Aboard the ship, circus workers milled about among familiar faces. Most of the performers had left for London a week ahead of the *Massachusetts*. But a few equestrians and the dozens of people with "boss" as part of their work title took this voyage with most of the animals. Even on the ship, work did not stop. Before reaching the open ocean, the workers had already begun making their rounds to check on the six hundred animals, whose lives became even more confined at sea. As for the animals, life on the ship was nearly as bleak as life on a train. Animals in the circus had been traveling their entire captive lives, whether it was on trains or in caravans across Africa, boats from Europe to the United States, or trains and wagons as they embarked on circus seasons across the States. These passages were dangerous for human and animal workers, whether because of freak accidents like trainwrecks, or more mundane dangers, like a lack of fresh air and clean water.[6] The turbulent waters took a toll on Barnum's animals in 1897. The elephants seemed noticeably rattled as they struggled to stay on their feet. Gorillas began suffering from sea sickness. Workers treated the illness with whiskey, a common remedy among circus employees. As animals fell ill on ships or land, whiskey became the cure. In 1902, for example, a Ringling Brothers employee claimed to keep a sick horse alive for an additional ten hours because of a steady intake of whiskey.[7] Tigers, lions, and other wild cats found a home in the ship's darkened forward hold. Workers wearily squeezed past the cages of the disgruntled animals while inevitably being thrown against the metal bars with each wave. By the third day, Daisy the giraffe, a regular in the advertisements for the London opening, had broken her neck and died in her stall. Like with Jumbo more than a decade earlier, Daisy's hide was quickly stripped and then her body disposed of. After all, the beautiful coat could still draw a crowd. Before the show reached London, three additional horses would be buried at sea.[8]

For hundreds of circus workers, both human and animal, this was a return trip to Europe. Even though the shows were based in the United States and exclusively toured the North American continent for more than a decade, the show's workers hailed from all parts of the world. Manual laborers often came from small US towns and ran away to join the shows as they traversed the country, but some were first-generation immigrants who joined the shows on the East Coast. The circus also boasted of its international cast of performers and billed them as top acts. And many of the animals had made an arduous journey across the ocean before, as they had moved through the animal trade business that brought them mostly from Africa and Asia.[9] But as Daisy and a growing number of other animals were born into show business, and as winter quarters moved away from urban immigrant centers by the twentieth century, a new generation of worker experiences marked the tented shows.

These two snapshots of trips across the Atlantic occurred in the opening decades of the circus's Golden Age. The scene on the Brooklyn pier captures the intersections of labor and performance, as audiences scampered to watch menial tasks performed by men, women, children, and animals. They also caught glimpses of uncontracted family members who made a home in the backyard and animals as they remained caged. As the history of the circus world demonstrates, even these truncated versions of circus experiences meant something for the public. Although primarily remembered as a source of entertainment, the circus was also a single workplace that held many trappings of a developing site of capitalism, colonialism, constructed gender roles, and labor. Yet the circus was most important and unique because of its undeniably cosmopolitan workforce of people and animals from around the world. It was part of a tented entertainment industry that redefined what constituted work and who counted as a worker.

This book examines the circus as a workplace during its Golden Age, from the 1870s until the 1960s. It is not focused on one particular circus. Instead, it considers the circus world—the wider collection of traveling shows on rails, wagons, steamboats, and cars each year—and the human and animal workers who created it. While some of the narrative threads in this book move through staged performances, *Circus World* demonstrates that laborers and their work infused all parts of the tented show. More broadly, this book exists on a continuum of scholarship that has considered nontraditional work and nontraditional workers.

The shows traveled at a near-constant pace, captivating small towns across the country. The big top tent had up to five rings, which simultaneously held excited acts like bears, elephants, acrobats, horses, and clowns. Prior to the show, audience members meandered around the circus lot, venturing into the menagerie tent to see caged animals, then checking out the sideshow tent to watch people on display on small stages. These performers and their onstage labor in the circus tents were integral to the popularity of the shows. Behind these tented performances of people and animals, circus workers performed menial tasks, also under watchful eyes.

This fuller circus experience meant that the daily lives of workers were inherently part of the circus experience. The circus regulated employee behavior both in and out of the tent.[10] Workers even conflated their own labor and leisure. They often organized their own internal Sunday baseball games and accepted the normalization of reporters getting scoops on their daily lives. The most attended performance in 1898 for the Forepaugh & Sells Brothers show was a gratis performance. During an off day in Des Moines, Iowa, the show announced that its elephant herd would be bathing in the local river that afternoon, drawing thousands of people to the impromptu performance.[11] These moments, which seemed so special for the audience, were part of the labor for circus workers. Animals in the shows needed baths, and these treks to local rivers offered elephants some semblance of species-typical behavior. This intimate viewing of animal care became so ubiquitous with shows that it also made headlines when elephants did not end up bathing in local rivers.[12]

Despite the public nature of their work, circus laborers maintained an insular view of their world. They referred to their workplace as the circus world, which created a networked sense of belonging and identity politics in an otherwise transient space. Despite their varied backgrounds, the "pot pourri of workers" found cohesiveness in the circus world.[13] Articles that

Elephants with the Ringling Brothers Circus bathe in a river with their trainers, probably at an Iowa stop, 1915. Robert L. Parkinson Library and Research Center, Circus World, Baraboo, Wisconsin. Image CWi 7194.

attempted to shed light on this world filled local newspapers in the days leading up to a show, but circus workers would still insist that "towners" could never understand them. Although the shows made temporary homes in the middle of towns, the worlds of "towners" and "circus folks" often remained separated. Shows often regulated this separation to ensure that their thousands of workers did not cost them needless amounts of money. But the rule also had the effect of further isolating circus folks. Circus workers rallied around one another, and although the circus season lasted only half the year, the circus world identity remained constant. The close-knit community of the circus world created a sense of family, kinship, and identity, reinforcing the idea that towners could never understand the circus life.[14]

An examination of the entire circus workforce—from uncontracted youth who swung hammers to men billed as living skeletons to globe-trotting tigers—provides insight into cosmopolitan and transnational workforces. The circus actively sought out diversity each season, strengthening its appeal and sometimes undermining the wishes of the circus magnates. Barnum & Bailey's "congress of nations" always drew more respect and earnings than a midwestern dog and pony show. Although the shows themselves were working-class forms of entertainment, the laborers ran the gamut from working class to highly paid professionals. Even beyond its transnational workforces, the circus also employed men, women, and gender nonconforming people for a variety of jobs. The relationships that circus workers formed with one another included both legally recognized and informal families. This brought to the circus world an influx of children, who began training at a young age and followed their parents' footsteps as members of circus dynasties.[15]

The diversity of the workforce demonstrates that an expanded definition of labor is necessary to fully understand how the circus world functioned as a workplace. The circus offers a view of physical, performance, and emotional labor.[16] Circus workers performed physically challenging tasks, whether they were practicing their acts, hauling hay bales to the equestrian stock, making coffee for thousands of people, or sewing sequined costumes. But additional kinds of labor proliferated on the circus lots. Contracted center-ring stars clearly engaged in performance labor each day as they dared to do feats that seemed impossible before paying audiences. But as the Brooklyn scene demonstrates, no circus worker escaped the role of performer. Teenagers who jumped on circus trains at the age of sixteen immediately became performers. This sort of performance history also intersects with the tourism industry. As other members of the working class performed physical labor under the eye of curious tourists, so did circus workers.[17] Whether in the center ring, under the sideshow tent, or simply on the circus lot, workers performed emotional labor. They flashed smiles and left their personal lives exposed. Families squabbled behind curtains seconds before flashing smiles in the center ring, and all circus workers knew that every offstage moment on the circus lot was part of an unscripted performance. By doing this work, which was sometimes sincere and sometimes disingenuous, circus workers tacitly endorsed corporate paternalism in the shows, which portrayed the workforce as a happy family.

The circus offers a unique site to view the intersections of these labors. Although historians most often view circus performers through cultural lenses, performers also saw themselves as workers who negotiated contracts and collected paychecks each week. As one circus worker noted, "even the bird-like 'queens of the air' descend to draw down a thick yellow pay envelope every Saturday afternoon."[18] The blending of labor and performance, from highly paid contracted stars to lowly paid workers, makes the circus an important site to examine performance labor and to rethink what defines work, while the shows themselves provide new insights into the corporatization of the United States. In this way, the circus is pertinent to rethinking who we view as laborers and how corporations brand themselves.[19]

This study aims to contribute to a labor scholarship that is beginning to ask questions about interspecies workforces and the multitude of paid and unpaid labors on any given worksite. Scholarly examinations of interspecies workplaces have included analysis of stages, cages, and factory floors. Kendra Coulter has explored multispecies relationships, tensions at worksites such as zoos, and a wide range of activities under the rubric of work. Sharon Sharp's recent scholarship on film sets as interspecies workplaces argues that the circus played a critical role in the treatment of animal labor in film. She focuses on animal trainers, a subset of workers with which this book also contends. Using different language, Peta Tait has examined a similar part of shows.[20] While the circus world identity drove much of the activism and social formation in the shows, human workers also embodied a host of other identities that determined where a worker labored on the lot, how much they were compensated for that labor, and what their job prospects looked like outside of the tented shows. This study deals squarely with the histories of child labor, women's work, global workforces, and labor within colonized spaces.

Circus World seriously interrogates the role of animals as actual workers that disrupted performances and had their lives uprooted in captivity. Similar to their human counterparts, animal workers had a variety of demands placed on them. These demands, which might have included pulling heavy equipment or interacting with the public, were dictated by the age, sex, personality, or level of fame for each animal. While shows proudly spoke of their giant herds of elephants, on the lot those herds would be separated into smaller groups to best fulfill the needs of the shows. Baby elephants, for example, were sometimes displayed with their mothers in the menagerie. But they could also be part of the baby nursery. This separation became especially common for big cats because the youngest members of the group could be handled if apart from their mother.[21] The constant flux of animals being imported, sold, retired, and born meant that animal workers faced an ever-changing workplace. Infant animals were most likely to be imported, while older matriarchs might stay with a show for a lifetime as part of the circus's breeding efforts. In 1922, for example, the Sells-Floto Circus combined with Buffalo Bill's Wild West Show for a three-day event in Saint Louis. The circus already had a herd of nine older elephants that had been traveling several seasons. But just two weeks before the Saint Louis stop, the Sells-Floto Circus received a shipment of thirteen baby elephants from Germany. This journey would have been thousands of miles between boat and train, yet the tiny elephants were expected to march in the parade at the Saint Louis opening.[22] This immediate expectation to perform and

Baby elephants in the Ringling Brothers Circus gathered together in preparation for the Candyland spectacle, 1953. Special Collections at Milner Library, Illinois State University, Normal. Image BSP2665. Used with permission.

integrate into the existing herd is indicative of the larger experiences of animals in the circus, which sometimes ignored group dynamics in a given herd. Like their human counterparts, circus animals were defined by the work that they did both in and out of the ring.

A Labor History of the Circus in the Golden Age

Although the circus is primarily remembered and studied as a place of entertainment, it was also a workplace, and its history informs how we understand labor movements, business history, and nearly any industry tied to colonialization throughout the late nineteenth to mid-twentieth centuries. As a mobile workplace, it contended with local, national, and international events and laws each day. The circus operated in preexisting worlds, local economies and societies, and global trade networks. What happened in places like Oshkosh, Wisconsin, affected the way that the circus workplace operated. But with a transnational roster of employees, what happened in places like Cape Town, South Africa, also affected the shows. The circus, therefore, is a window into larger moments in labor history, and for nearly one hundred years its relevance as a premiere entertainment site meant that workers understood their own work as essential.

While circuses that took up acres of land, traveled in more than a hundred railcars, or offered miles-long parades became the figurehead of the industry, many shows had much more humble beginnings. The five Ringling brothers, who would come to dominate the industry within decades, were second-generation Americans and self-described jacks-of-all-trades in their early shows. John Ringling noted that they were "able to do almost anything, from leading the band to doing an equestrian act," though later "it became necessary to specialize and divide the work."[23]

But as the Ringling Brothers and other shows grew, they capitalized on growing industries and were able to outsource their labor. Business practices in the American circus stayed in step with, and at times led, the rest of the corporate world. Like other Gilded Age robber barons, circus owners practiced unscrupulous business and labor tactics. Mergers, behind-the-scenes trusts, monopolies, and profits drove business decisions in the tented shows—even as circuses maintained an outward circus world appearance of benevolence and paternalism. Through decades of popularity, circus owners acted in accordance with other big businesses that faced similar economic depressions, labor disputes, and market effects. Although the workplace itself was undeniably unique—sequined costumes, man-eating work hazards, and an always-moving workplace—its back-of-house operations were indistinguishable from those of corporate America.[24]

Despite high start-up and maintenance costs, the shows produced significant dividends. In its first season, the Barnum & Bailey Circus grossed more than $1 million and profited just over $350,000. By the next season, that number had nearly doubled, with the newly minted circus kings profiting more than $600,000. These high profits were not spread evenly over the given season. Instead, shows could expect profits to vary wildly from place to place. Variables in each town, like weather, could contribute to poor attendance.[25] Even while competing with newly created circus giants such as Barnum & Bailey, smaller shows still turned a profit. The Adam Forepaugh Circus kept up with its larger competition from its debut in 1865. Within fifteen years, the circus had moved from a wagon show that served predominantly rural communities to a rail show that rivaled the Barnum & Bailey Circus. The show even led the way in circus world innovations, like with its introduction of a cookhouse tent for employees in the 1870s.[26]

Terms such as *show business* and *showman* emerged in the mid-nineteenth century to describe entertainment like the circus and owners like P. T.

Barnum. Yet *mass culture*, a term that has its roots in the 1930s, captured the American circus at the turn of the century. The circus utilized the new culture of advertising and plastered small towns across America with lithograph posters. The advertising business had reshaped people's relationship to entertainment. Almost all facets of mass culture relied on this cutting-edge technology and capitalized on growing nineteenth-century literacy rates. But the circus, with its iconic color lithographs, did not depend on literate audiences. Instead, it used images to attract all walks of life.[27]

Circus owners faced high start-up and maintenance costs, especially among the bigger shows. Costs, particularly for animals, were almost always exorbitant but could vary greatly depending on the year and location. Lions, for example, did not have set prices, but instead varied by sex, age, temperament, and place of origin. This fluid market operated under the control of animal capturers, traders, trainers, and sellers. When animals made their debut or were rare under the big top, their prices stayed high. A rhinoceros, like the one in the 1912 Barnum show, went for about $10,000. However, if traders had happened to place more on the market, that value could have dropped by half, and the short shelf life of most shows meant that once the Golden Age was underway the circus market was constantly flooded with surplus equipment and animals. Human labor, in contrast, was not always a significant business cost. Aside from the star attractions, who most often opted for larger operations, the circus could get away with paying employees very little.[28]

While Barnum, the Ringling brothers, and other early magnates perhaps attract attention for their marketing genius, they also operated in a world that offered them myriad ways to exploit underpaid workforces. In order to populate circus workplaces with thousands of human and animal workers, circuses leaned on colonial networks. Shows began as transnational and global companies, and they banked on cosmopolitan and "foreign" workforces.[29] "Foreign acts" brought value to shows, which billed themselves as a window for American audiences to view faraway places from the comfort of their own hometown. Larger shows, like Barnum & Bailey and the Ringling Brothers, often billed themselves as having more foreign performers than Americans. Country of origin often dictated what labor looked like for circus workers.[30] This transnationalism was a draw for circusgoers, who yearned for glimpses of "never-before-seen" animals and people.[31] In the earliest years of the shows, circuses depended on swaths of immigrant workforces to perform the manual labor. Census records from 1880 offer a look into immigrant labor in the shows. While people listed as "circus performer" from countries like Mexico, England, and France are in the census, so are people listed as "circus man" and "keeps horses in circus" from places like Bohemia and Ireland.[32]

The logistical efficiency of railroad shows mirrored assembly-line innovations in factories, including a history of work stoppages. Workers worked at dangerous paces for the sake of efficiency. Aside from occasional worker sabotage and organized strikes, they also lacked any control over their work pace, lest they interrupt a carefully controlled daily schedule of performances. The circus resembled growing factories even more closely as it used an underpaid working base for increasing profits. Although these manual laborers remained nameless in the public eye, their lives and labor did not go undocumented as circusgoers read about their unscripted performances.[33]

The mobile tented cities of circuses operated in a similar manner to the company towns that cropped up in the late nineteenth century in industries like railroads and lumber. Paternalistic circus owners kept workers clothed, fed, and housed. Overt paternalism characterized circuses of every size. While larger shows, such as the Ringling Brothers, provided nicer living quarters and more food options, smaller shows relied on paternalistic measures to compensate for the lower financial stability they provided for workers.[34] Paychecks could prove elusive. Workers received salaries rather than hourly pay, further allowing shows to blur the lines between work and home life.[35] The circus's business and labor practices continued to resemble those of America's corporate landscape into the mid-twentieth century, with similarly staged labor showdowns in the public eye and increased corporatization behind the scenes.[36]

While the paternalism of circuses resembled that of company towns, its later control of the labor supply looked like twentieth-century government-sponsored immigration. When circuses offered employment to people overseas, like when Barnum attempted to secure a German tuba player in 1890, they did not escape investigations.[37] Even as the government began cracking down on immigration and movement to the United States, particularly in agriculture, the circus provided a space for a different immigrant experience. Guest worker programs, ranging from the Bracero Program, which drew Mexican workers, to the H2 visa programs, which capitalized on Caribbean migrants, depended on outsourced labor. For employers of guest workers, the deportability made those particular laborers desirable. While international circus workers had appeal for different reasons, circuses still leveraged control over their employees as deportable people.[38] Paternalism also played a role in immigration. Like their Jamaican guest worker counterparts as explored by Cindy Hahamovitch, international workers in the circus world depended deeply on their employer because they were constantly away from home. They lacked close family and community ties outside of the circus. This, in turn, created an even stronger circus world identity.

The circus also provides a way to view processes of legal and illegal immigration, which, in the case of the circus, were highly visible. As notions of illegal and legal immigration surfaced and borders seemed to tighten, circus workers constantly moved across otherwise carefully controlled boundaries.[39] Show business created an array of legal exceptions to worker protections. Relationships between government and business that define the landscape of transnational corporations remained intact for the circus. Yet the circus business also defied industry standards by practicing carefully controlled migration. Instead of attempting to lure migrants in large numbers and outside of government protection, circuses openly changed what immigration looked like. Workers navigated local, national, and international labor laws that determined the appearance of circus labor at any given time. In later years, circus workers born outside of the United States labored in American circuses with P1 visas, designed for show business folks.[40]

Even in the inner workings of the tented shows, similarities existed between the circus and other industries. Industrial relations in the circus looked like those of any large workplace. Workers negotiated contracts with their employers and leveraged their skills to get better pay and working conditions. But the circus world identity often dictated the course of union formation and labor activism.[41] Circus workers interacted with national labor unions sparingly in the early decades of the Golden Age. Instead, workers negotiated the terms of their labor within their workplace. They formed internal organizations that framed their circus world identity. This work is also on the periphery of animal labor studies and the nascent field of animal autonomy, where industrial relations scholarship is part of larger work on animal husbandry. Rather than viewing animals as cogs in the circus business, this work views their labor as indispensable to the larger circus working class.[42]

The circus provided more than a job for its workers, which affected their approach to union building. The circus world acted as an inclusive working, political, and social identity for employees. Circus labor relied on both formal contracts and informal agreements to keep the show running. In many ways, circus workers found themselves in a strict social contract with their fellow workers and management, where loyalty to the circus world trumped individual claims.[43] The efficiency needed to maintain an entire tented city demanded intense worker devotion, both to complete their own jobs and to pick up the slack on other people's jobs.[44] This requirement cultivated a unique kind of identity politics that sometimes blurred the lines of race, class, or gender. Even though employees recognized circus paternalism, they sometimes spoke fondly of it. Workers recounted the homecooked food and free, albeit flea-infested, sleeping quarters. Despite their meager pay, they remembered circus world paternalism as a system of free benefits, without any "taxes or takeout money."[45] But while workers navigated in and around the circus world to get better contracts, management projected a narrative that employees were content with the unpaid compensation and difficult work. Even as the circus bragged of international performers, personnel boss Pat Valdo reported that the circus recruited its best women workers from American farms because "they are healthy, pretty, they like animals, and they don't expect circus life to be easy."[46]

The notion that circus life was difficult and that some people were just built for it helped cement a circus world identity that often ran counter to labor organizing. Yet circus history is still filled with isolated strikes and examples of social unionism prior to the 1930s. Some of these shifts in labor poked holes in the cohesiveness of the circus world. At other times, circus management welcomed the changes. Advance men, who plastered towns with circus posters a few weeks ahead of the show, were often the first indication for a small town that a tented show would be coming. Like the rest of the circus world, advance billing jobs were filled with a skilled workforce: this one had to be fluent in sales and have an eye for best marketing practices. A competent advance team meant that a show could nearly guarantee a full house, and even be able to boast about turning people away at the gates. Although directly employed by their given shows, advance men created a craft union well ahead of the rest of the circus world. In 1903, several circus world outfits noted that they employed a fully unionized advance team. While unionizing often worked in direct opposition to management's goal of cheap unregulated labor, the organizing of the advance car facilitated additional oversight over employees. Union advance men reportedly adhered to strict sobriety during the season.[47] This aligned with existing practices in shows like the Ringling Brothers, which insisted on maintaining oversight over billposters by sending out hired route inspectors to report on the billposters' work ahead of the shows.[48]

A unified circus world identity dictated life in the tented shows for workers, but just as in other industries in the early twentieth century, this did not mean that fault lines did not exist. National identity often remained strongly rooted in the circus world. Workers hailed from all around the world, but part of their appeal sprung from their place of origin. Particular skill sets were expected to be associated with certain nationalities. Circuses advertised Japanese workers as acrobats, Frenchwomen as the most death-defying performers, and American women as the most profound trick riders. Even though most larger shows wintered outside of southern states throughout most of the Jim Crow era, segregation still affected the labor in the shows, particularly with service jobs. Circus workers spent most of the season on the train, which held living accommodations of varying comfort levels. Like with other passenger trains, the sleeping cars were staffed by porters, which were most likely to be Black men. The route book for the John Robinson Circus in 1924 included caricature drawings in the margins of the department rosters. A Jim Crow caricature appears only next to the sleeping car roster of eight men.[49]

The inclusive circus world identity, which perpetuated the idea that all workers had the same opportunities and accommodations, often broke along racial lines.[50] White circus workers organized around race, and through direct protest they held power in shaping the demographic of the workforce. When the Barnum & Bailey show hired a "considerable number" of Black canvasmen for its 1907 season, white workers in the mechanical department successfully lobbied management through threat of walking off the job to "drop the colored battalion from its payroll entirely."[51] Route books and newspaper accounts provide some other chilling details about how blatant racism may have affected the safety of Black circus workers. Redlighting, the practice of stranding workers rather than paying them, was a documented part of the circus world. And in the late 1890s, two separate accounts of Black men reportedly drunken or half-asleep falling from a railcar and losing limbs are documented in the Ringling route book.[52]

The power of white circus workers aligned with that in other entertainment industries of the early twentieth century. The American Federation of Musicians perpetuated racism and nativism among its ranks, while the Actors' Equity Association was well known for admitting only white members.[53] Other industries, like vaudeville, also saw the formation of unions in the early twentieth century. As cultural historian Kerry Segrave has noted, the White Rats vaudeville union was "very non-aggressive" and "not radical." It was also racially exclusive, creating a Black auxiliary.[54]

These labor practices outside of the tented shows became critical in the formation of the circus world because workers often crossed imagined boundaries between stages—sometimes even during a single season.[55] Workers often spent decades in the circus world, despite unemployed winters each year. When a circus headed back to winter quarters, hundreds of employees had to find a way to make ends meet for months before the show started back up in the spring. Performers such as Ruth Budd seamlessly took their acts from vaudeville stages to circus center rings. Mary Rawls, a nearly fifty-year circus veteran, remembers her family making a career out of busking.

Like Budd, Mary Rawls's mother tried her hand in vaudeville, working as a juggler before the entire family embarked on a long circus career.[56]

Caged animals also moved between various entertainment stages. As animals began filling big top and menagerie tents, they also filled zoos and natural history museums. Animal husbandry and care practices were refined for each species after decades of practice in captivity. But while these institutions were learning how to keep a hippopotamus or polar bear alive, they capitalized on a network of animal traders who offered large and expensive, though increasingly less rare, animals from colonized spaces. And just as circus performers updated their act and changed their stage names throughout their career, animals could undergo a similar metamorphosis, which is explored in the second chapter with elephant trainer Eph Thompson. As one circus worker put it, "Elephants are renamed, rebranded, and resold. Bad elephants are disguised and sold for good elephants."[57]

The mobility of entire shows and individual performers was made possible by rail travel. Circuses turned the biggest profit as railroad shows, and the number of train cars required to move the circus often became a stand in for calculations of the size of the show.[58] Railroads allowed the proliferation of the circus and became intrinsically tied to this workplace. They facilitated rapid transportation between cities, and, through the early twentieth century, this sort of travel was also relatively cheap and reliable. But the busy rails were also dangerous places and could prove disastrous for shows. The high-speed travel on the rails brought danger alongside sought-after efficiency. Train wrecks lived in both circus workers' memories and circus folklore. They posed an incredible threat to the livelihood of circus workers and circuses themselves. When the Hagenbeck-Wallace Circus train collided with a government train in the middle of the 1918 season, leaving 86 people dead and another 175 injured, the show faced a significant financial loss and was forced to change hands the next year.[59]

The circus negotiated relationships with multiple national governments, local residents, and private enterprises. The US government at times provided benefits, like labor for circuses. Buffalo Bill's Wild West Show, a subsidiary of the Sells-Floto show by 1908, gladly accepted bonded Indian laborers to perform in its western pageantry.[60] As a mobile workplace, the circus owned its own labor, animals, and equipment, but not the land. Shows, then, were usually at the mercy of landowners who were willing to have a circus on their property. Smaller circuses that showed in a single state, like Mollie Bailey in Texas, circumvented this issue by buying dozens of small tracts of land across the state. But this was the exception and proved impractical for more mobile shows. Instead, circuses had to contend with securing and showing on a different piece of city or private property for each show. Sometimes residents gladly opened their land to the shows. To secure this land, however, circuses usually depended on knowledgeable advance agents, who scoured small towns weeks ahead of time, guaranteeing that land, permits, and resources were ready for the tented cities, and compensating landowners with free circus tickets.[61]

Larger international events continually shaped the circus. The Allied blockade during World War I drastically cut into the animal trade business under German entrepreneur Carl Hagenbeck.[62] The war also created the first major labor vacuum for shows, as nearly five million men throughout the United States joined the military. Draftees and volunteers poured out of various US industries, including the circus, to serve. The Sells-Floto show lost more than one hundred men at a California stop when the workers enlisted in the Army. The lost labor nearly halted the show. The John Robinson Circus proudly claimed that most of its laborers had served in World War I and that it had gladly welcomed back the animal handlers and roustabouts after the war. The war also left a shortage of available land for the shows. Circus agent E. P. Wiley remembered contracting out a private residence for workers during an Oxnard, California, show because most of the lot had been reserved for victory gardens. And, as he recalled, although the circus horses trampled through manicured gardens, he compensated the families with fifteen dollars and ten free tickets to the show.[63]

World War I affected the circus and its reliance on immigrant labor. The Barnum & Bailey show had dozens of German performers on its payroll for the 1918 season, all of whom had to file a $1,000 bond "to ensure their good behavior and respect of Government restrictions" before setting out on the season. When news of this bond requirement came, at the outset of the season, circus management scrambled to keep their workers legal. The Barnum & Bailey show activated its legal arm as it sent counsel to Washington to settle the matter.[64] But for smaller outfits, the required war bond shifted labor prospects. Fritz Brunner, a German animal trainer, was also affected by the required bond in 1918, but the Sparks World Famous Show could only get him a local permit to stay at the winter quarters and work during the season.[65]

The convergence of World War I and the flu pandemic in 1918 also shifted the built environment and physical landscape of the circus. Although the Ringling and Barnum shows had merged more than a decade prior, the outfits had maintained separate public images. But 1918 marked the decision to combine their winter quarters as the Ringling show officially joined the Barnum winter quarters in Bridgeport, Connecticut. The season closed early because of abysmal attendance numbers during the final few weeks and the finding that many cities on the route were "closed to performances." The move doubled the size of the winter quarters, as well as the number of human and animal workers living in Bridgeport until the opening of the 1919 season.[66]

The Great Depression also changed the circus landscape, with the sudden addition of government-subsidized shows under the Works Progress Administration (WPA) of the New Deal. In many ways, the WPA shows foreshadowed the shows that would follow the demise of the big top a few decades later. The Circus Unit of the WPA Federal Theatre Project toured the United States during the latter half of the 1930s, with hundreds of performers. Its audience remained much the same as that of traditional traveling circuses, as it geared its shows toward families and children.[67] The more than sixty performances included some fan favorites, including aerialists, wire walkers, and clowns. Although the shows also contained animal workers, their numbers were substantially fewer, including just one elephant.[68] The press noted that "it is full-fledged minus only a menagerie." Indeed, WPA circusgoers would encounter "peanuts, pop corn, hot dogs, and pink lemonade on sale. Balloons, too."[69]

Despite audiences seeing many of the same ticketed performances, the workforce and workplace for "Uncle Sam's first and only circus" were noticeably different in WPA shows.[70] The shows had dogs, ponies, and monkeys who performed under the big top, but they scrapped draft animals who would normally do the performative manual labor. The WPA did not carry its own tents, but instead showed in local buildings, like armories, making much of the gratis setup performance irrelevant. Labor remained more secure with the WPA shows as hundreds of "unemployed actors" took jobs in the shows, quickly garnering the support of the American Federation of Actors.[71] Sideshow labor also looked different. While the shows employed workers billed as "a giant of seven feet two inches tall and a midget of three feet," the WPA circus did not employ a full staff of sideshow performers. The most drastic change in the WPA circus was the pay scale itself; each worker, no matter their position, pulled in the same paycheck.[72] In the first season, more than half the workers in the shows were big top performers. But manual laborers still faced more precarious labor conditions. Despite high audience turnout, a dip in attendance in late June led to nineteen layoffs before those affected were reinstated a month later.[73]

The cohesiveness of the circus "cosmopolitan canopy" was remarkable, given its constant flux of workers during periods of war. During World War II, several workers joined the show as refugees. Arthur Konyot, a horse trainer, fled Poland with his wife and two children before joining the Ringling Brothers show during its stateside tour. And while trapeze performer Elly Ardelty found her way into US shows during World War II, her husband remained captive as part of the French Resistance.[74]

In 1943, the Ringling Brothers detailed the adjustments that war had brought to the largest tented show in the country. It coordinated with the Office of Defense Transportation, cutting the number of miles during the season to limit time on the railroads. Stops became longer in the larger cities, and fewer stops made the cut. The show coordinated with the US Department of the Treasury to offer nearly two hundred thousand free tickets to folks who purchased war bonds. Nearly thirty-seven thousand members of the military also took up the offer of free tickets that year.[75]

As circuses continued to tour into the 1950s, several things looked different from the peak of decades earlier. Magnates had modernized labor processes in the shows, largely in response to a series of strikes and ties with labor organizers outside of the circus. This meant that circusgoers were just as likely to see tractors on the lot as they were to see elephants. Even before the big top folded in 1956 and transitioned to shows in newly built arenas, circuses had begun to change their relationship to rural parts of the country. While fields were transformed into circus lots in the early twentieth century, paved fairgrounds and even airports became the venues by the 1950s.[76]

Even as some of the most visible parts of the circus world collapsed in the 1950s, people still lived and worked in the traveling (but no longer tented) shows. Throughout the history of the circus, workers found communities in which to put down roots, despite near-constant mobility. Winter quarters for the larger shows, such as Peru, Indiana, and Baraboo, Wisconsin, had become a winter home for many workers as the circus world began to organize. But Sarasota, Florida, became even more synonymous with the circus when the final two Ringling brothers moved their formerly midwestern winter quarters to the warmer climate in the late 1920s. With less fanfare, workers found a more permanent home in nearby Gibsonton, forming a familiar, insular community that outlived the traveling circus.

$\bullet \quad \bullet \quad \bullet$

While the history of the circus world that consolidated under Ringling has declension narrative appeal—from the humble beginnings of a band of brothers in Wisconsin to the dramatic moments when the show folded its tents—the experiences of individual workers are perhaps best understood through a topical approach that reconstructs the world from the ground up. Within the larger narrative of the circus world lie the stories of people and animals who signed contracts, or had contracts signed on their behalf, as they spent anywhere from days to decades as workers in the tented shows.

The workers who fill these pages often spent time on different kinds of stages, from vaudeville to Wild West shows. While centering the circus, this book also engages with these additional workplaces as performers moved between them. Owners, too, dabbled in investments across entertainments. And as Henry Bedow's contract to perform clowning for Ringling Brothers demonstrates, circus management explicitly saw Wild West shows as spaces that housed circus workers.[77] Today, as scholars comb through the historical traces of these pasts, sources from various traveling entertainments, including circuses and Wild West shows, often sit in the same collections.

By considering the daily labor of workers as a performance, this book recovers a larger history of the circus and considers previously overlooked sources that proliferate in circus collections around the United States. Everyone, it seems, has a circus memory. The magic that came with turning empty fields and quiet main streets into exciting cities within hours captured the public's imagination. Circus fandom caught men, women, and children, who not only frequented the shows each year, but also collected souvenirs. But a particular circus enthusiasm developed in the twentieth century, in response to the visual appeal of the shows. Model builders formed clubs and networks, trying to capture the circus on a miniature scale. They consulted multiple sources to ensure that their models accurately captured a moment in circus history. Although photographs often provided invaluable information, they could not offer enough details. Builders, then, sought circus workers to fill the knowledge gaps about the colors of the calliope wagon and the number of bars on the tiger cage. Within this correspondence, workers also complained of pay or working conditions, recalled interactions with audience members, and told of their lives between the shows.

Museums and libraries boast of their circus collections, which are often among their most exciting holdings, and these letters between model builders and workers often fill the collections. They are often tucked away in "miscellaneous correspondence" folders. Curated circus collections have been combed through by cultural circus historians who have focused on contracted performers with scripted acts under the big top and sideshow tents. The same collections contain, too, untapped glimpses into other parts of circus life. But uncovering these voices is still tedious. Voices from working-class transients, whom scholars have called "the most elusive social group," are notoriously difficult to find.[78]

In addition to curated collections, this work relies on newspaper reports from small towns across the country. Barnum made New York City an early hub for circus excitement, but as the shows realized the financial gains and cultural relevancy of focusing on less populated areas, they quickly moved out of metropolitan centers. Winter quarters and daily shows became the mass culture of small towns. For this reason, larger national news outlets do not provide the most intimate look into circus life. Instead, daily reports from local newspapers in towns that the shows visited provide a more complete picture of how the shows were welcomed and understood. So, while the *New York Times* reported on the season opening and larger events deemed newsworthy, papers like the *Oshkosh Daily Northwestern* provide a better look at the real relevance of circuses. The circus world hit its peak in attendance and popularity during what was perhaps also the height of Jim Crow. Black newspapers during these decades sometimes tell a different story of those circusgoers who lived "behind the veil" in the southern towns the circus visited.

While existing scholarship has broadly looked at segments of the workforce, including women and animal trainers, they have been analyzed as performers rather than workers. These earlier studies are crucial for understanding how particular identities or jobs determined how circus workers experienced their workplace. This book builds from this scholarship, looking at the circus work within the larger circus world by examining various cross-sections of identities and jobs on the lot. But the workers described in each chapter also appear elsewhere. While women and their gendered labor roles and unique experiences, for example, are discussed extensively in chapter 3, they are also part of discussions on animal training in the second chapter and sideshow experiences in chapter 5. This book is also filled with significant moments that happened in and around the shows that inevitably pulled circus workers in as more than just bystanders. Whether parades, strikes, or elephant baths, the circus was filled with moments and people that have lived in the memories of circus fans. Each chapter starts with one of these moments.

The term *circus world* is employed in intentional ways throughout this book. Rather than use academic jargon to describe life as a circus worker, I use a term that was and is actually used by circus people in historical and contemporary spaces. As someone who has not worked for tented shows, I feel most comfortable allowing the language of those who lived and labored in these workplaces to be foregrounded. In addition to its common usage, it is the name of a space that holds what is probably the most extensive circus collection in the United States: the Circus World Museum in Baraboo, Wisconsin. As will be explored in this book, this phrase is also associated with a failed theme park that sprang up after the big top folded.

This work rests on the shoulders of circus and cultural historians who have offered detailed and analytic chronologies of the tented shows. In her first book, *The Circus Age: Culture and Society under the American Big Top*, Janet Davis argues that the circus itself is a "cultural window" into larger historical changes. She adds to the historical context of circus labor by framing the work of roustabouts and other laborers as performance. This analysis is crucial for understanding the changing labor conditions in the circus in the early twentieth century. Scholars of entertainments that intersected with the circus world have also offered analysis on traveling shows as part of growing mass culture industries. Robert Rydell's work on world's fairs, as well as his more expansive scholarship in a similar vein with Rob Kroes, demonstrates that the mobility and popularity of these shows tied them to developing industries and entertainments.[79] Some of the most innovative looks at the circus have stood still geographically to understand how this mobile entertainment affected one particular place. Circus histories in New York, Wisconsin, and Georgia all demonstrate that shows shifted appearance and practices as they made single-day stops in hundreds of cities and small towns.[80]

The book is divided into parts, with chapters that move topically and investigate relationships within the circus world. The first part of this book, titled "The Circus Migrant," organizes around ideas of mobility and movement. The first chapter, "Making Circus Day," grounds this study in labor history by considering the work it took to put on a single circus day. It provides an overview of jobs through the lens of a 1912 Barnum & Bailey show in Wichita Falls, Texas. By centering this single day and its place in the larger circus season, it offers a glimpse into the remaining chapters, demonstrating how these other themes that emerge in the book were ever-present in the circus world. Chapter 2 asks about the unique mobility of animal trainers and their migrations, and the way that mobility afforded them new labor and performance opportunities. It argues that much of their control rested on their ability to own capital, and their success depended on their knowledge of global trade and labor markets.

The next part, "The Circus Lot," is organized spatially as it departs from the analysis of individual worker mobility to examine larger swaths of circus employees who worked in various spaces on the circus lot. The topic of underpaid labor permeates the book, but this part also highlights unpaid work on the lot through intersecting lenses of gender, species, age, and race. Through looks at women workers, animal workers, and sideshow workers, these chapters examine nearly every type of contracted labor on the lot, and three very visible categories of laborers that did not always receive financial compensation. Much of this labor exploitation was explicitly connected to age, as babies and children found themselves at the receiving end of unpaid care work or on the stage themselves. Chapter 3 explores the role of women in the shows. While many women performed side by side with men under the big top and sideshow tents, their labor and experiences differed.

Audiences expected women to perform a particular emotional labor onstage, and their gratis performance played out in behind-the-scenes newspaper stories rather than during the tent setup at each new town. The history of women workers also demonstrates how the circus world intersected with larger social and political movements happening in the places the circus visited, such as the women's suffrage movement. Chapter 4 examines the circus world's reliance on a constant influx of animal workers to stock the menagerie and center ring. It focuses on animal mothers, who constantly labored through their motherhood, which included birthing, fostering, or raising their young. Chapter 5 considers the adults and children who labored in the sideshow and focuses on their unique labor and activism. Their work was some of the most contested on the circus lot, as audiences alternatively cast them as performers or otherwise unemployable workers.

The last three chapters, in the book part titled "The Circus World from the Outside," zoom out to look at how circus management and audience participation affected circus labor. These chapters explore how changes to business and labor directly led to the decline of the shows. Chapter 6 takes a top-down perspective, digging deeper into the business of the circus and examining how workers felt about increasing corporatization. The seventh chapter looks at how circuses created celebrities out of their workers and what effect this had on the unmaking of the shows. The final chapter explores the role of circus audiences; it asks how they interacted with and affected shows, and how they understood worker autonomy. The conclusion briefly examines the concept of a circus afterlife by considering cohesiveness among a diverse and transient group of laborers, the decline of the circus as a cultural institution and workplace, and the ways that human and animal workers navigated the world after their time with the shows.

PART I

The Circus Migrant

Mabel Stark stood outside the Chicago Colosseum in 1929 with her performing partner, a Bengal tiger named Rajah II. That year, the Sells-Floto Circus showed in Chicago for a four-week opening stand.[1] Although that month saw some unseasonably warm days of eighty degrees in the city, the temperatures averaged in the upper forties. This snapshot, captured by circus photographer Harry Atwell, was likely taken on one of those cooler days.[2] Although Rajah II wears a harness in the image, the posture of both tiger and trainer appears relaxed; they are aware of each other's presence while seated with a Hudson car, but also acknowledging Atwell and his camera. The Chicago-based photographer, who captured decades of circus photographs both on and off the circus lot, was likely a familiar face to both Mabel and Rajah II. He had also captured photos of the two wrestling in the ring, photos that served as an introduction to the act for audiences who read the *Chicago Tribune* in the days leading up to the season opener.[3] Stark swore that like elephants, tigers have long memories.[4]

Both Stark and Rajah II were circus migrants who spent most of their adult lives traveling. Like other circus workers, Stark worked her way into her position, contracted with a variety of shows within the circus world, and transitioned to other entertainment venues after the decline of the big top shows. Rajah II's journey to the Chicago sidewalk on a chilly spring day in 1929 took a similar path. Despite Stark's reputation for training "savage jungle bred animals," Rajah II had never known life outside captivity.[5] The young female tiger had been born in a California zoo. Her seemingly sweet disposition, including purring when Stark came near, made her a good replacement for the

Tiger trainer Mabel Stark with her tiger Rajah II, 1929. Robert L. Parkinson Library and Research Center, Circus World, Baraboo, Wisconsin. Image CWi 1987.

big cat wrestling act when Stark's beloved tiger Rajah died. After John Ringling sent word to Stark that he had found a replacement, Stark said she could work with her for a new wrestling act. Ringling paid $1,800 and had the zoo-born tiger shipped to Stark. The cross-country trek in a steam-heated car during the winter months meant that Rajah II had only six weeks of practice performances with Stark before the duo moved to New York City for that season's opening stand.[6]

This image of the performing duo reveals a similar relationship to the one that audiences saw under the big top. When she reflected back on her career in a 1940 autobiography, Stark noted that of the dozens of cats she trained and worked with, Rajah and Rajah II were the smartest and most lovable. That's likely why those two tigers wrestled with the trainer in the ring, displaying high levels of trust between the two performers.[7] Like other women trainers, Stark leaned into the assumption that women were kinder with animals, but even without the whip or pistol that her male counterparts often wielded, she showed immense bravery in the ring by fending off the pouncing cats. The wrestling between the trainer and the cats that characterized her act left her with a litany of scars that became synonymous with her appearance.

But the photograph is also striking because the setting is perhaps unexpected. The circus world appeared to be a self-contained city, as it was designed to be by the industry's magnates. Workers did not need to leave the lot to have their needs met as the shows traveled throughout the country. And yet, as explored in this section, some workers did wander off the lot, move through a variety of circus troupes, and even drift between entertainment stages. During the opening stand, like the one happening in the moments surrounding the picture of Rajah II and Stark, workers were stationed in a large city that could support a long running show for upward of a month. Chicago, then, became in 1929 a temporary home to a flurry of animal residents, including Rajah II.

Tigers roaming outside of the jungle, on sidewalks, and with harnesses around their shoulders should have perhaps been an unnatural sight. But because of the animal entertainment industry that Americans were frequenting, seeing a tiger in Chicago was not completely unexpected. After all, that same year, just a few miles away in Lincoln Park Zoo, Prince the tiger was nearly twice Rajah II's size and seemed to enjoy his diet of "fresh slaughtered pigeons" that supposedly saved him from stomach ailments.[8] Americans encountered migrant animals in a number of ways in the early twentieth century. Zoos increasingly became scientific in scope and better at curating their collections of captive animals, as explored in Daniel Bender's *The Animal Game*.[9] Jay Kirk and Rachel Poliquin have explored the ways that people interacted with taxidermy forms of those same animals.[10] But even as the zoo and natural history museum offered some semblance of the wild, Atwell snapped an image of Rajah II on a busy street filled with the sights and sounds of the modern city. His photographs seemed to perfectly capture the circus as a city within a city.

The animals and people in part I of this book offer varied experiences of the circus migrant. It begins by examining the movement of an entire show and then shifts to individual migrations of the human workers most closely associated with animal costars. The circus migrant was, and is, a labor category that often operated in legal loopholes. To migrate with a show, between shows, or as a solo act inherently meant crossing a barrage of borders. The legalities of migration and labor constantly shifted in these spaces during the peak decades of the circus. Collectively and individually, circus migrants navigated not only the circus lot, but the spaces around the tented cities during and between seasons.

1

Making Circus Day

On the morning of September 24, 1912, residents of Wichita Falls, Texas, found an exciting announcement in the local paper: the Barnum & Bailey Circus billing crew had arrived in town. This group of two dozen men drew paychecks from the circus, but they were never present on circus day. Like their 1,500 coworkers, the billing crew rode the rails across the country, jumping between small towns for short stays. But rather than fill the railcars shared with acrobats, clowns, elephants, and snake charmers, the billing crew rode "up ahead" of the show in an advance car.[1]

Although unreported by the Wichita Falls press, the car also carried contract men, who secured land and food for the circus and its workers. Sometimes called "fixers," these men would typically pay for necessary licenses, talk to police, and secure any additional resources for the shows.[2] Later in the Golden Age, contract men would be increasingly responsible for cutting through red tape. These workers, who made humble incomes even at larger shows, could spend their entire circus career in this job, working their way toward the well-respected role of "boss poster."[3]

By day's end, before the big top even arrived in Wichita Falls, the town would look different. Wichita Falls residents would not see elephants that day, but they would see circus workers plastering advertisements in a thirty-mile radius. They knew that circus day would be a familiar sight, with a parade and two shows. As always, the show was bigger than ever. Barnum & Bailey had reportedly spent more than $3 million that season. At least some of that bankroll was spent on a plethora of performers who were "making their first tour of America."[4] As the billing crew pasted colorful posters in conspicuous places throughout the town, Barnum & Bailey performed a show in Tucson, Arizona. The people of Wichita Falls would have to wait nearly three weeks. In the meantime, they might catch glimpses of several more advance cars carrying dozens of other circus employees whose job was to ensure that the show would run as smoothly and efficiently as promised. Even hours before the arrival of the circus, the traveling agent kept an eye on the weather and gave one final approval for the show, while the "twenty-four-hour man" delivered contracts to local businesses for food and secured the required fifty thousand gallons of water.[5]

The 1912 circus day in Wichita Falls, Texas, offers a window into the circus world. For Wichita Falls residents, circus day was a single-day event, but for the Barnum show, it had been months, or arguably years, in the making. The multifaceted forms of labor needed to put on circus day were on display in Wichita Falls, just as they were in the other 152 cities that season after the opening at Madison Square Garden. This chapter uses the Wichita Falls stop on the Barnum route in 1912 to explore these various forms of labor and the array of workers both on and off the lot. This single moment in the longer history of the circus world also offers insight into the thematic analysis in subsequent chapters of this book. Through the circus stop on October 14, 1912, this chapter offers grounded examples of how immigration, animal training, women's work, infants in the menagerie, unpaid labor, worker celebrityhood, and the show's business tactics functioned in the circus world. Taken as a whole, these examples demonstrate how the threads of this book were woven together.

Routing agents worked on calculated decisions rather than luck. They had carefully chosen Wichita Falls as a circus stop for the season. While some towns bragged that their true fandom made them a premiere destination for the shows each year, in truth, seasoned routing agents made calculations based on local economic markets. The show wound its way through the southern states each fall to wrap up its season. During the late nineteenth and early twentieth centuries, the agents turned "to thoughts of the cotton picker's money," particularly among southern Black circusgoers. Good routing agents knew the cotton reports from the South and the wheat reports in Texas, claiming that "when the cotton crop is big it is as lucrative as a circuit of gold mines." Show agents also familiarized themselves with the presence of boll weevils, lest they "eat into the receipts of the circus."[6] Seasoned routing agents knew that sharecroppers collected their paychecks of up to two dollars per day in August or September. Their attendance would be "a mainstay of the circus on its Southern trips" if the route was calculated correctly.[7]

Circus historians Fred Dahlinger Jr. and Stuart Thayer have asserted that the increasing complexity of circus advertising demonstrates a marked difference between the early years of Barnum's show and the later Golden Age of the circus, particularly under the Ringling brothers. According to

Dahlinger and Thayer, while P. T. Barnum and some of the other early magnates were attuned to various populations that would attend the shows, the Ringling brothers understood harvest and planting seasons and production schedules in factories and mines.[8] Indeed, in the 1890s, the Ringling brothers spoke of their fondness for pulling into the South amid "the wavy fields of cotton with their white plumes nodding you a welcome" and Black sharecroppers "picking the fleecy substance." The Ringlings knew that those same laborers in the field would be circusgoers the next day, trekking into town to make a "conspicuous majority" at circus day. The impact of Black circusgoers was echoed in newspaper accounts, recollections, and even an insert story in the Ringling Brothers route book.[9] Circus workers also knew that their southern leg of the season meant the sweet appearance of snack carts run by Black circusgoers.[10] These sorts of regional expectations marked the experiences of the circus as a traveling workplace.

Much of the work to put on a single circus day began prior to the start of the season. Many workers stayed with the show for multiple seasons, with some essential employees also working in the winter quarters between seasons. Circus veterinarians worked one of the most necessary behind-the-scenes jobs in the shows during and between seasons. They drew on previous experiences with less exotic animals, but they also faced additional challenges. Doc J. Y. Henderson, Ringling veterinarian, described some of these difficulties, particularly in the winter quarters when preparing to go out on tour. The animals themselves also had an adjustment period. According to Henderson, newly acquired "animals were frequently irritable and weak with vomit because of the ocean trip, and nervous because of their new surroundings." Like his zoo counterparts, Henderson was also on the front lines of care work for animals that otherwise had only been observed sparingly, in the wild or postmortem. Henderson recounted several autopsies he performed on circus animals. He described in stunning detail an autopsy that he performed on a polar bear that had seemed to decline overnight. "As I plunged my knife into it, the [intestine] wall burst and worms sprayed into the air like water from a fire hose. . . . I jotted in my notebook the first of hundreds of routines: *Test every new bear for worms.*" Job hazards also shaped the array of injuries that circus vets had to treat. In his first week on the job, Henderson witnessed a lion fall from a steel pedestal and break his jaw, leaving the new vet to experimentally try to fix the break.[11] As workers, animals faced the risk of injury often. The lion with the broken jaw had stood at heights typical of lions in other shows. Its tiger counterparts also faced potential burn injuries from jumping through hoops of fire. And, as explored in subsequent chapters, unnatural mixed groupings of big cats sometimes meant vets were treating attack wounds.

While many circus veterans rejoined the tented shows for the 1912 season, it was not always with their former employer. The mobility that characterized the circus world affected nearly every circus that year as workers moved between outfits. Jack Phillips moved from Barnum's show to head the music department in the Downie & Wheeler Shows. The behind-the-scenes mergers that had brought several shows under the Ringling banner in the first decade of the twentieth century also created a different sort of forced mobility. Jake D. Newman in the advertising department, for example, was transferred from the Forepaugh & Sells Brothers show to the Barnum show for the 1912 season. Other workers moved out of the circus world that season, including John White, who retired to a stock farm in Baltimore after decades in the circus world, including a stint with the Barnum show.[12]

This mobility characterized the Golden Age of the circus more broadly, as workers rarely stayed with a single show. Harry "Cookhouse" Kelly made a meager paycheck preparing meals on the circus lot. But he stayed in the business for more than thirty years with nine different circuses and traveled throughout the United States and Europe. William Fraser experienced similar mobility among circus outfits throughout the United States. During a career that lasted more than twenty years, Fraser spent most of his time traveling. He was employed with multiple shows during that time, laboring "in every [manual labor job] on the show except ticket seller." He had even been a supervisor as an assistant boss animal man.[13]

Quick start-ups and closures were a reality for most circuses. Barnum and the Ringling Brothers were notable exceptions in profit and longevity. Even when smaller shows could guarantee salaried paychecks for workers, they sometimes did not have the capital to finish a season. In what was called "closing ahead of the paper" in the circus world, shows would pack up and liquidate when that yielded bigger profits. In these cases, worker paychecks were hardly guaranteed. When a small Texas show went under midseason, a family of jugglers and tightrope walkers ended up broke and stranded in Missouri. Throughout their careers, veteran circus workers quickly joined other circuses. Having enough money in their pockets, too, could be a problem.[14] Circuses notoriously withheld pay from employees, reportedly because otherwise "they'd all get drunk and leave the show. That was the way they held onto them." The remaining half of their salary was often paid out at winter quarter, after the season.[15]

For high-paid performers, a closed circus simply left them as temporarily unemployed performers. But circus closures made the circus working class indistinguishable from otherwise unemployed hoboes. When Albert Zeno went before a judge in South Chicago after he allegedly stole rides on freight trains, he did not deny the charges. Instead, he justified his illegal cross-country journey from Philadelphia to Chicago by claiming his status as a circus worker. He claimed to have been stranded in the Northeast. If the report and Zeno's claims were true, he was probably a victim of redlighting, the underhanded business tactic of leaving unpaid workers behind at rail stops when shows fell short of cash to pay them. Redlighting had a long, yet largely undocumented, history in the shows. Circuses became famous for leaving uncontracted workers behind in towns rather than keeping them for the season and paying them for work they had already completed. Without their back pay, these workers immediately entered local communities, much to their dismay. Although circuses never officially spoke of the practice, workers recounted memories of themselves or others being redlighted during the season.[16] But Zeno defended his actions by telling the judge that he had traveled around the world with various shows. Despite his hobo appearance, Zeno—like other members of the circus working class—was well traveled, cosmopolitan, and employable.[17]

The coordinated practice for Barnum & Bailey performances in 1912 began weeks prior to the opening date. On March 10, the show had made its way from the Bridgeport, Connecticut, winter quarters and had settled into Madison Square Garden—where it premiered each year—by ten o'clock that evening. In the winter months, the show had been kept up by a regular skeleton crew of workers, including twenty-one blacksmiths, twelve wagon repairmen, and sixteen painters. Many acts were still in Europe or on their return route from other overseas performances, but full rehearsals began three days later.[18] On March 21, New Yorkers purchased tickets from the box office, entered through a side door, and walked past the menagerie of thousands of animals before reaching the tiered rings on the main stage. They passed a sign that read "Don't Touch! Wild Animals! Danger! Danger!" as they walked along cages of nervous mother animals with babies and anxious animals in solitude.[19] Much of the labor required to assemble the Garden shows was done behind the scenes for the month-long opening stand. Each day before the performance, the New York arena was filled with high-paid performers practicing their daring stunts and handlers feeding formerly wild animals.[20]

Following the New York City opening, the show traversed the entire length of the United States and back again on eighty-five double length railcars carrying "twelve hundred birds of passage forever on the wing."[21] By the end of the season, the show would travel more than forty thousand miles.[22] The entire performance troupe traveled together, but people working in the show knew that each person's job dictated which railcar they could call home. Despite the claim that "each man has a wide berth to himself," the circus working class of roustabouts shared cramped quarters.[23]

The well-paid center ring performers usually attracted a few newspaper headlines, as did the lesser-paid sideshow performers.[24] In keeping with public curiosity of circus life, local papers also investigated other labor in the circus world. A network of behind-the-scenes laborers, the so-called animal trappers and jungle hunters, existed to put on a show with thousands of "exotic" and "never-before-seen" attractions and workers. Circuses portrayed themselves as benevolent employers and paternalistic environmentalists. The public read about animals who "take kindly" to nomadic circus life and "show signs of unrest and ferocity" when they are away from the big top for too long. The "blazing heat" of the summer seasons had "the touch and homelike feeling of the jungle." The work hazards associated with training and performing with wild animals were recast as "courageous," "brave-hearted," and "longing to thrill the public."[25] Circuses also boasted of their collection of "strange people" and their unique ability to procure them from equally strange places.[26]

The *Wichita Daily Times* continued the work of the advance men by keeping the circus in the headlines in the weeks leading up to the show. The words "bigger" and "better" became synonymous with the show each season, lest somebody argue that they had already seen the circus the previous year.[27] Often, newspapers would also post the circus parade route so people could prepare for the traffic-blocking excitement on each street.[28] New performers hailing from twenty-two countries were on the payroll, promising a true "congress of nations." The *Daily Times* announced individual costs for acts, and gave people sneak previews and behind-the-scenes looks. Anticipating that people would be excited for the ornate wagons that would be pulled down the street, the newspaper told readers that they were crafted in Europe, "in the foreign workshops of the circus for many months, both day and night." But it also reported on other back-of-house labor involved in the performances.[29]

Newspapers reported on additional details that demonstrated the transnational nature of the circus world and the people who worked in it. In many ways, as the 1912 season demonstrates, the circus was an immigrant workplace. Every sequin in the shows seemed to catch the attention of circusgoers, who marveled at a show that reportedly had $3.5 million in upgrades. For the 1912 Barnum season, the costumes were sewn in Paris, the laces in Ireland, the scarves in Japan, and the tapestries in Turkey. The harnesses and mechanical parts were created in the United States, while the wagons themselves were designed and built in "foreign workshops" in England. Many of the performers themselves had first debuted on foreign stages, before signing contracts with talent agents in the Barnum show.[30]

Ringling Brothers seamstresses work on costumes at the winter quarters in Baraboo, Wisconsin, circa 1910–17. Robert L. Parkinson Library and Research Center, Circus World, Baraboo, Wisconsin. Image CWi 29134.

Year after year, newspapers analogized the shows to the Tower of Babel for the dozens of languages spoken on the lot by the workers.[31]

As the circus finally pulled into Wichita Falls in the early morning hours of October 14, crowds gathered to watch an array of people, animals, and equipment exit the train after a full night. As one newspaper later stated, the always staggering number of curious onlookers might have meant that many people "would rather see a circus train arrive than witness one of its performances."[32] Those onlookers who lived in the surrounding areas might have come to Wichita Falls that morning via the special circus day commuter train, which connected whistle-stops. This ensured that visitors would be spending an entire day on the circus lot.[33] Upon arriving, circus people immediately went to work. The speed at which workers unloaded the trains drew praise and curiosity. The *Wichita Daily Times* made special notice of how seemingly easy it was to unload the show. The first section of train, nicknamed the Flying Squadron, held only equipment. Even though crowds saw only tents and poles emerging from the cars, they could hear

Circusgoers watch the stock cars unload, 1937. Special Collections at Milner Library, Illinois State University, Normal. Image BNP3825. Used with permission.

the trumpeting of elephants anxious to depart from their railcar. Handlers began unloading caged animals. Finally, "led" animals emerged from the train car. The trainyard now contained a motley crew of elephants, horses, camels, gnus, and "sacred cattle." Each car was unloaded by workers who performed this labor nearly every day. With job titles like razorback and poler, these workers performed the skilled labor of unloading wheeled wagons, unwieldy equipment, and unruly animals.[34]

Excited onlookers followed the unloaded show to the circus lot. Workers referred to the often-grueling procession as the haul. By this point, workers had already spent hours unloading the train and preparing the animals and equipment for the short trek to the lot. Teamsters would use this time to hitch a few horses to a wagon and make their way into town to get hay and feed that had already been secured by the advance men.[35] Their work would continue, uninterrupted, until the train left later that evening. "Happy Jack" Snellen, a decades-long circus veteran and boss canvasman, oversaw this process at each stop. Snellen and his "corps of men" were experienced enough to navigate the array of snafus that could happen. Just a few years earlier, when the show set up in "a hollow at the foot of the hills" in Butte, Montana, a sandstorm had ravaged the lot. But as the show reflected back on this event in the annual route book that year, it gave credit to Snellen and his men for "staying at their posts" like "true soldiers" until the work was finished.[36] In 1912, the circus lot once again began to take shape under his direction. Thousands of human and animal laborers began pounding tent stakes into the ground, erecting poles, and pulling tents into their locations. A circle of nine men quickly and efficiently alternated swings with their sledges at a tent stake. Newspapers noted that "Barnum & Bailey employ a good sized proportion of colored helpers." Indeed, Black men performed much of the manual work of setting up the lot and laboring in the cook tent. Within two hours of the circus's arrival, coffee would be boiling in giant cauldrons while cooks fried eggs under the designated dining tent.[37]

The midmorning circus parade "would have made Noah jealous." It was led by nearly forty elephants, which the circus dared people to count as it made its way down the city's main streets.[38] More than seven hundred horses, from Clydesdales to Shetland ponies, followed closely. Criers, who seconded as sideshow talkers, used their skills to yell out directions, such as the famous "hold your horses!" This year, Clyde Ingalls, who would end up having a long and storied career in the circus world, joined the Barnum show for his second season as the sideshow manager. The parade promised to be more than three miles long. The stars of the show and the circus underclass were on display as they marched down the main streets of Wichita Falls. The parade was the first opportunity for locals to experience the sights and sounds of circus day, and larger shows like Barnum & Bailey spared no expense. The shows carried wagons just for the parade and treated it as a live index of their featured performers. The wagons pulled by horses on uneven roads elicited the roars and grumbles of caged big cats, to the delight of audiences. If anyone had missed the throngs of crowds that had already joined the show, they would surely hear the approaching sound of the brass band, led by Edward Brill. All parades, including the one that made its way through Wichita Falls, ended with a calliope wagon.[39] Circusgoers in Wichita Falls may have even heard that the Barnum show had paired with the growing suffrage movement. Several of the parades that season featured Votes for Women banners.[40]

For townspeople, the parade was not an isolated event, but part of a larger circus experience. They trailed behind the final wagons into the circus lot, watching each minute of work. People complained about the sweltering heat but showed less concern for the "crowd of working men" building the tented city. Instead, circus folks were considered lucky workers who could enjoy circus day every day, and viewers welcomed the smell of fresh sawdust. Animal laborers also remained in the public eye during the tent setup. Babe, a matriarchal elephant and center-ring star, dazzled people by performing manual labor. She "seemed to take delight" in doing so. Babe

Victoria Davenport, bareback rider and member of the suffrage movement, 1912. Robert L. Parkinson Library and Research Center, Circus World, Baraboo, Wisconsin. Image CWi 10963.

also reportedly knew every circus lot in the country since she had spent years with the show. This institutional and geographic knowledge, reportedly held by the animal laborers, added to the ethos around the circus as an insular community that included both people and animals. The designated circus lot quickly became a tented city, covering nearly fourteen acres.[41] The big top tent, with performance rings and stadium seating, was the final part of the lot setup. Its assembly happened while the dining tent was already serving nearly one thousand of the three thousand daily meals, by waiters who, according to the press, had to "double as linguists" to serve the entire circus world. In truth, separate interpreters were on the Barnum payroll.[42]

While the sights of the tented circus were surely something to marvel at, audiences also took part in the setup. They offered their own labor in exchange for free tickets or simply additional access to the circus day experience. Some of the larger shows made good on their promises so as to keep their reputation when they likely came back the next year, but smaller, start-up shows were more likely to become synonymous with grift. As one newspaper asked, "who has not broken his back in hard labor, spurred on by the promise of tickets only to be disappointed when the man who made the promise never could be found?"[43] Larger shows quashed any insinuation that circus workers were grifters. To help offset those connotations, the Ringling show kept detectives on the payroll to internally police the lot. It boasted entire seasons without any reported thievery and kept John Brice on payroll as its official chief of police for decades.[44] Yet employees notoriously conducted their own illicit gambling rings despite management oversight, noting that circuses were not Sunday schools.[45]

The circus working class had erected twenty-four separate tents before lunch. These housed performances, animals, and spaces for workers in their downtime. Within a thirty-minute time frame, the sideshow tent was raised, with interior stages in place and banner lines hung along the midway. Sideshow workers moved quickly, readying for their opening within the hour. Before the "flag's up" indication that the lunch tent was ready for circus workers, the grandstand was erected, marking the moment that "orderly chaos resolves into quiet and symmetry in steel, cordage, and canvas."[46] This work nearly always seemed to go off without a hitch as workers banded together to create the circus world. Whether or not circus workers were aware, shows blacklisted workers deemed unfit to perform this labor quickly and effectively. In a "strictly personal and confidential" memo to superintendents of all departments in the Barnum & Bailey show in 1901, a substantial list of workers was circulated with explicit instructions to deny them employment. Although a reason for dismissal was not given for most workers on the list, George S. Sullivan was cited as refusing to work.[47]

The "backyard," as circus folks called their living space, could provide some degree of privacy yet still attracted curious onlookers. During the setup, workers strategically placed wagons to block views of this private space.[48] The same year that the Barnum show played in Wichita Falls, a picture show in Kansas featured photographs of the Hagenbeck-Wallace Circus, with "nothing pertaining to the circus or menagerie left out." It explicitly advertised the backyard as an attraction. The small show encouraged people to witness the arrival of the train, attend the shows, line the streets for the parade, watch the putting up of tent poles with horses, and witness "750 people at breakfast" in the "scene of the kitchen camp."[49]

While the backyard belonged to the circus workers, certain areas remained further secluded and segregated by job. The 1912 Barnum show offered circusgoers three of the most iconic circus attractions: elephants, peanuts, and clowns. Elephants and peanuts were readily available, but clowns prepared for the show in an area of the backyard that would later be called Clown Alley. This space offered clowns a dressing room, but like other dressing rooms in the backyard, it became a home where workers would also wash their clothing, read mail, or simply relax between show time and rail travel.[50]

The elephant, peanut, and clown trifecta also invoked the wonderous mix of American and foreign. Peanuts were billed as crops of the "Southern soil," and elephants traveled from Africa and Asia. Clowns, like many other contracted big top stars, were often billed as European performers.[51] In the 1912 troupe, Barnum's clowns—who numbered more than fifty—reflected the multinational identities of the circus workers at large. James Duval hailed from France, with reportedly little understanding of English; Glen McIntosh and Will Scott came from Scotland; and the remaining troupe joined the show from eight additional countries.[52]

Some of the public curiosity on the lot was about the physical labor. People wanted to see the blacksmiths working and handlers bringing food and water to the collection of caged animals. But people were also curious about the more personal and intimate moments in the lives of circus folks. One newspaper in 1912 noted that "many peered into the menagerie tent to watch the animals eat or stood around the entrance to the cooking tent . . . where employees were at supper." The desire to see them eating, washing costumes, and interacting with one another meant that nearly all circus workers were constantly working and could not separate private life from public life.[53]

Circusgoers read that the women in the shows changed their outfits thirteen times each day. Although this gendered exaggeration probably did not hold true, it does illuminate the constant performances on circus day and the miniscule reprieve that the backyard provided, perhaps especially for women, who wore intricately sequined costumes before audiences and then doubled as caretakers in the backyard. During the 1912 season, seven hundred women joined the Barnum show.[54] Children also appeared on the circus lot as workers, often accompanied by women. As one newspaper reminded readers, "it is more than likely that the man who is tossing the little chap into the air is his father, or that the woman who holds some little girl suspended a hundred feet in the air, is her own mother."[55]

The circus world attempted to create an inclusive relationship among unrelated workers, but additional relationships between circus folks were often familial. As the Golden Age marched forward, performers often bragged about their place as a second-, third-, or fourth-generation circus star. This long-rooted history in the business solidified their loyalty to the shows.[56] Shows capitalized on this by boasting about their royal lineages in the ring. Performing families, either real or created, drew crowds. This practice legitimized the use of child labor as entertainment and created a

Performer Media Banta lifts her daughter Zemedia Banta in the backyard, 1947. Special Collections at Milner Library, Illinois State University, Normal. Image BNP6987v1. Used with permission.

financial opportunity for circus proprietors, especially when family units received a single paycheck.[57]

Race affected career opportunities in the circus, and the ability of workers to navigate these spaces with their families, particularly within the Jim Crow South. Newspapers ran syndicated stories of immigrant and white families on the lot but neglected to ask about the Black workers. While white workers, particularly contracted performers, often took their families along during the circus season, this was often not a safe option for Black workers. Gilbert Taylor, whose father played in minstrel bands in several circuses in the 1920s, recounted that his father "could talk about some of the horror stories that he experienced in the South. None of our family members could travel south . . . because he really forbade us going."[58]

Taylor's father understood that despite being an insular community in its own right, the circus world was dropped into the local community at each stop. In one route book, circus management noted that upon pulling into a town, workers witnessed a Black man being whipped at a whipping post.[59] Newspapers often acknowledged circus workers leaving the lot to explore the town. A newspaper feature in 1912 suggested that circus women were "intelligent tourists" between the performances. Although the claim was used to draw audiences into the lives of circus workers and highlight readers' connections to an otherwise odd occupation, it points to an important facet of the circus.[60] In many ways, circuses brought more than a thousand hoboes into a town. In the case of redlighting, these hoboes became longer and more unwelcome visitors. Even when the circus retained its entire workforce, its one-day stay could also prove disruptive. Sometimes, the large population of manual laborers clashed with local populations, leaving a wake of newspaper reports about uncivilized circus workers. Even more disruptive were the hundreds of exotic animals. Performances notoriously went awry, animals broke loose during parades, and shows dealt with rogue elephants and disgruntled lions.[61]

The fears that Taylor's father had are echoed in cases of Black circus workers being singled out among an outcast group of workers as especially criminal.[62] When a Black circus employee by all accounts mistakenly hit a young man with a tent pole, he ran, likely well aware of the implications of the accident. His decision to immediately flee from the lot likely saved his life, as a group of circusgoers "attacked the employees," whom they clearly thought were harboring the man, and demanded that he be "given up so they might string him to the center pole."[63] This was far from an isolated incident, as Black circus workers faced potential mob violence for allegations against townsfolk, with this violence sometimes ending in lynchings.[64] This potential outcome appeared common enough that it garnered only a casual mention in the 1898 route book of the Adam Forepaugh Circus. Even when a lynching occurred on the circus lot itself in Mayfield, Kentucky, Ringling Brothers noted it with only a quick mention in the route book.[65] Black circus workers also encountered law enforcement, who stepped foot on the circus lot often after an allegation had already taken place. Robert Lee, a Black worker with Ringling in 1905, learned this as police officers confronted him for "insulting a streetcar conductor"

Black roustabouts with Ringling Brothers on the circus lot, receiving a shave, playing craps, and sitting behind a wagon, 1917. Robert L. Parkinson Library and Research Center, Circus World, Baraboo, Wisconsin. Image CWi 7112.

in Montgomery, Alabama. The altercation ended in shots fired and Lee's arrest.[66] Most infamously, three Black circus workers, Elias Clayton, Elmer Jackson, and Isaac McGhie, faced a lynch mob in Duluth, Minnesota. The well-documented event in 1920 indisputably demonstrated the particular dangers of circus work for Black workers.[67]

But the presence of Black circus workers can be found in more than just records of racial violence. While the violence demonstrated in Duluth and feared by Taylor's father during the seasons loomed large, this was not the totality of the Black circus experience. The circus offered a radically varied worksite that is perhaps easiest to explore through the lives of contracted performers. Vanessa Toulmin offers such a study on Black British performers. As Eph Thompson's migration demonstrates in chapter 2, Black big top performers crossed country and continental borders to live and make a living. But Black workers with less power over their contract negotiations, like the three roustabouts in Duluth, made up a significant portion of the circus world. Beyond Thompson and the workers Toulmin describes as "lauded and applauded," Black workers operated as the cocreators of the worksite as they skillfully attended to the grueling and fast-paced work of erecting the tented city daily.[68] Their necessary inclusion in this history requires us to cast our gaze beyond scripted performances. While images of Black workers in moments of leisure are less prolific in circus photo collections, they are still there. They provide a window into some of the communities formed within the circus world.

Circus workers interacted with townsfolk off the lot, but most of their time was spent on the circus grounds. Although private life was viewed by the public, circus folks still constructed backyards and filled them with things that were necessary to circus life beyond entertainment value. Veterinarians set up shop and crossed behind the Do Not Touch signs in the menagerie. Doctors spent their mornings on the lot helping sick circus folks. Then they patiently waited in their tented offices near the dressing room during big top performances for the slew of injuries that would need their attention. Just a few months before the Wichita Falls show, audience members at the Barnum show had witnessed the death of Prince Youturkey, a high-wire performer. Following his death, Barnum workers raised $300 for his wife, which was typical of the social unionism that characterized the circus world. Audiences often saw the injuries that brought workers to near death, but performers more often left the ring in pain or "suffered physical torture in order that the act may go on."[69] Circuses intermittently had a variety of priests, nuns, and other religious leaders traveling with them during the season. Reverend Doc Waddell did not travel with the Barnum show, but by 1912 he was a known chaplain and minister in the circus world. His career took place in the backyard and included service on Sundays, Sunday school for circus children, counseling sessions, weddings, funerals, and baptisms.[70]

As a traveling show, the circus also had a tremendous effect on local economies. While some critics complained that the tented shows drew income away from local businesses, most acknowledged that the circus drew in large populations from surrounding areas, filling local pocketbooks. In 1912, the Hagenbeck-Wallace show received a month's worth of back pay just before its daylong stint in Chanute, Kansas. Locals reported that it was a "good day for . . . merchants" as workers splurged on shoes and other goods.[71]

At Wichita Falls in 1912, circusgoers made their way through the menagerie tent as they waited for the two o'clock show. The massive display, kept up by workers called menagerie men, served as a mobile zoo and pseudomuseum. The menagerie promised to provide "with few exceptions, every beast, bird and reptile mentioned in natural history. . . . No country has been too remote to frustrate the great travelling zoo's search for rare and curious animals."[72]

Circusgoers likely knew what to expect in the menagerie tent as they had seen many of these animals when the train unloaded and during the free parade, and read about the few animals that attracted extra press.[73] Usual menagerie animals, like the hippopotamus and rhinoceros, continued to be a draw. John Patterson, the head of the department, had a pet dog who frequented the backyard. Given that giraffe keeper Andrew Zingara "practically lived with the strange animals," he might also be found around the menagerie.[74] Like zoos, circuses created and promoted their new nursery departments, which cared for and displayed their array of new baby animals each year. Of the 110 cages under the menagerie tent, the crowd favorite was the new baby giraffe (named Suffrage by circus women), whose birth and survival seemed to defy odds. The Barnum show had invested $14,000 in two giraffes eight years prior. Their eight years in the tented shows had set a record, and their new baby was only the second born in captivity in the United States. But litters of big cats, including lions and tigers, as well as baby elephants and camels, also filled the stalls in the nursery.[75]

The circus played two ticketed performances for packed houses, with nearly fifteen thousand seats. Any manual laborer working in the big top officially fell under the property men department. Venders, called butchers in the circus world, hawked sweets and programs to the incoming guests, who began streaming in one hour before the show started, after purchasing a ticket from the sellers outside the tent.[76] As people made their way to their seats, a military band of seventy musicians played in the center ring. The usual array of acrobats, clowns, and trained animals spilled out of the big gates at one end of the arena.[77] But the $500,000 Cleopatra opening spectacle made promises of being "the greatest spectacular, theatrical, and circus event in the history of amusements in America." It did not disappoint, featuring "a cast of 1,250 characters, a grand opera chorus of 400 voices, an orchestra of 100 musicians, a ballet of 350 dancing girls, 650 horses, five herds of elephants, a caravan of camels, and an entire trainload of scenery, costumes and stage effects."[78] Viewers understood the opening spec to be one of "oriental splendor," which was another nod toward the ways that the American shows offered performances that carried a non-American identity.[79] The impressive number of bodies required to put on the spectacle included several well-known people in the circus world posing as Egyptians for the show. James Wolfscale and his experienced crew of circus minstrel performers donned Egyptian dress, and teenage roustabouts posed as palace guards.[80] These grand spectacles, like Cleopatra in 1912, became a mainstay of circuses in the Golden Age. As historian Jacob Dorman notes in his biography of Noble Drew Ali, the frequent opening specs with African aesthetics and Orientalism made use of the many Black laborers, who were costumed for the grand performances. While the working-class job category can be impossible to track fully in the circus work, these performances give insight into the significant presence of Black workers on the lot.[81]

The two o'clock and eight o'clock shows looked identical on paper, but circusgoers might choose to attend both shows. With multiple rings under the big top, no single seat could give circusgoers a good view of every performer. Three rings and two stages filled with seventeen separate acts. The newspaper's afternoon review encouraged people to view it again under calcium lights.[82] The labor involved in putting on the Cleopatra spectacle, as well as the other ring performances, was intense. Additional big top performances drew press and praise, like the Siegrist-Silbon family of aerialists, a circus dynasty of gymnasts who had reportedly been practicing circus acts since they could walk. The stars commanded public adoration. High-paid stars, like Australian equestrian May Wirth, drew applause, as did the novelty of a jujitsu demonstration.[83]

The performances given by these workers were the culmination of decades of practice in an industry that required constant physical labor to remain top-billing stars. As usual, elephants garnered attention for their center-ring performance, which demonstrated the best the circus had to offer. In this performance, three elephants—named Taft, Roosevelt, and Wilson—competed in a lively baseball game. Newspapers gave a play-by-play with thinly veiled political commentary, and audiences reveled in the seemingly gentle giants.[84] As with most elephants in the tented shows, this small herd had undergone years of extensive training before center-ring appearances. The baseball gimmick was two years in the making, under the direction of head elephant trainer Harry J. Mooney and other backstage trainers and handlers. Although training methods and trainer effectiveness varied, a commonly held belief persisted that "elephants love applause as much as a chorus girl does."[85]

The labor continued between the big top shows. Between the performances, circusgoers stayed on the lot, often making the most of their cheap ticket. The circus lot provided some candid moments with its baby animals in the menagerie during this time. Ponies seemed approachable and were often crowd favorites. Even when a mother pony acted uncomfortable around the hordes of people, she reportedly "decided it was hopeless and ate her hay while little tots patted her baby."[86] If circusgoers had already visited the menagerie, there was still plenty of activity to fill a few hours. Candy butchers, like the ones they encountered under the big top, stood behind stands. Pink lemonade, an invention of Barnum & Bailey circus employee Henry E. Allott, was "an almost sacred institution" in the tented shows.[87] Peanuts, popcorn, and cotton candy sold in high volumes. Souvenir venders, such as balloon men, also found steady work during the season. The circus compensated this labor with a small salary and commission.[88]

This nonstop entertainment, under several tents, provided the circus with constant income throughout the day. Sideshow tents lured thousands of circusgoers for just a few more cents. "Silver-tongued" barkers gave quick pitches about marvelous, never-before-seen, exotic, once-in-a-lifetime "freaks of nature" available for viewing. The massive canvas banners that hung outside the tent gave a caricatured preview of the top billing sideshow performers. In 1912, sideshow workers included the "smallest living woman" and the seven-foot-tall boy. A host of minstrel musicians performed just a few feet away from the sideshow entrance.[89] While top-billing performers in the big top appeared indispensable to the circus season, sideshow workers were often billed as replaceable; categories like "smallest" or "largest" people could always be refilled. During the first half of the 1912 season, a performer known as the Wild Man of Borneo, who had traveled extensively with the Barnum show during his lifetime, passed away at home. An untitled newspaper notice a few days later informed the public. But it also assured readers that show people "doubtless know where they can get one equally as good."[90]

As intentionally public as the setup was, the dismantling was much quieter. With no time to spare after the final performance, circus workers started loading the train before the performances even began. The cook tent was dismantled, rolled, and packed onto the train following the six o'clock meal. The stable tent, which housed nearly seven hundred horses, was the next to come down, followed by "incidental tents," such as the hospital and blacksmith shop. As people filled the big top for the final show of the day, circus workers began disassembling more of the circus lot. The menagerie and sideshow tents came down, and caged animals began their trip back to the train. By half past nine, as circusgoers sat under the calcium lights, workers had cleared the entire lot, save the big top and dressing room tents. By ten o'clock the first section of train had departed. With a length of 580 feet, the final tent was the most daunting to disassemble. One hundred fifty canvasmen got to work minutes after the final circusgoer left the big top. Within thirty minutes, the big top was down, packed, and headed back to the train.[91] Workers laid down to rest, knowing that "tomorrow is another day, another circus day, in another town."[92] The circus departed for its final month of its forty-first season, before ending in Meridian, Mississippi.[93]

This is what created and sustained the circus world. These labor conditions allowed the circus to thrive as a growing corporation for nearly eighty years, but the workers sustained a variety of networks that had more longevity than the industry itself. The people and animals who performed this array of labors in the Barnum show in 1912 were part of a transient community that stretched across traveling shows and connected cities around the world. These underpaid, unpaid, and, occasionally, highly paid workers built a new city to live in each time the circus train stopped, and they lived within a networked circus world. The mobility of the traveling shows defined how the workplace looked. But for workers themselves, mobility affected them on a much more personal level, as they made individual decisions regarding the spaces where they worked and lived.

2

Human and Animal Circus Workers and Their Knowledge Networks

While circusgoers marveled at all the sights on circus day, none was perhaps more iconic than the animals on the lot. For many people, this would have been the first time seeing this array of animals, which were most likely imported. People who worked with these animals seemed indispensable to the shows. Somebody who could do daring tricks or manage an entire herd was a commodity in the circus world. But finding people who had the training and ability to break into this profession and have a long career in it was difficult. These workers often had enough power and capital to negotiate the terms of their labor and attract audiences in ways that other folks in the circus world could not always do. These human workers are also a window to the animal workers themselves, creatures who stood by the sides of their trainers, tamers, and keepers in and out of the ring. Mobility defines these stories, as it precipitated captivity for animal workers and increased financial freedom for the people who worked alongside them. This chapter tracks not just the movement of people and animals, but also the movement of ideas in the circus world, particularly around people who worked with animals.

Ships that connected the circus world across oceans are some of the most important spaces in which to examine this mobility. A crowd of spectators gathered at Earle's Shipbuilding in Hull, England, on August 10, 1880, to witness the christening of the HMS *Assyrian Monarch*, with toasts to the "success to the trade of Yorkshire," and "the success of our American cousins." The impressive crowd came to celebrate the ship that the Royal Exchange Shipping Company (or Monarch Line) touted as the largest ever built at that port. This foreshadowed an impressive career of more than twenty years of trade between the United States and Great Britain. The builders fitted the ship to carry 1,500 immigrants across the Atlantic on each trip. Following its maiden voyage, thousands of immigrants boarded the steamship in London and Glasgow and made a permanent home in New York in under two weeks. The steamships of the Monarch Line offered regular routes and safe passage to the United States for no more than twelve pounds. For each return voyage, the ships' hulls were filled with American goods bound for British shores.[1]

The *Assyrian Monarch* took its most publicized voyage in April 1882, as P. T. Barnum awaited the arrival of his already famed African elephant Jumbo. Reporters joined Barnum on the uncomfortably cold morning at the Castle Garden Pier and watched the ship anchor offshore. Reporters described Barnum's mood as unusually light, despite his not knowing how Jumbo had fared on the transatlantic journey. While they waited for the ship to dock, the showman spoke to the crowd about his other transatlantic stars, reminding them that Jumbo was just the latest proof that he knew how to procure talent. He also boasted that he had personally spent more than $30,000 on the trip, which included buying out the ticket price for the immigrants who would have instead been on the ship. He bragged about how well he could strike a deal, noting that the secretary of the treasury was foregoing a duty on this import because of his excellent negotiation skills.[2]

Upon docking the ship, Captain John Harrison assured Barnum that Jumbo had "behaved grandly throughout the voyage." Barnum seconded this notion, claiming that elephants do not get seasick. This was likely an exaggeration; the ship's books described Jumbo as "under the weather" throughout the trip. Barnum gave a hearty congratulations to William "Elephant Bill" Newman for surviving the voyage with Jumbo, but then immediately began shouting "Where's Scott?" Matthew Scott, a man described as modest, particularly in the presence of Jumbo, quietly appeared. To the delight of the crowd, Scott produced a photograph showing that he was taller than the baby Jumbo when they first began working together. Indeed, Scott had worked as Jumbo's primary caretaker at the Royal Zoological Gardens in London for nearly twenty years, and both elephant and keeper reached the United States for the first time as the *Assyrian Monarch* docked.[3]

From animals to goods to people, the HMS *Assyrian Monarch* was central to several migration and trade networks that would intersect with the circus, demonstrating the circus industry's multifaceted dependence on importation and immigration. Thousands of animals and animal trainers undertook this same transcontinental journey to perform in the sawdust rings of the American circus. Barnum's decision to bring Jumbo to the United States with his longtime keeper by his side signals that even the self-proclaimed savvy entrepreneur knew that the expertise required to train animals was not built on generalized knowledge. Instead, trainers cultivated long-term relationships with their animals and continued to land jobs in the circus world, based on their first-hand experiences of maintaining docile animals. Circus management was quick to assure audiences that the formerly wild animals were "perfectly lamb-like" and easily managed, but the decision to arrange for trainers to migrate with their animals acknowledged a different reality. Most keepers and trainers would also just as quickly disagree with the circus's public stance on animal docility. On the trip across the Atlantic, Scott was, he later admitted, too fearful to enter Jumbo's shipping crate to clean it.[4]

Like Scott and Jumbo, most human-animal pairs crossed multiple national boundaries and types of stages because circus management understood that animal trainers carried their own knowledge and training styles. Stylistic differences became rightly associated with where any particular trainer began their career, and trainers increased their value to the shows with their previous associations. Scott's career with the Royal Zoological Gardens, the only scientifically based zoo in the world at the time, positioned him not only as an expert in Jumbo's well-being, but also as a keeper who possessed knowledge only available through specific connections to London.[5] The press also seemed to pick up on these nuances, noting during Jumbo's arrival in New York that Scott never even used a whip and that he gently assured the elephant while the crate was moved. Yet Newman, the American trainer on the scene, used an infamous bull hook, leaving the animal "astonished."[6]

Keeper Matthew Scott, trainer Eph Thompson, and tamer Frank Bostock each made these migrations, demonstrating the interconnected nature of these physical and intellectual networks. The constant mobility of both individual workers and the workplace itself meant that the shows were connected through networks of knowledge.[7] The lives and routes of these circus migrants demonstrate the complexity of late nineteenth- and early twentieth-century migration, particularly in the Atlantic world. Taken together, censuses and other public records, along with circus and media records, provide a unique look at migrant entertainers. This history shows that migration moved in multiple directions, sometimes offered the best opportunities across the Atlantic, and carried an intellectual history of animal training methods along the way.[8] Analyzing this history though sources such as census records, ship passenger lists, port of call records, ships' logs, and memoirs, while historicizing the sources themselves, demonstrates that the circus industry worked within larger conversations of race, migration, and labor in the United States, with animal trainers on the front lines of those conversations.[9]

Tracking Circus Workers through the Census and Other Public Records

Circus workers engaged in labor that was seasonal, unstable, sometimes uncontracted, and inherently migratory. The circus's performance season stretched from March through October, leaving many workers out of a job during the intervening months.[10] As seen in the 1912 season discussed in the previous chapter, it was during this time that performance equipment, circus parade wagons, and menagerie cages received repairs and upgrades from a skeleton crew of workers.[11] This was also the time that animals stayed in the winter quarters, learning new performance routines or nursing their new spring babies. Keepers stayed on the payroll and continued to work with their animals, monitoring their health and offering an environment that was less performative than the big top. Higher-salaried performers could pull in a twelve-month salary by turning to different markets.[12] Although workers deemed indispensable by circus management were employed under regulated contracts, the show's working class often joined or left midseason with no guaranteed payments.[13] The larger shows, such as Ringling Brothers and Barnum & Bailey, dominated both the headlines and the historical narrative, but at the height of the market, more than one hundred circuses operated throughout the country, making quick start-ups and liquidations just as common.[14] With winter quarters in the Northeast and Midwest, most shows recruited heavily from those areas at the start of the season. Just weeks into the season, though, even those local workers were hundreds of miles away from their home, and performers often hailed from much farther away as the circus intentionally featured international acts on all its stages. Performers who headlined the posters and worked under the big top, like equestrian performers from France or Australia, commanded hefty, guaranteed salaries that were negotiated individually or under the protection of their agent.[15] In contrast, workers under the sideshow tent often came from colonized places and worked under a group contract signed by someone employed as their manager.

Even beyond animal departments, each job in the circus was skilled labor, as demonstrated by the inability of the shows to use scab labor during large-scale strikes.[16] Circus workers learned on the job, while also bringing knowledge with them to the circus lot. Candy butchers created and perfected recipes that became synonymous with circus day; lion tamers boasted of the mentors who had taught them how to bring the ferocious animals to heel; and equestrians assured circus fans that they had begun riding horses before they could even walk.[17] Those internal knowledge networks within the circus world were not bound to any particular show.

Instead, they crossed between shows as workers brought their tips, tricks, and trades to their new jobs. Moreover, people walked into the circus with their own ideas of labor and community. As part of a jobsite demographic that required immigrant labor, circus workers were part of a globalized workforce whose diversity was reflected in both people and ideas.[18]

An examination of these qualities of circus labor, then, requires multi-faceted methodologies and multiple sets of sources. Circus workers might spend anywhere from a single season to a decades-long career in labor-driven migration to a new country. Some chose to naturalize while others returned home; some kept close ties with the circus world while others quietly slipped into obscurity. Because circus communities continued beyond the season and beyond a worker's career, certain cities became synonymous with large populations of circus folks. City directories in Bridgeport, Connecticut, and later Sarasota, Florida, offer insight into a worker's decision to retire among other people from the circus world.[19] While censuses offer snapshots of immigrant populations at the turn of the century, they cannot track the movement of circus workers, who could be traveling abroad during a census year. But major life events for these workers around the world still appear in documents like marriage licenses and passport applications.

Beginning in 1880, the United States saw a steady uptick in the number of immigrants arriving each year, from more places than in previous decades. In response to the influx of new groups of people, politicians began shifting and expanding the categories of questions on the census. This rise in detailed census taking also coincided with the rise of the American circus industry. The division of labor and performance in the circus indicates prevailing ideas of scientific racism and colonialism—ideas that abounded among US policymakers in their conversations about immigration and national origin. By 1900, political ideas about race and national origin had become intrinsically linked to the mass influx of immigrants that entered the United States each year.[20]

The decision to use the census to track labor centered on several fears, including the possibility that immigrants would undercut wages.[21] But as a historical source in the history of the circus, the census also allows us—through its detailed categories of nationality and job skills—to better track people who continued to take migratory jobs. Census records capture a snapshot of the circus working class, which garnered a notoriously transient reputation even within the circus world. For the thousands of workers in the circus, their place of employment was an all-encompassing space where they worked, lived, raised families, and passed down intimate knowledge of all these things. People who worked on the circus lot, visited it as a ticketholder, and wrote about it in the press recounted similar memories and observations about the culture of the circus world. As the tented shows traveled by train to towns across the US countryside, they brought a cosmopolitan workplace with them.[22]

The circus operated as a mobile tented city, and a "community in itself."[23] While vaudeville, burlesque, and other traveling forms of entertainment integrated their performers into each city they visited through the use of local food and lodging, the circus required that circus workers stay on the lot—sleeping in the railcars and eating in the dining tent. But even on the lot, circus workers could not escape the prying eye of the public. Wandering fans and curious reporters often slipped into the dining tent and "backyard" living quarters because viewing the array of eating habits and social structure of circus people from around the world became part of the entertainment. Circuses capitalized on this interest and put seemingly private time on display in the sideshow, which resembled human zoos in Europe. In American circuses, this became particularly true for Native American performers, who held babies tight while they ate meals of "strange foods," as described by the outside press.[24] But even during events created for and by circus people themselves, national identity remained at the forefront. At one of its first annual dinners, the circus's benevolent society "tastefully decorated with the national colors of the United States, England, Germany and Austria."[25] Such expressions of national identity in spaces occupied exclusively by circus workers were celebratory in nature, yet they also replicated power dynamics at play in colonialism.

The American Circus as an Immigrant Workplace

Circuses depended on a near-constant importation of people and animals to ensure that ticketholders would not be disappointed by the promises of never-before-seen entertainment. Aside from the center-ring stars, who commanded enormous salaries and had celebrity status, performers understood that their allure came from how new and unique their performance seemed. This meant that performers would often cycle between circuses and even through other stages, like fairs or vaudeville theaters. For circuses themselves, recruiters kept an eye out around the world for talent that they could procure for their shows, leading to a constant stream of immigrants into US shows each season. For animals and people who worked in the sideshow tent, descriptions like "fresh from the other side of the world" had the biggest draw, creating an even deeper pipeline of labor that exploited colonized people. The circus justified the expense of contracting individual performers or groups of people because assumptions that race, nationality, and skills or abilities were intertwined proliferated among American circusgoers. Even the circus working class of mostly seasonal laborers was incredibly transient, though for different reasons. The paternalistic nature of the circus corporation often substituted room and board for actual wages. Circuses notoriously redlighted workers when they were due back pay, leaving them in a small town as the rest of the circus quickly packed up for the next show, hundreds of miles away.[26] Seasoned workers were privy to this tactic and avoided the circus's false promises of advance pay if they waited outside the train. Newer workers, however, fell victim to the ploy.[27]

The circus also depended on lax labor laws that directly affected immigrants. As a workplace, the circus nurtured a diversity that was likely not seen anywhere else at the turn of the century. The labor force on circus lots included workers with a range of skills, ages, genders, nationalities, and even species. Child labor laws in the United States lagged behind their European counterparts, and at a time when more than one million children per year faced death or injury in industrial employment, child tiger trainers became a somewhat normalized form of entertainment.[28] The tented shows also welcomed entire families on the payroll, or allowed them to tag along during the season, allowing first- and second-generation immigrant families to stay together during the working season. The 1913 season of the Hagenbeck-Wallace show included fifty workers' children, although some were described as apprentices.[29]

The circus itself nurtured a work and social culture that encouraged its immigrant workers to hold on to their Old World ties while still asking them to assimilate into the larger circus world identity. The press's colorful language in circus reports, including references to a "nomadic melting pot," held some half-truths. Workers continued to speak their mother tongue and maintained long-standing customs, but the circus world also offered larger social networks that transcended national identity, like labor unions and benevolent societies.[30] Circuses fed into this contradiction and capitalized on the diversity of their workforce because it was a draw for circusgoers.

The Keeper, the Trainer, and the Tamer

While any reputable circus could have boasted about having an entire herd of elephants at its disposal, and most audiences were thrilled to see elephants of any size, Barnum's business model dictated that he have the biggest and most renowned elephant in the country. Jumbo found himself in the Barnum & Bailey Circus because of his extraordinary size and reputation.[31] The sheer physical power of Jumbo and other large male African elephants placed their keepers and trainers in some of the highest-risk jobs in the circus. The animals' human counterparts often described a moment around the age of four that male elephants would "go rogue," indicating a personality change that would usually include an attempt to kill a human companion who had been with the elephant since its infancy. The Royal Zoological Gardens likely sold Jumbo for this reason.[32]

Despite the dangers of the job, most trainers did not undergo professional training at a centralized location. Circus workers prided themselves on having been born for that line of work, often citing themselves as part of a long line of entertainers who had "sawdust in their veins" and some sort of natural intuition about animals.[33] Carl Hagenbeck's animal training school in Germany became the exception, prompting the most expensive trained animals and trainers themselves to be networked in Hamburg. Hagenbeck, often described as a "collector and exhibitor of wild men as well as wild animals, with hunters and agents at most of the points of contact between the savage and civilized world," prided himself on the belief that all animals could be trained.[34]

Hagenbeck's network of trainers and animals garnered respect in the circus world, and he became the primary supplier to zoos and circuses. His renowned school, and his even more influential training method of "gentling," demonstrated real migration networks at work in the circus. Gentling took hold throughout the circus world and opened the door for women animal trainers in the United States. Showman W. C. Thompson reported that a woman in the circus told him, "Women are more patient, and it is quite a mistaken idea to suppose that rough methods are necessary in training animals. One sees many more woman animal trainers abroad than in this country, but a number of them have been celebrated in the United States. I think it is the mother instinct in women which enables them to command the obedience of animals."[35] But even as Hagenbeck's training method opened the door for women to enter the animal training business, it also reinforced several stereotypes about countries of origin that often determined social mobility in the shows.[36] Snake charmers presented themselves as Hindu from Southeast Asia, bear trainers were most likely to claim that they hailed from Russia, and camel riders donned turbans.[37]

But when a keeper or trainer was working with animals, the key to success seems to have been that person's deep-seated knowledge, combined with luck. Keepers likely had knowledge of animal husbandry and participated in tasks with the animals that were less performative. Scott's background, as a former zookeeper and longtime human companion of Jumbo, made him an especially attractive figure to accompany the elephant. Animal keepers like Scott maintained physically close relationships with their charges. The nature of a traveling workplace meant that trainers and keepers often slept in the same train car as their animals. Scott described the journey

Jumbo's skeleton toured with the circus after his death, circa 1888. Robert L. Parkinson Library and Research Center, Circus World, Baraboo, Wisconsin. Image CWi 2318.

with an anxious animal as especially exhausting, claiming, "I no sooner get just nicely off into a doze than his trunk is groping into my little bed, feeling all round my body to find my face, to ascertain if I am there, so as to awake me to talk to him. Sometimes he is so fidgety during the night that neither of us get any sleep at all. Jumbo gets worried by this mode of travelling to such an extent that if I do not get up to talk to him when he calls me, as above described, he begins to lash his trunk against the sides of the car, and to save the car from being broken to pieces I have to get up and play with and talk to him."[38]

The final few months of Jumbo's life, in 1885, likely put Scott under intense stress and scrutiny. Barnum notoriously sought to profit on his performers even after their deaths.[39] Letters dating back to 1883 show that Jumbo's taxidermized body would likely still be a source of entertainment and a profit center for Barnum. The elephant had reportedly become sick, although Barnum denied it and filed a lawsuit.[40] But in a private letter written just weeks before Jumbo's death, the taxidermist Henry Ward claimed, "Today I want to ask you a word about Jumbo. He was here lately and his keeper told my cousin (quietly) that he does not think he will live long, that it is now nearly a year since he has been able to lie down."[41] When Jumbo died in a train accident in 1885, conspiracies abounded about whether

Barnum had set up the death, as well as whether Scott's caretaking had played any part in the elephant's health.[42]

Days after Jumbo's death, Barnum pensioned Scott. The press latched on to the relationship that Scott had cultivated with Jumbo, reporting his difficulty coping with the death even years later. Scott stayed with the Barnum show for a few years, until management said that it "would have no further use for him" and advised him to go back to England."[43] Although Scott had accumulated decades of knowledge and had overseen the caretaking of one of the most famous animals in the world, his knowledge was intimately tied to the livelihood of that single animal. Jumbo's death made Scott irrelevant in the circus.

In the public records of the years that followed, Scott's presence demonstrates several likely paths that circus workers might take following their retirement. Scott shows up in the records of Bridgeport, Connecticut, where Barnum kept his winter quarters and where Jumbo had spent his offseasons. Circus workers spent their career in relatively odd jobs that often left them feeling more at home among other people in the industry. While Barnum's show was headquartered in Bridgeport, the town became a familiar haven for former circus workers more broadly. Although Scott never left the United States, he did not naturalize. The only US census in which he appears is 1910, where he is listed as a head of household, although unemployed, and recorded as living with two other men.[44] Like many other animal keepers and trainers who worked high-risk jobs, Scott struggled with alcoholism, particularly after Jumbo's death. Just three years after the 1910 census, Scott appears again. This time it is in the Bridgeport City Directory, where he is listed at Lakeview House, the local poorhouse. Scott would stay there until his death.[45]

Turning back to circus records, we find in Scott's death evidence of the role of the circus world in formulating collective identity. As a hub of circus activity, Bridgeport served as the annual meeting place for the Benevolent Order of American Tigers, a mutual aid society of circus workers that, by 1910, had gained so much popularity in the decade since its inception that local circus fans also honorarily joined.[46] Scott had made a complete break from the tented shows years prior, and seemingly had little to no contact with other circus workers in his later life. Yet, when the local newspaper announced his death and subsequent burial in the poorhouse's pauper graves, the Tigers publicly declared that they would fund the funeral and burial. With his procession led by current Tigers, including Barnum's elephant trainer that season, Scott was laid to rest "among circus men" in Park Cemetery.[47]

Scott's career—from a zookeeper to a famous animal keeper in the circus—followed one of many paths that people took in the circus world. Often, animal trainers, like Moses Ephraim "Eph" Thompson, apprenticed in the circus world to acquire knowledge and skills. Thompson was born to a free Black family in Philadelphia in 1859. He first appears in the 1870 census, where his father is listed as a day laborer, and his family of seven had moved to Michigan.[48] Thompson began his career at a young age, probably in his late teenage years, which was not uncommon for lower-paid roles in the circus. Even though he was not performing in the center ring, newspapers began taking note of him as a keeper with the Adam Forepaugh winter quarters in 1880. They often noted him as *the* Black elephant trainer, while also referencing his seemingly sound expertise about the twenty-one elephants in the herd.[49] When Forepaugh faced a lawsuit after a woman fell from an elephant, she directly cited a comment she overheard Thompson make about the elephant's disgruntled disposition.[50]

By 1883, although not yet a center-ring star, Thompson had secured a position as an elephant assistant performing in the third ring, which still put him in front of ticket-holding circus audiences to perform his own act with ten elephants. He also headed the elephant and camel tent in the menagerie, with fourteen men under his watch. During the free street parade, Thompson teamed up with two other trainers to oversee the elephants on their march.[51] This supervisory role demonstrates that he had earned a level of trust. The close audience interactions in menagerie tents and in circus parades created inherently risky situations that required well-versed trainers. Loud noises, quick movements, and crowds all contributed to the animals sometimes breaking free.[52] These emergencies could often be avoided through the efforts of astute and quick-acting handlers.

As a nineteenth-century Black performer in an American circus, Thompson had limited options.[53] The Forepaugh circus gladly entered the "elephant wars," which pushed every major American circus to obtain a rare white elephant.[54] As with most circus publicity stunts, the origin and description of the elephants were likely exaggerated. The Forepaugh show put its young white elephant, named Light of Asia, on display. But as he began to gain darker pigmentation, similar to the rest of the elephant herd, as he aged, his value in the circus diminished. Forepaugh management announced that the elephant had passed away, but the press claimed that Thompson brought the elephant into his trained herd as the feature act. Now named John L. Sullivan, the elephant wore a boxing glove on the end of his trunk and sparred in an orchestrated boxing match with Thompson. American audiences seemed delighted to see the "pugilist" elephant. The boxing match featured the elephant taking swings at Thompson until the elephant came out victorious.[55] Training an older elephant from the ground up would have been considered a feat by anybody in the circus world. But Thompson's status as a Black American inhibited his ability to climb in the American circus world ranks. News reports nearly always centered his race and even referred to his act as "pickaninny."[56]

Likely realizing that he would have greater opportunities in other markets, Thompson utilized the mobility of the circus world and networked his way to Europe. In June 1884, he quietly boarded a boat to Germany to collect a $5,000 foreign commission as a trainer. Although his employer was not named in the press, his later association with Hagenbeck likely puts his destination at the Hamburg epicenter of animal training.[57] In 1892, Thompson filed for an emergency passport at the US Consulate in Bordeaux, France, which provides a glimpse into his migrations. He cited both travel to the United States and within Europe as the reason that he needed the quick document. Although his migration from the United States had been to Germany, by this point he was living in France with his wife, also an entertainer, and his son, Leo Thompson, who had been born in Russia nearly four years prior.[58] On that 1892 passport application, Thompson listed an intention to return to the United States within the year, as well as a permanent residence in Philadelphia. But he filed another passport application in 1895 with the sole purpose of traveling Europe and no residency in the United States, but instead a home in Russia. He listed his intention to return to the United States in another two years, though that still would not happen.[59]

For nearly two decades in Europe, Thompson found fame and wealth, reportedly amassing $250,000. The level of success that he reached within the fickle world of show business was likely because he had expertly cultivated a novel act that played to audiences wherever he performed. He left his comedic boxing act behind and replaced it with a militaristic uniform and acrobatic feats from his elephants that left his audiences amazed rather than amused.[60] Thompson's popular performance pulled from both American and European elephant acts at the time, while also demonstrating why the animal training world deemed him one of the best trainers on either side of the Atlantic. His herd of elephants, which ranged in number from three to seven, somersaulted, played bells, and participated in games of jump rope as he headlined shows on theater circuits throughout Europe.[61]

Thompson did eventually return to the United States with his herd, but he retained more autonomy over his career and found himself billed differently in the press. Often, though not always, he was not identified by his race. Instead, advertisements for his performance included descriptions like "not to be compared with elephants seen in the circus." These advertisements also highlighted the exorbitant value—$15,000—of the herd. A newspaper advertisement for a show in Canton, Ohio, shows a man of light complexion directing a musical band of elephants with his back slightly turned. Those silences on race may have fueled advertisers to assume that he was white.[62] Adding to this possible confusion could have been the billing that described the show as fresh from Europe. Like in Europe, Thompson retained a top billing spot in theater advertisements, even ahead of Harry Houdini when both performers were featured on the same night. His performance was billed as "high-class vaudeville," which was a departure from where his career began, in the working-class sawdust rings of the circus.[63]

At the height of his career, his own voice appeared more in the historical record as the press clamored to get interviews with the trainer, who recognized the knowledge networks that he both utilized and led. The press described him as a Forepaugh protégé, and he did not seem bothered by the connection. He reportedly told the press, "I learned the rudiments from Addie Forepaugh, but my methods are largely my own. I have introduced most of the elephant tricks in vogue today."[64] While his point about original tricks was likely true, his time with Hagenbeck had a profound impact on his training methods, which clearly stemmed from gentling practices. When asked about how he could possibly train an elephant to do a somersault, he replied that "the trick took nineteen months to learn, but that patience—and carrots—will always win in the end."[65]

The circus world existed as a worker-constructed space, and the training methods that took hold also point to animal cocreation within these processes. Gentling methods worked because animals submitted to them. Susan Nance has explored the intricacies around elephants who went rogue and killed their trainers in entertainment industries, noting that their actions demonstrate that they "rejected the conditions of their experiences in captivity."[66] What Nance argues, and circus workers understood, is that elephants and other animals in the tented shows actively dictated the terms of their captivity. When elephants performed on cue, attacked trainers, or acted lovingly toward former trainers, circus workers pointed to their sharp memory.[67] But, as explored in chapter 7, transgressions were met with harsh punishment, including execution.

Because they were associated with animals that the public perceived as gentle giants, Scott and Thompson faced relatively little backlash for their caretaking and training methods. Trainers of big cats and other animals known for more ferocious behavior, in contrast, faced a more fraught situation. These trainers focused their knowledge networks of training methods not on attaining the best tricks, but on finding performances that would be deemed acceptable by the public. Because circuses crossed state and national boundaries within a single season, they had to constantly contend with a barrage of laws and social norms around animal training. Animal trainers, who often acted as individual owners of those animals and always acted as the public face of animal treatment in the circus, became central in these disputes.[68]

While Hagenbeck cornered much of the animal trade and training markets, he still faced competition, particularly with Frank Bostock. Born into a family of animal trainers in England, Bostock entered the training business in college. He grew up with "his father's instincts" toward animals but felt pushed out of the family business and pursued college. After witnessing a cruel lion tamer under his father's employment who was almost killed during a performance, Bostock entered his first cage.[69] When Bostock arrived in the United States, his business tactics mirrored those of the rest of the American circus world. In 1900, he filed a charter for the Frank C. Bostock Wild Animal Importing and Exhibition Company, which gave him significant power in the importation business in both Europe and the United States.[70] Like circuses at the time, Bostock had begun the business practice of vertical integration by controlling the supply chain at several steps along the way through his importation venture. Tensions between Bostock and fellow importer Hagenbeck seemed to escalate quickly. Within two months, Hagenbeck had filed an injunction against Bostock, claiming that he had used the Hagenbeck name in his show to garner more legitimacy.[71]

Bostock's training methods did share some similarities with Hagenbeck's, even though he had never been part of the Hagenbeck empire of trainers. Bostock used calming methods and did not attempt to incite ferocious behavior during the performances. This led the press to describe his performances as "more than mastery" over the cats; he instead demonstrated education.[72] But Bostock also cultivated a unique performance style that presented big cats in large open areas, rather than in the more familiar "pyramid poses" on stacked stools.[73] Bostock took his familial knowledge and personal experiences from traveling menageries in England and applied them to the increasingly popular realm of theme parks and carnivals. He arrived in the United States in 1884 and moved into a space in Brooklyn before setting up his menagerie at Coney Island. The self-proclaimed "animal king" brought an array of animals that his company had procured.[74] Bostock believed that wild-born animals were the easiest to train, and he readily admitted that not all animals could become stage performers. He articulated a difference between the practice of taming and training. Tameness, according to Bostock, depended almost solely on the individual disposition of the animal. By controlling the market and maintaining a constant flow of importation, Bostock, like Hagenbeck, was able to focus his finances and energy on animals that he deemed most tamable and trainable.[75]

Bostock's migration across the Atlantic, as well as his silence in American public records, demonstrates the porous boundaries of the American circus. Coney Island and traveling carnivals rose as American enterprises, but one of their largest draws, the wild animal show, was derived from counterparts in England and Germany. Prior to his US migration, Bostock listed himself in the 1891 English census as a menagerie owner.[76] His migrations to and from the United States appear in ship passenger lists. He initially migrated as a "showman" with his children, aboard the *Etruria*.[77] Bostock never appears in census records in the United States, however, likely due to his constant movement across continents. He migrated back to Europe in 1898 and immediately began soliciting musicians for his menagerie, which was preparing for a tour of France.[78] By 1900, he was advertising in the *Era,* a newspaper in England, and touring the principal cities of the United States and Mexico. By 1908, he had established Bostock's Arena and Jungle in England, bringing Americanized ideas of traveling carnivals back across the Atlantic.[79]

• • •

Matthew Scott, Eph Thompson, and Frank Bostock found varying degrees of success with their animal costars in and out of the circus world on both sides of the Atlantic. Scott's career came by chance. When Jumbo arrived at the Royal Zoological Gardens, he did not come with fame. But his enormous size, and sometimes troubling behavior, landed him and his head keeper in the Barnum show. Jumbomania spotlighted Scott, as he coheadlined posters and advertisements with the elephant. But that spotlight also tied Scott's expertise to a single elephant, rather than pachyderms more generally, ultimately contributing to the end of his career. Thompson retained much more control over his career following his migration out of the United States. His knowledge networks positioned him as an expert on training any elephant as he built his reputation on both his US and German connections. Details around Thompson's death remain undocumented, aside from references to a possible tuberculosis diagnosis and mention that he decided to go to Egypt—a decision that is worth noting to understand his identity as a circus performer in the African Diaspora. A note in *Variety* following his death indicated that his doctors may have advised him to seek treatment in Egypt.[80] Bostock's career in the circus world included physical migration, but his pioneering concepts in big cat training, as well as in amusement park and carnival entertainment, connected menagerie successes in England with American spectacle.

Scott, Thompson, and Bostock crossed paths with thousands of animal trainers who each carried unique migrations and experiences. These three animal handlers hailed from the United States and Europe, as did most handlers, which speaks to the colonial framework of the circus world. But trainers also joined the shows from places and peoples colonized by the United States and Europe. Chief Blue Horse and other Native American men joined Wild West shows as horse experts, Suresh Biswas of India found fame in Europe as the "Hindoo" cat trainer, and Martini Maccomo of Angola toured England as the African lion tamer.[81] As explored in the next chapter, women also worked as handlers, often offering some of the more popular big cat shows. As a collective workplace that included hundreds of shows that moved through cities daily, the circus thrived on global workplaces. Trainers sometimes hopped on the train to join the shows, carrying their identities and normalized labor practices with them.

Despite the fact that animal trainers lived in the public eye for decades, their real experiences often appear only sparingly in circus records. Circus biographies are challenging because circuses made a business out of exaggerated tales of animal capture and tried to capitalize on the trainers as well. Stage names, birth dates that made trainers appear younger, and countries of origin that made their backstory compelling (casting them as natural-born trainers) all mark where and how trainers gained their knowledge. But when paired with narratives from the press and circuses, public records such as censuses and immigration documents allow historians to track globalized migration and to insert into the narrative voices that were overshadowed by Barnum, Hagenbeck, and other giants of the field.

PART II

The Circus Lot

Jenny Wallenda Zoppé, pictured here standing in the strapless outfit, was part of a circus dynasty. Four generations of circus workers came before her in the family, including her perhaps more famous father, Karl Wallenda. Following her parents' divorce, her mother married Doc Henderson, the vet who traveled with the 1912 Barnum show, as explored in chapter 1 of this book. Between seasons, Doc Henderson and family lived in Sarasota, Florida, with Sweetheart, a leopard who doubled as a house pet. Jenny found herself on a familiar path for circus stars when she married Alberto Zoppé, the famed Italian equestrian pictured here standing in front of Jenny. Their baby, Tino, who appears gleefully balancing in his father's hand, would go on to represent the sixth generation of Wallenda circus stars.[1]

Jenny mothered behind the scenes, worked through and after pregnancies, and later watched her children perform in front of audiences. Later, in 1965, after giving birth to her daughter Tammy, she complained that her weight as an aerialist was higher than she would have liked, though she seemed sure that she could lose "the baby fat." When asked where the new baby was amid a two-week engagement in New York, she replied, "We brought her up in our camper that Andy [her then husband] fixed to sit on a truck. Tino, my 14-year-old son by my first marriage, took off from school to baby-sit. . . . So he's back there studying and I hope Tammy is sleeping."[2]

The other people in the image, who can be found seated in a semicircle, conversing under a tent, or busying themselves in the backyard of the circus lot, represent a mix of workers and family members. The juxtaposition of casual attire and spangled outfits demonstrates the

Jenny Wallenda Zoppé (*standing, background*) and others look on as her husband, Alberto Zoppé, holds their son, Tino, 1951. Special Collections at Milner Library, Illinois State University, Normal. Image BSP2097. Used with permission.

mix of labor and leisure that characterized this space for circus workers. In this way, the photo seems to capture the circus lot in a single snapshot. It is a scene that could have been captured on any given day during the season as performers and other workers gathered with friends and families between public spectacles.

But the people missing from this image also provide some insight into life on the circus lot. An overwhelming number of circus backyard photos in archives feature European and white American big top performers. As explored in part II of this book, the circus world was incredibly diverse, but that diversity was largely predicated on colonial networks. Those networks often funneled workers—both human and animal—into uncontracted and highly exploitative roles. Historian Janet Davis argues that the shows celebrated an "illusionary" diversity that was a reflection of the world in which they operated.[3] Put another way, the circus as a workplace was incredibly diverse, but it operated under colonial systems. Ideas of migration, as explored in the previous chapters, are central to understanding the experiences of people and animals engaged in various degrees of unfree labor on the circus lot. And although movement characterized the circus world, the lot itself as a workplace remained physically static between the setup and takedown of the tented city, making it a necessary site of exploration.

While gender is the primary lens in this section, each of the following three chapters takes an intersectional perspective. The magnifying glass on gender within this workspace reveals the centrality of intersecting experiences associated with race, age, class, and species to the analysis. The act of mothering is also a central thread in these chapters. The ways that it was simultaneously made necessary, useless, invisible, and performative are paramount for understanding how these intersecting identities informed the circus world experience for workers. Moreover, motherhood is a category that cuts across species, allowing a more robust analysis of the space as an interspecies site of labor, and it demands a reexamination of questions surrounding what constitutes labor in a worksite and a community. For circusgoers, the circus lot was a place of leisure and entertainment. It was a one-day event each year that would have been attended by almost the entire town. For circus workers, the circus lot was a mobile worksite and a home.

Women's Work and Gendered Circus Labor in the Tented Shows

Circusgoers could not step foot on the lot without seeing women. Some of the big top's most impressive physical feats, like equestrian work and trapezes, were dominated by women. They were also under the sideshow tent, defying whatever beauty standards and social norms existed. Women billed as bearded ladies, fat ladies, tattooed ladies, and armless wonders filled the sideshow tents as they interacted closely with audiences. The backyard was sure to be a space where spangled costumes rested in trunks (which might also have a toddler sitting on them), underwent repairs in the hands of a circus seamstress, or were worn on the body of a performer preparing to once again risk her life in front of tens of thousands of people. The workers examined in this chapter navigated the circus world as gendered workers. Unlike men in the tented shows, they did not engage in the unpaid labor of manual work during the gratis performance. Instead, they often graced posters and newspaper headlines that drew in audiences. Always serving as contracted workers when actually employed, women in the tented shows operated in a circus world that presented a unique set of job opportunities and stages.

Some women, like Josie De Mott, occupied several of these stages and brought their work beyond the circus lot. As a political activist, De Mott became a high-profile name in 1911, but as a circus performer she had been dominating newspaper headlines for decades. She began her career as a child, traveling the tented shows with her parents. Equestrian performances came naturally to her, and she quickly developed an impressive tumbling routine atop a horse. Her parents' show traveled across the United States on horse-drawn wagons, but it never gained much traction. After the show folded in 1883, the De Mott family immediately joined the Orrin Circus on its tour of Mexico. Her equestrian skills brought her under the banner of the Ohio-based John Robinson Circus and eventually the Barnum & Bailey show.[1]

By the turn of the century, De Mott had faded out of sight of circus fans, as she had opted for an early retirement as the wife of Charles Robinson, a business manager in the circus world. Circus folks admonished the couple as "gillies," and the press stopped reporting on the former circus personalities. The couple quietly spent their earnings on a farm in Hempstead, New York, and later trekked through Alaska to make a living taking censuses. De Mott reportedly chose love over work and "left the circus to preside over the home of her generous husband."[2]

When De Mott returned to the circus world in 1906, fans in and out of the arena eagerly awaited the woman who had left the profession as a renowned figure. In her first center-ring appearance, the horse threw her to the ground. But she climbed back on to finish the act, reportedly with some torn ligaments. Her tenacity brought delight to the audience and reaffirmed the "artistic instinct that gives circus women their individuality." Her dangerous somersaulting act on a galloping horse remained a headliner; she was the only woman in the circus world performing the feat.[3]

Although details of an unhappy marriage would later emerge, the public saw her return as a sign of the circus performer's addiction to the limelight. She reportedly could not find happiness outside of the circus world and in "the pleasure of society." Following this reasoning, De Mott's return to a circus career seemed an easy choice—after consulting her husband, of course.[4]

But De Mott returned with more than just a flashy performance. She began publishing articles and letters about women in the circus world. In the *Washington Post*, De Mott asserted herself as a worker. She stated that "if there is any glamour to the circus, it is not apparent to the woman, who by virtue of her profession, is always behind the scenes." She claimed that for women in the tented shows, a circus career "is a very practical thing—a means of making a living—usually a very good one." De Mott framed circus women as stronger than their "towner" counterparts because they lived in the "narrow confines of a Pullman car" rather than "a cozy bedroom." But she noted that any woman could manage a circus life.[5] Other publications seconded this notion, claiming that anyone who "had an ounce of circus blood. . . . pities stay-at-homes with their modern conveniences."[6]

While acknowledging that circus women's lives looked unique, De Mott framed her coworkers as relatable and idyllic models of American womanhood. She emphasized the second shift of women cleaning costumes and the costs that women bore in buying costumes. Leisure time, according to De Mott, meant that circus women could finally get to their book groups, needlework, and the exclusive "Young Women's Tea Table." Reiterating the concept of unity, she made clear the place of women in the circus world. With very "little bickering or jealousy," the women worked and lived "in close intimacy." She credited strong women for the relatively low divorce rate in the circus and praised their typical decision to stay in the workforce after marriage, despite her own experiences.[7]

De Mott's progressive views toward women's equality and work derived from her experiences in a mixed-gender workplace. But that same sort of progressiveness did not touch all aspects of De Mott's worldview. Despite the diverse backgrounds of circus employees, De Mott assured readers that they "need have no fear" about race suicide. Her comments tugged at a prevalent fear in the early twentieth century: that white birthrates were being outpaced by people of color and new immigrants. Other columnists seconded this notion and praised (white) circus women for raising families despite their ardent schedule.[8] The xenophobic and nativist sentiment that colored De Mott's commentary demonstrates another fault line in the circus world identity, one that was most evident between the big top and sideshow tents. De Mott's contradictory stance mirrors that of other entertainers. In her study of union formation and nativism in entertainment industries, Krystyn Moon argues that this contradictory attitude among US entertainers was informed by the politics of national origin and racial distinction.[9]

Although De Mott gestured toward mainstream nativist conspiracies, she continued to advocate for circus women as workers and feminists, promulgating the image of the New Woman in the tented shows.[10] Her political work culminated in suffragism when she cofounded the Suffragette Ladies of the Barnum & Bailey Circus. Following her circus career, De Mott stayed connected to the circus world. She started a stock farm, bought retired horses from circuses, and trained young women in equestrian acts. But her postcircus life spoke more to her feminist activism than it did to her place in the circus world. De Mott noted that "the woman before the public is always on display." She sought to establish a refuge for ordinary women to regain the athleticism lost in the everyday monotony of turn-of-the-century American life. Her life in and out of the circus created a particular idea of feminism for the circus star. As De Mott subtly insinuated and blatantly stated in her shows and writings, life as a circus worker made her tougher, while society made women outside the circus world softer. While she advocated for fellow women, she also spoke of the strength of the entire circus world workforce, claiming that "you rarely hear of circus people complaining of being tired."[11]

Josie De Mott and other sought-after stars retained circus world fame and fortune decades after leaving the ring, while women in the sideshow tent were more exploited. But no matter their tent, women performed obvious emotional labor. Many women workers played the role of performer in the ring and then wife and mother or idealistic single woman behind the scenes. Both sets of performances were in the public eye. The public consumed the celebrity of both their staged and unstaged work. Rather than performing dazzling and daring feats, sideshow women often performed stereotyped representations during the ticketed shows. And while big top women sometimes hid pregnancies and motherhood, sideshow women undertook the grueling emotional labor of performing these processes for the public.

Women carved out their own spaces and formed networks of solidarity yet often clung to the larger circus world identity. Through their performances, writings, and political activism, circus women showed their solidarity to one another and their fellow circus workers. The mobility of entire shows put circus workers in contact with burgeoning political and social movements. Given the gendered dynamics of labor, the women in tented performances and unpaid roles performed a double shift to ensure that the show would go on.[12] Circus women also pushed on gender constructions, which helped provide job opportunities.[13] Their activism on- and offstage demonstrates the permeability of the circus world, growing consciousnesses outside of their labor identity, and a long history of political activism among circus workers. Yet they also operated within patriarchal and colonial spaces, where their labors and fates were often tied to those of the men in the tented shows.

Re-Creating the Wild West

Because women workers in the circus performed an array of paid and unpaid labors, they could be found in every tented touring show in the country. Wild West shows, which often toured in conjunction with circuses and included performers who skirted between the two stages, offered some of the most blatant stereotyped performances in the industry. For women, this meant taking on familial roles, like wife and mother, as part of their performance. The public infatuation with Wild West shows stretched far beyond American shores. Like business-savvy circus owners, Wild West show owners realized significant profits overseas. William "Buffalo Bill" Cody dominated the industry and made several trips to Europe prior to 1900. With his large workforce of Native American and white men and women, Cody provided battle reenactments and skill demonstrations that claimed to transport audiences to life on the American frontier.[14]

During Cody's 1891 European tour, the public seemed most interested in the twenty-three prisoners of war whom he had acquired just after the

1890 Wounded Knee massacre from Fort Sheridan, Illinois, where they were incarcerated. These bonded laborers were not actually Ghost Dance participants, but the publicity materials and performances told a different story. Through song and dance, the prisoners showed audiences what they wanted to see—seemingly authentic Native American otherness. Audiences in Germany, Belgium, and Britain witnessed singing and dancing that appeared to give a nearly live play-by-play of the conflict between Native Americans and the US government.[15] Like other circus workers, conscripted Native Americans often appeared in the public view as happy and lucky to be under the paternalistic care of the shows. Newspapers cast Native Americans as "privileged" to do circus work, and said that it was an indication of the "great men" in the tribe, who were "especially favored."[16]

Most workers in Cody's show were men. But Cody understood the intrinsic value of women in his Wild West shows, and he featured Native American women as well. Like big top circuses, Wild West shows contained a host of sideshow performances that were available to audiences as they awaited the main attraction. As one example, Lakota women demonstrated more mundane parts of life on the frontier, such as bead making. The press and audiences raved about this display of home life.[17] Importantly, Louis S. Warren has noted that these domestic displays offered women significant income: one Native American woman in the show, for example, took home a $112 salary and an additional $260 in sales. Moreover, this work offered women control over their craft, and the craftwork that is now in museum exhibits demonstrates that, at least at times, the product reflected "minimal craftsmanship."[18] In other words, Native American women in these moments offered a performance that was as authentically representative as they wished it to be.

Cody carefully drew up contracts with Native American women. Unlike the men, Native American women were not contracted as individuals. Instead, they joined only if their husbands had also joined the show. Contract stipulations from the Office of Indian Affairs directly addressed the role of women, with the objective of keeping them fed and cared for. This narrow interest in only certain workers helped craft the particular way that audiences consumed the image of Native American women. Their image reinforced their roles as spouses of warriors and caretakers of the home.[19] Because Native Americans were often contracted in groups rather than as solo performers, this large workforce also set conditions for worker pushback, as happened when Smooth Quiver, a Native American performer with the John Robinson Circus, was killed off the circus lot during the season, and her body immediately shipped to the nearest large city. Other Native American performers were reportedly "in an uprising" over the

A Native American woman sits with two children in the Miller Brothers 101 Show, 1926. Robert L. Parkinson Library and Research Center, Circus World, Baraboo, Wisconsin. Image CWi 292.

handling of her death, claiming that they were not notified until after the next ticketed show.[20]

When Cody returned to the United States in 1907, his shows gave similar performances. The 1907 season included nineteen battle reenactments, demonstrations, and exhibitions that showcased men on the western frontier. Audiences saw Cody's sharpshooting skills, an Indian attack on an emigrant train, a Pony Express reenactment, Rough Rider impersonators, and train robbers. In the "Battle of Summit Springs," cowboys hunted down Native Americans who had been accused of murdering settlers in Nebraska and Kansas. True to events in the 1869 conflict, Cheyenne Dog Soldiers were shown performing a pivotal role in the resistance against the US government. However, Cody's depiction of women's roles was markedly different than reality. In his version, warriors were killed, Indian women and children were captured, and two white women prisoners were saved.[21]

In the real story, one white woman prisoner was injured and another died, while Indian women and children were massacred.[22] This creative retelling of Summit Springs positioned the US government and American cowboys as protectors over womanhood. By engaging in this new narrative in front of audiences, Buffalo Bill turned a story about the real role of women into an idealized story with rigid gender roles.

Cody's show depicted Native American women as savages who were staunchly different from their white counterparts, even as they also embodied universally relatable mothers. As Buffalo Bill's show toured Europe, Indian women performed in the sideshow, alongside fire-eaters and magicians. Like the popular bead-making women of earlier decades, the Native American women on this tour had more to offer the public than simply battle reenactments. When Luther Standing Bear's wife, Laura, gave birth to their daughter while on tour in Birmingham, England, Cody saw a publicity opportunity. Just as with circuses that advertised new attractions, the mother and her two-day-old daughter became a media sensation. In the moments that European audiences passed by the mother and baby, the private labor of motherhood became public.[23] Native American women also attracted the public's attention between shows. When a contracted Native American performer walked back to the railroad tracks with "her brave," carrying a baby on her back, it attracted "considerable amusement and interest."[24]

Indian rights activists criticized the savage imagery on display and the potential moral corruption that workers faced.[25] An array of reports claimed that the shows had introduced gambling, alcohol, and abuse to the Native Americans. In response, US secretary of the interior John Noble began refusing permits for the show. But silence surrounded the emotional labor that women performed in sideshows and other circus performances. Activists pushed back against the corruption of Western influences but took less issue with workers being contracted to perform intimate moments, with motherhood often at the forefront.[26]

Wild West shows also showcased a different labor of motherhood. Pawnee Bill's Wild West Show always seemed second rate next to Buffalo Bill's. Unlike the more famous Buffalo Bill, Pawnee Bill, whose real name was Gordon William Lillie, claimed to have "drifted into show business."[27] He began his show business career under the direction of Buffalo Bill when he signed on as the Pawnee translator, hence his stage name. His behind-the-scenes work transformed into a starring role. Within five years, Pawnee Bill and his wife, May, introduced their own Wild West show.[28] Several years later, when Buffalo Bill embarked on his two-year tour of Europe under the urging of co-owner James A. Bailey, Pawnee Bill modernized, updated, and enlarged his own Wild West show to capture the American market.

The investment paid off, as evidenced by his $15,000 weekly receipts in 1906. His battle reenactments, trick riding, sharpshooting, and glamorized portrayal of life in the West attracted audiences. His wife, too, found fame as one of the show's stars.[29]

Pawnee Bill enlarged the careers of his performers and capitalized on one of the circus's most beloved traditions—the free circus parade. Folks lined the streets to see the costumed stars stroll by on horseback or foot, or in wagons. Audiences seemed captivated by the women, who stole headlines. And yet, after parade watchers viewed May and other "cowgirls" on horseback, they walked the circus lot to witness Native American women caring for children in so-called Indian villages. Onlookers sought a peek inside the constructed tepees as the women worked under the supervision of Native American men.[30] Unlike her Native American coworkers, May did not have to put her family life on display for gawking audiences. And the stars who seemed to transgress gender norms on horseback stood in stark contrast to the Native American women who performed the emotional labor of mothering for eager audiences. Yet May's private family life was also scrutinized by the public, most notably her struggles with fertility.[31] Like Josie De Mott's experience, May came under scrutiny for what appeared to the public to be the prioritization of paid work.

Women's Work in Tented Shows

Even beyond the Wild West shows, the circus had long employed women in visible public work. Women populated big top shows in the early Golden Age, performing flashy and dangerous feats that appealed to audiences. Women were the equestrians, dancers, and acrobats under the big top, as well as the bearded lady in the sideshow tent. Women also stepped outside of these roles and occasionally dazzled audiences with animal acts. Although each of these acts demonstrated a unique feature or skill, they also lived up to certain gender expectations. Scholars have documented the role of women in early shows. Literary scholars Katherine H. Adams and Michael L. Keene provide a detailed look at early circuses and the increased opportunities and roles for women toward the turn of century. Historian Janet Davis provides a larger cultural analysis of the tented shows in her book *The Circus Age*, but the book also makes substantial gendered analysis.[32]

Snake charming, in particular, became associated with women workers in the circus and Wild West shows. Women snake charmers either hailed from faraway places or were made to appear so. One feature story described the typical snake charmer as a "tall, majestic woman garbed in gorgeous Eastern costume with raven tresses and an imperious gaze, who smokes cigarettes, wears strange jewels, and sits all day with boa constrictors, cobras and rattlesnakes entwined around her shapely form." When undeniably white women played the role, their title was more likely to include "snake-ologist" than "charmer."[33] Like the animal trainers explored in chapter 2, snake charmers seemed to possess an unknowable skill that the public was desperate to understand. The "secret" for these snake charmers came from real or imaged ethnic ties, as well as some innate essence of womanhood. Whether or not they really charmed the animals, snake charmers spoke of their own gentle nature as the key to their success.[34]

Snake charmers and other women workers did not avert danger in their staged performances. As snake charmer Mademoiselle Octavia noted in an interview, "Nowadays the act where there is the greatest possibility of your being taken straight from the stage to the mortuary is the one that is the most sought after." Octavia described her multitude of snakebite scars as medals, which she supposedly earned through her successful treatments of morphine, a caustic pencil, and a shot of whiskey.[35] Other women also found injury or death in daring stunts during the parades, sideshow acts, and big top performances in front of live audiences. Shows did not shy away from placing women in dangerous working conditions. Audiences seemed accustomed to women handling snakes, stunt cars, and trapeze bars. But circuses also assured audiences that even as these women risked their lives, their morals and chastity were protected. As one Barnum employee noted, "the unmarried [girl] who does a daring act in the air has never gone through the streets of New York alone." The same sentiment surrounded the ballet girls who premiered in the opening Cleopatra spectacle in 1912. The feature, which included dozens of young, unmarried women, prompted particular regulations by the circus that more strictly limited fraternization between men and women.[36]

Audiences could find Octavia and other women workers in the sideshow tent, but they were much less likely to see women milling about the lot. While working-class circus men readied for the show during the gratis performance, women were noticeably absent. Yet audiences still yearned to catch a peek at their roles behind the scenes. Women filled these desires in newspaper articles and behind-the-scenes glimpses published in the show programs. Much of this work would have been invisible otherwise, and it broadened their role beyond the tented performances. Their offstage performances included social gatherings and domestic labor. In 1906, the *New York Times* dedicated a full-page spread to the internal social lives of circus women. Aside from the scattering of costume trunks on the outskirts of the meeting place, the reporter noted that the room looked rather ordinary, with women "crocheting or writing down a cookery recipe." Even more notably, a woman went from one of the "circus girls" to an "ordinary-looking" woman as she changed from "yellow tights and pumps" to a "brown cloth dress [and] a modest hat to match."[37] This, again, echoes De Mott's comments on the circus world and the ability of most women to undertake this labor.

The press noted that circus women often handled familial obligations behind the scenes. While Cody regulated Native American women more heavily and only hired those who were married, circus proprietors often had more lax rules. Both single men and single women worked for the show. However, single women's offstage time included more regulation, such as the requirement that they return to their sleeping cars "at a reasonable hour" after the nightly show.[38] Even if women performers were contracted individually, their ability to obtain a contract could still depend on their networks with men. As circus agent Frank Miller said, "No manager of a circus especially if his show be a first class one, will engage a female performer in any capacity unless she is accompanied by some male relative."[39] Exceptions abounded, but his words still indicate what sort of spaces were available to women on the circus lot. The paternalistic nature of the circus world, too, had special implications for women workers on the lot. According to one newspaper report, "no woman could live a more protected life," with a strict curfew one hour after the final show ended.[40]

The labor structure of the circus led to many women being viewed more as charges than as independent workers. Aside from being contracted under spouses or hired because of preexisting networks with other male relatives, women were under the oversight of a "circus mother" in larger shows like Barnum & Bailey. Hired to look after women and children, the circus mother served as the "matron of the women's dressing room" and as the teacher of children attached to the shows.[41] Emma Talbot worked as the circus mother on the Barnum & Bailey show through the first few decades of the twentieth century and could often be found sitting just outside the women's dressing room tent sewing before the first big top show.[42] Officially employed by the wardrobe department, circus mothers like Mrs. Talbot oversaw the upkeep of the aesthetic parts of the shows.[43] While still given more freedom than many of their sideshow counterparts, big top women thus had circumscribed freedom of movement as regulated by the management.

Most women who joined the show did so with their spouses and extended families. Privately, these celebrity women played mother, wife, and daughter. The public became enthralled not only with how women played these roles, but also with how similar their family lives looked to those outside the circus. For instance, the train car, otherwise part of the mobile workplace, also served as a home, whose decorations "suggest[ed] the feminine instinct

A performer pushes her child in the backyard while clowns converse behind her, 1947. Special Collections at Milner Library, Illinois State University, Normal. Image BNP6746v1. Used with permission.

of homemaking."[44] Under a similar pretense, reports assured audiences that the body modifications of Padaung women, who performed as the giraffe-necked women of Burma, did not "interfere with domestic duties." On the contrary, they told circus fans that "the more brass, the better the bride."[45]

As a functioning city, the circus also employed back-of-house workers who washed and sewed uniforms. The daily performances in sawdust rings meant that circus uniforms needed constant upkeep. During the season, circuses maintained a staff of wardrobe mistresses or seamstresses that readied and repaired costumes for daily use. As W. C. Thompson noted during his travels with the shows, "the whir of sewing machines is never absent from the wardrobe tent, and seamstresses work with needle and thread from light to dark." This hard labor also continued throughout the winter, making these women more akin to permanent workers. Thompson wrote: "all through the winter a corps of women is busy on new uniforms and trappings for man, woman, and beast." Mrs. White, the head wardrobe mistress for the Barnum show in the early twentieth century, kept a staff of twenty women in New York during the winter months. Her sewing talents required her to do measurements and fittings for the elephants, camels, and human performers, thereby blurring the requirements of human and animal labor.[46]

The repeated emphasis on how circus women resembled ordinary women obscured the unique reality of life on the circus lot, which stretched beyond sewing costumes. With the usual exception of very young children, circus families constituted a group of workers. Despite the multitude of families and children on the circus lot, only sixty-five "pretty, young girls" did not have a place in the tented performance in 1942. Yet even these young women still acted as uncontracted, probably unpaid, "fill-ins" by riding on elephants and floats in the spectacle. According to circus workers, bareback riders had to begin working as children if they ever wanted to look graceful. Part of the skill, they claimed, was "the feel" for the horse, which had to be mastered at a young age. Famed equestrian Lizzie Seabert echoed this notion when she recounted her own experiences as a child in the circus. She was a third-generation circus worker, and when she was still at a young age, her "father was beginning the lessons of [her] life's work." She traveled with her family during the season and spent the winter months at a riding academy in New York "from morning til dark." The difficulty of her somersaulting job was not lost on Seabert, who noted that other women had been "exhausted by the strain and violence of the performance and compelled to abandon their careers in their early prime."[47]

The reality of child labor loomed large for circus workers who defied danger nightly. And the double burden that married circus women faced did not exactly mirror the situation of noncircus women, since their familial obligations were circumscribed by their professional roles. Married circus women were partners and parents who did not cook or clean. Rather, the circus world created a different home and work life for women within a larger circus world family. The press was unwilling to see the difference, praising women for preparing additional meals outside the cook tent or providing a quick stitch to a uniform.[48]

Women composed a substantial part of the workforce and forged their own space in the circus world. Their experiences are a swath in the larger fabric of women's history. But the circus world also offered unique social norms, boundaries, and expectations. Unlike for most early twentieth-century women, career often trumped marriage for circus workers. Pregnancies could shorten, alter, or end their careers. Tightrope walker Mary Rawls remembered how her father disapproved of her impending marriage because he would "lose her" in his act. Sure enough, she formed a new act with her husband. When she became pregnant soon after, she sewed new costumes to hide her belly and continued to perform; ruffles around her midsection adequately hid her five-month pregnant belly.[49]

Raising children on the road presented more challenges. Mary recounted rushing to the center ring for her act after unsuccessfully trying to change

Left to right: Beppi De Canter, elephant trainer Virgil Seagraves's child, and a clown in the backyard. Special Collections at Milner Library, Illinois State University, Normal. Image BNP8140v1. Used with permission.

her toddler's diaper and clothes. Minutes into the act, her naked son also made his way into the ring, in front of thousands of laughing audience members. Famed bareback rider Ernestine Clarke made waves in the circus world as a premier performer by the age of fourteen. Her life in the circus world, however, began when her mother returned to the big top when Ernestine turned five months old. She proudly claimed that she slept in her mother's costume trunk during performances.[50]

The New Woman

Aside from the gendered backstage performances, life as a circus worker also presented opportunities to represent women that transgressed gender norms. When British circusgoers attended shows during the 1897 season of the Barnum & Bailey Circus, they witnessed a cast that included men and women. As the circus entered the town, circusgoers rushed to the railcars to see working men unload their animal stock. Per usual, men dominated the gratis performance. Women, however, would soon populate the circus lot as sideshow and big top performers, behind-the-scenes workers, and family members readied for the show. Women modeled for the posters that the shows plastered on walls and served as spokespeople in the advertisements that filled the program pages, while also serving as real workers in and out of the ring.[51]

Under the big top, women worked under the banner of the New Woman, a term of empowerment created and popularized in the 1890s. The New Woman represented, among other things, a career-driven and athletic ideal.[52] The image described circus women well, and management capitalized on the seemingly perfect fit. From 1895 to 1898, the Barnum & Bailey Circus offered audiences a feature called the "New Woman" under the big top in an all-woman performance. One of the three rings was dedicated to a female cast that included a ringmaster, clowns, and chariot drivers. Famed equestrians looked different in the ring as they jumped hurdles in outfits more conducive to horseback riding. Other circuses, like the John Robinson show, also capitalized on the New Woman trend with similar gimmicks.[53]

The female-led "New Woman" performance contained a sense of novelty, but it also signaled a degree of feminism among circus workers that existed outside of that scripted performance. This feature brought a new image of women to the performance stage, and it carved out new employment opportunities for women in the tented shows. Following the end of the "New Woman" feature in 1898, women retained several high-profile performance jobs.[54] The years-long performance was also significant because of its timing. The transatlantic performance debuted in Europe and continued in the United States.

Even after the shows abandoned the "New Woman" performance, the term continued to be applied to female performers under the big top. Katie Sandwina, born Kate Brumbach, bent gender conventions in the arena in the years following the short-lived "New Woman" spectacle. The Barnum show advertised Sandwina as a beauty with brute strength. She had already made a name for herself on European stages and the Keith vaudeville circuit, earning fans and substantial paychecks. Her popularity earned her a center-ring promotion by 1911.[55]

Like Josie De Mott, Sandwina pushed her celebrity status into the realms of political and social activism on behalf of women. Her newly earned center-ring celebrity status gave her a platform, particularly within the growing movement around women's suffrage. Newspapers made quips about Sandwina's participation in the movement since her onstage persona included feats of strength, such as lifting men off the ground. Reporters noted that her physical equality with men meant that women could perhaps have voting equality too. Articles written in response to the movement still had headlines like, "Barnum and Bailey's Circus Is One of the Greatest Beauty

Shows on the Road."[56] But Sandwina and other circus women used their unique career and social positioning to further suffragism.

In 1911, as women's suffrage campaigns were in full force around the country, the circus brought immense publicity to the larger movement.[57] As the Ringling Brothers Circus pulled into Los Angeles in the final months of its tour, it entered a politically charged arena that was weeks away from deciding on a measure that would give women the right to vote. Women activists in Los Angeles had been campaigning in immigrant neighborhoods and holding tea parties with elite women in an effort to attract supporters and members.[58] The popularity of the circus offered a unique platform for the Los Angeles activists to continue their campaign. At nine o'clock in the morning, as the circus began its march down Washington Street, people lined the streets to view a glimpse of the performers. Elaborate wooden wagons rolled down the streets, filled with big top celebrities and magnificent animals behind golden bars. The suffrage movement had politicized this typical scene, which preceded every circus show. At the urging of several local activists, a brightly colored Votes for Women banner hung around the neck of Jennie the elephant as she walked in the usual procession.[59]

Although Jennie's politicized walk is an early example of both activism in the circus parade and support for the suffrage movement among women, it was not the last example of either. Women were a visible presence in the circus and became increasingly active in the campaign for the vote. Aerialists, animal trainers, costume designers, and equestrian performers banded together to form their own faction of the suffrage movement, the Suffragette Ladies of the Barnum and Bailey Circus. With more than eight hundred members, including stars such as Little Lizzie Hanneford, the organization garnered significant attention from both the press and the activists in the larger movement.[60] As the activism surrounding women's voting rights grew within the circus world, male and female performers donned suffrage sashes on several occasions, brandished banners in parades, and distributed literature to willing patrons. Even the Buffalo Bill show carried a Votes for Women banner to promote the cause. In the short offseason, the political stirrings gained momentum. When the show opened in Madison Square Garden in 1912, circusgoers were again treated to a growing women's movement within the circus world.[61]

This political activism promoted a sense of solidarity among women, further shaping their circus world identity. Their use of circus parades as legitimate political expressions reinforced women's desire and ability to include true political activism within their performance. Recounting her time in the movement, Josie De Mott remarked, "I could ride Comet and make him stand straight in the air, while I waved a suffrage banner with a firm hand and a high arm. I could lead a parade."[62]

When the suffrage movement broke into the circus world, it capitalized on a significant female presence. The circus had a large, cosmopolitan female workforce, as well as women who traveled along as family members. Married manual laborers often left their spouses at home, but high-paid performers traveled with their families.[63] The circus was reportedly home to "husbands and wives, mothers and babies, sisters and cousins and aunts."[64] Women who joined their families on the circus route could also find paid employment opportunities doing back-of-house work. Ringling band director Merle Evans embarked on circus seasons with his wife, Nena, who also served as a personal secretary for the Ringling owners. Her labor included leaving the lot each day to get a meal from a local diner for show co-owner Henry North.[65] Men dominated most jobs in the circus, but the number of women employed grew to nearly half of the workforce by 1910.[66]

The public appeared infatuated with the community of women workers on the circus lot. Aside from emphasizing their domestic duties and connections to housewife identities, the press also lauded the seemingly strong community bonds that women workers formed with one another, despite their multiple national identities.[67] The public praise of circus women was deeply embedded in the ideas of womanly work that Josie De Mott pushed. The *Washington Post* called these working women "an honor to their sex." Despite their public work, their less-scripted private life, which adhered to more rigid turn-of-the-century gender norms, made the uneven balance between home and career more acceptable. That the lot was also populated by men (described by the press as "protector" of that honor) did not overturn those rigid gender norms.[68] Although circus workers interacted with one another at various times on the lot and during the shows, a significant portion of their day occurred in the sex-segregated space of the dressing room tent. The men's dressing room tents went relatively unreported in newspapers, but women's tents remained a public fascination, a space where the more relatable and mundane parts of the job were performed. Women workers enjoyed tea and fixed their costumes to satisfy their "very strong" "domestic instinct."[69]

There were gendered realities to starting a circus career. Individually, some circus women had stories about becoming captivated by the circus lights and running away from farm life to join the shows.[70] But the more prevalent stories about running away to join the circus came from the circus's transient population of workers—the uncontracted, underage, and often underpaid male manual laborers. Women on the lot, whether a contracted performer or a family member of someone under contract, were more readily described as being "born into the business." And Cody's publicized policy of accepting female performers only when accompanied by a husband tracked with Ringling policies that placed additional behavior constraints on unmarried girls.[71]

Because women were themselves contracted or else were able to bend the ear of a contracted performer, their political activism occurred on a larger stage. Activist work such as that of the Suffragette Ladies gained significant attention, without much pushback. As moneymaking workers, circus women were less vulnerable to the circus's unscrupulous tactics in dealing with increasingly autonomous workers. And the shows themselves benefited immensely from circus women's involvement in feminist causes. As easily as shows could spin stories about circus women living under the paternalistic protection of men, they could also demonstrate that women workers had unprecedented control over their lives. Either way, shows gained the press attention that sustained them.

Circuses, then, seemed immune to bad press about their women workers. But for women themselves, the grueling, abnormal, and often life-threatening work did not completely escape critics. As exemplified by the narrative surrounding Josie De Mott, circus reviews that centered on women touched on anxieties over their roles as wives and mothers. Reports assured audiences that a circus woman would work only "as long as maternity did not interfere with her profession."[72] At a show in Raleigh, North Carolina, the equestrian was "as graceful as wreathing smoke . . . [and] poetry in motion." But it seemed odd that she was performing, given her very recent wedding. Her success in the ring did not exempt her from being seen as a "failure as a wife."[73]

• • •

The lives and careers of women complicate the overarching circus world identity of the tented shows. Women had different opportunities, duties, experiences, and sites of oppression than did men. Their behind-the-scenes work—what was an invisible second shift for noncircus women—was consumed by an eager public. Meanwhile, their staged and scripted work under the tents emphasized gendered labor while toeing the line of femininity. And despite the hokey press coverage of their labor and politics, women took real measures to practice activism and solidarity.

As the most visible snapshot of this activism, the Suffragette Ladies of the Barnum and Bailey Circus promoted feminism and a vision of gender equality that had emerged among circus women prior to 1910. As workers, De Mott and her predecessors had labored, organized, and fought alongside their fellow circus workers for decades. They had asserted their places as workers and women within the circus world.[74] The relationship between circus women and first-wave feminism demonstrates the permeability of the circus world, links between circus workers and "towners," and the social and political ramifications of mobile workplaces. Women in the circus found themselves in competing identities that became entangled with movements and people as they moved around the world.

As the circus declined in the 1950s, many jobs had been mechanized or popularized out of existence. The behind-the-scenes obsession and celebrity status of circus women, however, remained an important part of the circus's appeal. The next chapter moves to nonhuman workers as it explores larger constructions of motherhood among animal workers and the ways that this identity became just as popular. Gender constructions were not bound to human workers, and circus women were not free from the 1950s stereotype of the middle-class housewife. Harking back to Josie De Mott's parallels between circus women and their noncircus counterparts, midcentury publications emphasized the multiple roles that circus women played: circus star, mother, wife, and "simple housewife" who performed while "gritting [her] pretty teeth."[75]

4

Animal Motherhood and (Re)Constructed Circus Families

Animals occupied most spaces on the circus lot. They were one of the first things circusgoers laid their eyes on when the train stopped. Fantastical illustrations of the creatures graced lithographs and advertisements. Animals marched in the parade, carried people on their backs, and pulled other caged animals. On the lot, literal horsepower and brute elephant strength made the lot into a tented city. Animals also filled the backyard as they awaited the opening spec in their herds and with their trainers and keepers. But baby animals offered something different to circusgoers and held a higher value for the shows. They were proof of a show's mastery over nature, ability to create and cultivate families, and financial investment. The circus nursery, which held the show's baby animal collection, became a frequently visited part of the circus lot, even if it did not offer the thrills of the big top. This chapter considers a historical view of motherhood and the ways in which ideas of mothering were transposed onto animals who lived captive lives on the center stage. It examines how motherhood was both exploited and rendered useless by circuses. In doing so, it aims to understand how nonhuman animal mothers have been central to patriarchal and colonial discourses on motherhood.[1]

The 1908 circus season offered significant competition to the cute antics in the nursery. That year, the Barnum & Bailey show, under Ringling Brothers management and production, promised new and exciting acts under the big top tent. Wotan, the horse balloonist, stood in a hot air balloon and flew one hundred feet in the air over a "baptism of fireworks" in a thrilling act for guests.[2] Witnessing dangerous spectacles like these under the big top became a central part of the circus experience, one that openly put animal workers on the front lines of precarious working conditions, as explored more extensively in chapter 7.

But paternalism was also embedded in the circus experience, and management bragged about taking care of their own. The circus nursery of newborn baby animals served these ends rather perfectly. Between big top performances, circusgoers on the Barnum & Bailey lot crowded inside the nearby menagerie tent in "throngs" and "mobs" to see the infant animals in the circus nursery. The press described the nursery as an "animal kindergarten." Like with a human kindergarten, the infant animals often found themselves away from their parents. A baby elephant, described as the size of a Saint Bernard, stood alone on a railed pedestal. Infant ponies, llamas, and camels were nearby under the menagerie tent. A kangaroo mother also stood in the nursery, with her babies safely tucked in her pouch during most of the day.[3] Though unidentified by name in either the press or circus records, the timid mother could have experienced the death of a baby the previous year, when the show reported that both a baby kangaroo and camel died on the same July day.[4]

Baby animals provided a financial windfall for circuses, and show management willingly offered enough care to keep up with appearances. Although the primary purpose of maintaining a nursery was reportedly to "keep up the stock," shows also clearly had a separate agenda by opening the nursey for public viewings. This was particularly true when the infants were in their "cute stage and . . . the darlings of all who witness their antics."[5] The appeal of baby animals transcended species divides. The circus nursery contained elephants, who would grow up to be considered genial; pumas and lions, who were particularly prized as cute babies because it would be a stark contrast to their often-provoked ferocious behavior on- and offstage; and primates, often billed simply as monkeys, who performed many of the physical and behavioral traits of newborn humans to the delight of crowds.[6]

Circus management advertised the circus as a space where people could be entertained by performers in their re-created natural environments. This was often presented as a pseudo-scientific endeavor, where circusgoers could take real glimpses into the lives of people and animals from around the world. Shows cemented this image with scientific plaques on the sides of cages or in front of the sideshow stage, experts with imagined academic credentials acting as keepers, and a plethora of press and circuspublished materials that documented their lives prior to the circus. In the case of people and animals from colonized places, images of family life often remained central to the narrative.[7]

But the circus world, particularly the parts that relied on captive lives and labor, presented a curated view of what family looked like among its

An adult elephant pushes a baby in a spectacle, 1955. Special Collections at Milner Library, Illinois State University, Normal. Image BSP3069. Used with permission.

animals. Circuses separated and reconstructed animal families for aesthetic purposes, without consideration for the animal cultures at stake. Extinction studies scholars have been particularly active in conversations about animal cultures. Thom Van Dooren's work on endlings, the last remaining members of a species, demonstrates that extinction occurs prior to the death of these last few. Instead, the larger culture and social ties of the animal die when its social group is gone. Marcus Baynes-Rock explores this phenomenon in his study of Australia's fauna, calling domestication a "great unmaking" of animal societies.[8] Matriarchal-formed animal groups, like elephant herds, likely experienced more difficult separation periods when infants were removed.[9] Some animal mothers, like large cats, often could not escape their predatory reputation and had their infants preemptively removed upon birth and then fostered by gentler animals or people. When circuses cited safety concerns with these larger animals, discussion often centered on the dangerous nature of the mother rather than her protective response.[10] Other infants, like giraffes, found themselves grouped in immediate family units for menagerie display rather than in the female-heavy herds that they would form naturally.[11]

The decision to displace animal mothers and reconstruct animal families into groups that seemed more familiar to the average circusgoer ultimately came down to entertainment. Infant animals had an intrinsic monetary value for the circus world, whether they were born into captivity or the wild. Stories of their capture centered on traumatic removal from familial ties; descriptions of their births in circus winter quarters emphasized the observed inability of the mother to properly care for the infant. Each of these scenarios centered the role of the circus as a better caretaker for the welfare of animals. Even when importation was cheaper and perhaps easier (prior to late twentieth-century importation regulations), circuses still chose to engage in breeding programs. Yet throughout this long-standing history of circus nurseries, the language around why and how to care for animals shifted with changes in larger conversations around colonization and motherhood.

The justifications for circus nurseries offered by the press, and by circuses themselves, provide a window into how the circus reflected larger society, particularly as it intersected with prevailing ideas of womanhood, motherhood, and family.[12] In the same moment that the circus dominated the American cultural landscape of the early twentieth century with a curated version of animal families on display, ideas of scientific motherhood and best practices for human mothers circulated in medical communities.[13] This discourse attempted to overturn community knowledge and stripped autonomy from poor women and women of color in disproportionate numbers.[14] The New Woman ideal, explored from the human perspective in the previous chapter, pushed forth a feminist discourse on labor. It ultimately centered circus women and provided the means for them to displace animal mothers with their caretaking.[15] The roots to this feminine care in the circus are also found in early conversations around the innate ability of women to act as gentle trainers. Circus nurseries demonstrate that animal display in the early twentieth century rested on more than just colonial narratives about maternal care and knowledge. It also included the trappings of a mothering discourse that sought to displace long-standing knowledge systems.

Circuses blurred the lines of science, entertainment, spectacle, and conservation. Within this history, circus nurseries played an integral role in demonstrating the centrality of colonialism and patriarchal power systems. Circuses sought out baby animals because they offered better attractions. In doing so, circuses created a long history of relying on animal mothers in various circumscribed roles. According to circus workers, when introduced to the circus world as an infant, an animal would be more likely to acclimate. This made infants a commodity throughout the entire history of the circus. But more than simply taking care of seemingly abandoned young animals, circus nurseries put colonial and patriarchal frameworks on public display.[16] From capture to caged performances to behind-the-scenes life, the circus emphasized the displacement of animal motherhood in favor of human counterparts. Circus workers took on motherly roles, offering bottle-feeding and other round-the-clock infant care and companionship.

The circus was inherently cosmopolitan and diverse, with dozens to hundreds of animal species and separate animal cultures traveling with each outfit. To account for this diversity, and the circus's fairly monolithic response to infant care, this chapter takes a sweeping definition of motherhood, examining it in biological, adoptive or foster, transspecies, and nonmaternal (or allomothering) forms. Even given the variety of mothering methods that marked the many animal cultures on the circus lot, circuses engaged in a displacement model that mirrored scientific mothering. Examining the central role of animal mothers throughout the circus's history, from wild capture to controlled breeding programs, demonstrates the emmeshed colonial and patriarchal systems that underscored the circus. It also shows the permeable boundaries of the circus world and the ways in which social and political movements deeply affected the business of animal entertainment.

Mothers, Infants, and the Business of Animal Trade

Despite a reputation for claiming to have the "biggest" of nearly everything, shows also found a distinct niche by advertising that they possessed the tiniest and youngest animals in the world. This made even untrained baby animals an immediate revenue source for circuses. As the Dailey Brothers Circus prepared to embark on its 1948 season, it targeted its promotional campaign on the new arrival of Baby "Butch," a six-month-old elephant who stood three feet high and weighed two hundred pounds. Butch arrived as part of a ten-elephant herd, destined to join the twenty-five-elephant herd already with the show.[17] Despite Butch's young age, his mother went unmentioned by the Dailey Brothers Circus. Today, scholars like G. A. Bradshaw classify elephants separated from their mother under the age of two as orphaned.[18] If left with his mother, Butch likely would have nursed for years and would have formed attachment bonds with several female members of the herd.[19] Instead, Butch ventured across the Atlantic with a steady diet of rum, which animal transporters often used to quell anxiety and sickness. Once he arrived in Boston, his diet transitioned to Eagle Brand milk and pablum, a common remedy for human infant malnutrition.[20]

Butch's story was not new or unique to the circus industry. Animal importation to the United States for entertainment purposes dated back to the Zoological Institute in the early nineteenth century. This company, run by a group of former farmers and horse breeders, engaged in importation and breeding programs to stock some of the earliest animal entertainment industries.[21] For Butch, the absence of his mother likely indicates that she was killed upon his capture: the execution of the mother to obtain an infant was the most widely used method of obtaining wild animals during the height of the animal trade business. Circuses openly advertised this form of capture as their primary means of obtaining animals for their shows. Hunters, often subcontracted through a procurement company like the one created by Carl Hagenbeck, would "reserve their ammunition to make war on the mothers" in order to "carry . . . [the infants] off to captivity"—as an 1881 Barnum & Bailey souvenir booklet proudly proclaimed on a page about the mighty tiger.[22]

The narrative from this souvenir booklet speaks to the true nature of animal capture even as it overtly courts the coveted straight-from-the-wild label. But it also plays into several other motherhood tropes that plagued animal husbandry practices in the circus. Mothers, like the tiger described in the booklet, operated with a fiercely protective instinct that could only be countered with a gun. The image associated with the detailed text shows two snarling tigers with blood-stained mouths and a pictured kill. The text and image displace the mother as a necessary figure in raising the infant tigers, rendering her useless if human foster mothers emerged as a viable option.[23]

Such capture narratives provided the reader with colonial and patriarchal justifications for capture. In the case of the mother "tigress," her own instinctual ineptness made the capture possible, as she reportedly sent "her young family into a pioneer band" while she fell behind to stalk the potential predator. According to the circus, this dire mistake provided easy cover for animal bounty hunters to abduct the infants away from the mother. Still focusing on intensely protective mothering, the circus also boasted of its lion population, which it had obtained by entering a sleeping den and slaughtering all but the cubs. These stories align with most other capture narratives, where graphic details of the mother's death go unreported. Instead, the circus generalized the dangerous physiology and hunting prowess of the formidable mother predators to position the animal bounty hunter as superior in his capability to swiftly capture the infants.[24]

Even animals displayed for their more humanlike characteristics still found themselves in similar capture narratives. Seals, sea lions, and walruses performed in the traveling aquarium exhibits that often accompanied the larger shows. Similar to sea shows in the present day, their feats would involve impressive displays of critical thinking and problem-solving. Yet descriptions of their capture mirrored that of their tiger and lion counterparts. Mother seals who watched their newborns with "jealous care" on the coast found themselves at odds with animal bounty hunters after circuses deemed it financially viable to display marine mammals.[25]

Circuses delved into a range of colonial and contradictory justifications about the animal trade industry. With an image of "the now celebrated tiger babies," photographed without their mothers, the Sells-Floto Circus positioned itself above its animal laborers on religious terms. The accompanying text claimed that "the Sells-Floto Circus is a monument to courage; the courage of men who go into jungles, into tropical heat, into freezing cold; who faces disease and death to bring out for your edification the wild creatures over which man is given dominion by God."[26] But even as circuses projected this image of God-given rights over nature in magazine spreads, they claimed—in more intimate reports about relationships between human and nonhuman circus workers—that some animals, like elephants, shared the same range of emotions as humans. They refused to extend these conclusions to hippopotamuses, who instead earned the reputation of "lazy."[27] But virtually none of the animal mothers, regardless of their supposedly observed character traits, were protected from displacement from their infants. Even the elephant, who seemed so humanlike in her behavior, still had her infant removed to achieve a better aesthetic during public performances. And the "lazy" mother hippo fought to the death for her infants in nearly every hippopotamus capture story.

Like other captive animals in the spectacle industry, circus animals constantly interacted with a variety of workers. Daily feedings, except for big cats on Sundays, brought menagerie assistants in close contact with the animals. While animals with more ferocious reputations spent much of their time caged, others, particularly hooved animals, could be seen on the lot simply tied to a stake. Other animals, like snakes, were routinely exhibited on the shoulders of a woman connected to the sideshow tent. In general, the big top show was a space where animals had slightly more freedom of movement.[28]

Circuses relied on a mesh of labor networks to procure animals for their shows. W. C. Coup, Barnum's longtime business partner, explained the usefulness of the networks, despite their high costs. Independent, circus-operated hunting trips to Africa were "tremendously expensive" and likely did not end with as many captive animals as more experienced hunters could pull in. Instead, the "very large profits demanded by the established animal houses" made the networks attractive to Coup, since they could "employ educated Germans who delighted in the adventure, and they saved us time, anxiety, and money."[29] These networks were reportedly quick and reliable, a necessity for circus proprietors, who forced animals into risky working conditions. When the highly flammable big top tent caught fire, or the high-speed train that carried the circus derailed, shows stood to lose their entire menagerie. But when this happened, wealthy proprietors, like James A. Bailey, could order "a whole menagerie in one day."[30] Like manual workers (whom management thought were replaceable by scabs) or sideshow workers (whose slots could easily be refilled), animals fell under broad categories rather than being cast as individual, known performers and thus could be easily replaced as needed. With the exception of "firsts" in captivity, or animals that were unequivocally unique, like the oversize Jumbo, circusgoers were more concerned with the novelty of seeing a species than with the experience of meeting a specific animal.

Larger outfits, like the Ringling Brothers Circus, also maintained a corporate presence around the world. Offices in London, Paris, Hamburg, and Johannesburg provided the shows with a watchful eye on the procurement process. Coup's acknowledgment of the German presence on hunting expeditions speaks to the reality of the business. Germany's colonial systems in Africa superimposed economic trade networks, including cornering the animal trade market.[31] But as with other colonial enterprises, the animal capture business relied heavily on local laborers, who acted as guides, hunters, and animal handlers. The Ruhe family boasted that it hired "whole native villages" to engage in this labor.[32]

Even without a global presence, smaller circus outfits engaged in the importation of infant animals by tapping into existing trade markets. While these smaller shows could not afford the animals provided by market leader Hagenbeck—who trained them at his facility in Hamburg before shipping them to the United States—they were still able to get newly imported infants fairly regularly, especially from importers who did not train, like the Ruhe family. The Yankee Robinson Circus reported a new baby rhinoceros in 1915, and the Cook and Wilson show announced in 1916 that "three baby lions arrived several weeks ago, and more are expected in the near future. It is intended to make a feature of baby animals, wild and domestic."[33]

The death of mothers and capture of infants had resounding effects for both humans and animals. Although largely unreported by animal traders, the removal of infants and matriarchs affected entire herds of elephants, which would have attended the birth and remained invested in the infant's upbringing.[34] For the now-captive infants, PTSD likely developed, due to the community-shattering trauma of their mother's death and their capture.[35] The death of mothers also fed into larger economic markets. While the babies made their way to European training markets and American circuses, the mothers' bodies still pulled in profits. Coup engaged in these exploits. He explained, "the beautiful skins of the leopards, lions, and other animals we kill, the tusks of the elephant, the feathers of the ostrich, and all other similar spoils, go to the native chiefs and sheiks."[36]

Financially, this institutional practice of capturing infant animals made sense to turn-of-the-century US entertainment industries. Capturing and transporting the infants without their intergenerational family members financially benefited proprietors. These animals made center-ring debuts after rigorous training under Hagenbeck in Germany.[37] Often employing American-bound trainers and holding American-bound animals in captivity, Hagenbeck cornered the industry by offering circuses animals who had undergone the highest levels of training, as explored from the human perspective with Eph Thompson in chapter 2. Hagenbeck's system of "gentling," combined with increasing pressure from a highly organized burgeoning animal rights movement, meant that kindness—or rather the perception of kindness in the ring—became integral to animal training in the early part of the twentieth century. This displaced the image of a lion corned in a cage and a trainer with a whip and chair in hand.[38] Hagenbeck's training revolution opened the door for women animal trainers, but it also brought conversations about the well-being of animals to the forefront in the circus world. This new conceptional framework around training that centered less overtly violent means also centered humans as competent caretakers and the most logical mother figures for infant animals.

Circuses capitalized on mothers who would never see captivity to keep a constant stream of center-ring performers. A generally accepted view among circus folks and other animal trainers at the turn of the nineteenth century was that only particular animals had the right temperament for stage work. While animals caught in the wild were intriguing for circusgoers, who viewed them from behind a barred cage, animal trainers often viewed these animals as untrainable if they had reached a certain age before captivity. Instead, baby animals became a training commodity. As one of Barnum's early business partners stated, "we like to capture elephants when they are about 1 year old. Younger ones are too tender, and older ones know too much." The seemingly right age to capture an infant animal varied by species. He went on to note that for some animals, like hippopotamuses, the separation between mother and baby needed to occur early. After describing the mother hippos, who "die hard," he plainly stated, "We cannot get these babies too young to suit. One, I remember, was captured the very day it was born, and the hunters and attendants brought it up on a bottle."[39] Within the circus world, shows offered tongue-in-cheek commentary about the limits of docility an animal could exhibit when it formed early attachments with humans rather than its own mother. A cartoon in a circus trade journal showed a lion and a ringmaster, who beckoned an apprehensive trainer to stick his head in the lion's mouth, saying that "he was raised on milk!"[40]

For those animals that had garnered a reputation for forming attachments to humans, circuses found significant value in displacing the mother from her young in the early stages of infancy. Wolves in the circus, for example, found themselves in shows as pups, so that they would be more likely to display domesticated, doglike behavior toward their human caretakers. But circuses also acknowledged that not all young animals could ever be effectively trained and tamed away from their cultural behavior. Ostriches, which served as a novelty in the menageries, could reportedly be "rendered docile for a time" when captured at a young age, but would eventually resume their "natural, repulsive, belligerent disposition" with age.[41]

Circuses also operated within internal US trade networks. With more than a hundred outfits traversing the country at the height of the circus industry, quick start-ups and closures became a defining feature of tented shows. This led to regular auctions and sales that included not just wagons, tents, and hardware but also whole menageries of animals or individual animals. These quickly assembled auctions often saw representatives from Ringling, Barnum, and Forepaugh shows. Occasionally, entire shows with full menageries would trade hands at auction.[42]

The Development of Circus Breeding Programs

Even with these networks making animal trade easier and cheaper, circuses still engaged in a whole host of breeding programs. Early breeding programs themselves often became a commodity as shows bragged about their ability to not only successfully breed, but also keep alive infant animals. The programs had limited success in terms of viable baby animals, but significant success in terms of monetary value. The Coop & Lent Circus, a smaller show with a size less than one-fifth of the larger outfits that traveled, worked with mostly leased animals and equipment. Yet it still engaged in breeding efforts. It successfully bred monkeys but had less success with lions. In 1917, three of seven infant lions died. The show vowed to continue its breeding efforts.[43]

The advertisements broadcasting the success of these programs helped make them financially viable. After a baby was born, circuses immediately engaged in a marketing campaign by either allowing the public to choose the name in a contest or naming the infant after the city in which it was born.[44] Circus workers also capitalized on the public excitement of new babies. As alluded to in the first chapter, when a giraffe was born during the

1912 season, circus women who had organized their own suffrage campaign aptly named the baby Suffrage.[45] Capitalizing on the circus's headquarters, the Barnum show announced the birth of an elephant, Baby Bridgeport, just prior to the opening of its 1882 season. In the announcement, it provided intimate details to circus readers. Baby Bridgeport was only the second elephant born in the United States, despite the dozens of elephants that were touring in circuses that same year. The baby reportedly nursed from her mother every few minutes.[46] Barnum acknowledged and even capitalized on the difficulty of these early breeding programs, particularly among giraffes. Even prior to exhibiting successfully bred infants, the Barnum & Bailey show advertised giraffe families. An 1882 lithograph from the Barnum & Bailey show headlined "10 beautiful giraffes. From the 22-foot giant giraffe to the nursing baby." The picture invoked the same imagery, showing two infant giraffes, one nursing, with their respective mothers. The circus also advertised the herd in "native groups" on display in the circus lot.[47] Despite the limited success of attempts to breed giraffes and elephants, circus breeding programs also created surpluses of particular animals, some of whom could not labor under the big top. In 1910, the Barnum & Bailey show offered "no end of baby monkeys" in its nursery, along with the rarer tiger and lion kittens.[48]

To lure potential customers, circuses engaged in an array of false advertising, promising everything from mermaids to unicorns. The Al G. Barnes Circus claimed to have crossbred a zebra and a Shetland pony, though it really had an okapi on display. But breeding programs mostly propagated already existing species, rather than offering up hybrid species; circuses tended to see hybrid animals as "of little worth other than a curiosity specimen."[49] This sentiment likely centered on reproductive value, given that hybrid births came with sterility. When hybrid animals were wanted, circuses were more likely to simply purchase the animals. Ringling Brothers, for example, made an exorbitant offer for a lion-leopard on its animal roster rather than engage in a novelty cross-species breeding program.[50]

The history of large-scale importation and attempts at the domestic breeding of species overlapped by decades. Barnum's novelty programs were overshadowed by Ringling Brothers when it committed to an extensive breeding facility, first in Chicago and then in the Florida Keys. Neither of these facilities came to fruition, but its plans for operation still indicates the massive investment that circuses willingly made to have mothers and babies in breeding programs. In the initial justification for the program, Ringling management claimed that "by opening the breeding program we will save thousands of dollars, and not run the risk of bringing wild animals across the ocean."[51] Charles Ringling went on to say that "we are not in this business from motives of philanthropy. . . . It is a novel thing, I know . . . [but] there is a constant demand for wild animals at good prices, and it is much cheaper and easier to raise them in Florida" than to purchase and ship them from overseas.[52]

Even though the Ringling breeding farm did not materialize, and it would be decades before the circus moved its headquarters to Florida, other circus proprietors did successfully engage in similar programs. The Ruhe family created a lucrative trading business that headquartered its imported animals in Long Island.[53] By 1910, Billy Hall had established a successful Missouri-based breeding and leasing program after one year of operating his own traveling show. Like the founders of the Zoological Institute nearly a century earlier, Hall banked on his previous experience as a horse trader. Hall navigated lawsuits as he notoriously underbid and oversold, eventually earning a reputation for having "an interest in about every circus in the United States." Visitors to the facility described the close quarters that animals lived in, as well as the swaying of elephants.[54] Although circus folks chalked this up to a fairly common elephant behavior in the early twentieth century, it likely signaled deep-seated anxiety, as explored in Susan Nance's historical study of elephants in captive spaces.[55] Hall's operation created even more displacement between kin and familial ties, and signaled just how disorienting the animal trade business could be for young animals. Importation was still a financially viable way to get animals, and Hall boasted about his quick turnarounds, with dozens of elephants imported to his farm and then exported to US circuses within a week.[56]

Even as colonization in Africa maintained animal trade markets, importation took a nosedive following World War I. Hagenbeck's heavy-handed investment, particularly in German colonies, created a crisis for the industry as Germany lost access to its exploits through colonization and the Hamburg-based zoo temporarily closed.[57] This led to more attempts to create a domestic infant circus animal market. Citing doubled or tripled prices for imported animals in 1919, the John Robinson Circus announced plans for a new breeding program in California.[58]

No matter what continent a circus animal was born on, shows invested in marketing their collection of infant animals. But having the mother on the circus lot presented new complications. Often, even when mothers stayed with the babies between performances, circuses still pulled the infants onto the lot to interact with circusgoers. This led one onlooker to note, "Three lion cubs, only a month old, were taken from the mother's cage. It could not have been healthy for any of the party to have gotten within reach of the infuriated mother about this time. The newspaper men, after being assured that the cubs could not hurt them, fondled them for a time. Three months

Three lion cubs in a cage, with their birth date indicated on a sign, 1952. Robert L. Parkinson Library and Research Center, Circus World, Baraboo, Wisconsin. Image CWi 3114.

later they would not dare go within reach of them."[59] The mother lion served a larger purpose by birthing the babies, but she also obstructed the show's desire to turn the babies into immediate performers. The three-month time frame demonstrates the fairly small window that animals were cute enough to draw crowds. For its street parades, Ringling Brothers invested in "a score of dainty cages, carrying the baby animals of the menagerie."[60] Placing baby animals in the free parade was a lucrative form of advertising for the nursery. Sello Brothers likewise offered up its two baby lions in the circus parade, showing them in a small cage pulled by a team of horses.[61]

Although baby animals were a draw, this did not necessarily mean that mothers were part of those circus nursery optics. Circuses felt no qualms about admitting that mothers were not adequately taking care of their young. Larger shows, like Barnum & Bailey, traveled with elephant herds that was composed of nearly fifty individuals, including bull elephants. In the case of a new elephant birth, they removed the infant for cited safety concerns. In 1909, the Barnum show saw the birth of a baby elephant and immediately removed him from his mother, claiming that "although the elephant is of the most affectionate of wild animals, long experience has shown that a baby elephant breeds trouble in herds." The show kept the baby in a cage and fed him a diet of bananas, rice, and milk in between menagerie performances. In the case of the three-week-old lions that remained caged in the same nursery, the circus did not feel compelled to provide a justification for taking the infants away from the predatory mother.[62] Giraffes, in contrast, were allowed to stay with the mother for a time. These animals, although a longtime staple of circuses, did not undergo rigorous training for performances. Instead, their value to the shows was in their ability to remain docile when displayed. Training, in that case, involved allowing the infant to stay with the mother but leading the infant on a rope from birth.[63]

Even though circuses regularly removed mothers from their infants for nursery display or training purposes, their advertisement of newborn babies nearly always reflected the first few moments of the infant's birth. This centered the mother's role, not as a caretaker, but as a birth mother. The Cole Brothers Circus offered up images of several of its mother-baby pairs, including camels, elephants, and tigers. Rather than showing the safety concerns that circuses cited, the images reflected the types of relationships that circusgoers would have expected among noncaptive animals, with the infants playfully climbing on the mother's back, suckling milk, or standing under the mother's watchful eye.[64]

But following the birth, circuses positioned themselves as the ultimate caretakers, who had the knowledge to remove animal infants from danger, whether that was the wild or a seemingly inept mother. Circuses alternated between referring to animals as "inmates" and saying that they were "enjoying freedoms of captivity." Colonial justifications for capture and breeding programs favored the freedom narrative as a way to explain the exploitative trade market, claiming that "these babies will enjoy throughout their lives freedom from jungle fear; freedom from devastated feeding grounds; freedom from ticks and disease and native hunters."[65] Once again, the circus did not hesitate to adopt colonial language and justifications for capture as it positioned the tented shows as Western liberators of colonized spaces.

Because infant animals spent their young lives riding the rails with the circus for the purpose of entertaining the public, human interaction and intervention became inevitable. Mothers usually birthed infants during the last few weeks that shows were at their winter quarters or early in the season. This meant that within the first few days of an infant's life, it would be spending each day on the circus lot and each night on a train. The Ringling Brothers Circus took a four-day-old camel on the road, using two roustabouts to guide the baby on and off the train car, to the delight of the press.[66]

The New Woman and Circus Infants

To understand differences in mothering and infant rearing among captive animals, their lives and relationships should be put against the baseline of life outside of cages and stages. Chimpanzees, for example, have a long history in captivity and have also been observed in the wild. Jane Goodall's extensive studies of chimpanzees have included several examples of

Martha Hunter holds a baby gorilla as a young fan stands nearby, 1951. Special Collections at Milner Library, Illinois State University, Normal. Image BNP7656v1. Used with permission.

mother-infant pair behaviors. She has documented grief from the sudden end of a mother-infant relationship, breastfeeding behaviors that lasted years, allomothering of orphaned infants, shifting social statuses for new mothers, and lifelong unsevered relationships between mothers and female infants.[67] The historical treatment of chimpanzees in the entertainment world stands in stark contrast to that of their uncaged counterparts. Chimpanzees, perhaps resembling humans the most, nearly always landed in circuses as infants, with human caretakers. Shows boasted of behind-the-scenes human caretakers who were foster mothers and grandmother figures. They cured upset stomachs, set early bedtimes, and provided orange juice as a treat for infant chimps. Supposedly, too, affection went both ways, with the infants crying when removed from their female human caretaker.[68]

When infants were taken from the birth mother, circusgoers were assured that these foster situations provided the best experience for the baby. Humans often took on this role of fostering, using nutrition created for human babies. As a product of captivity, interspecies mothering—and not just by humans—became a common technique to keep infants alive in the circus. Although interspecies mothering also occurs outside of human intervention, the circus capitalized on mother-baby pairs that would be the most alluring for the public, usually offering up the circus dog to nurse newborn cubs.[69]

Circuses portrayed baby animals as well suited for human companionship, particularly women. The circus did not always cite the reason for removing infants from their mother, but instead bombarded the public with sought-after images of fostering behind the scenes. Women in the shows often served as the foster mothers for these infants. Some, like aerialist Harriet Beatty, were so swayed by their early attachments to infant animals that they changed careers, moving into animal departments.[70] But more often, women in other departments performed a second shift by fostering infant animals from the day they were born. Aerialist Dorothy Johnson acted as "best friend" to a newly born tiger cub in the Hagenbeck-Wallace Circus in 1934.[71]

Women like Beatty and Johnson performed the paid labor of their big top performance and the unpaid work taking care of baby animals. Other circus women did this while also caring for their own families, including children, who traveled with them during the season. For circus fans, this aesthetic was expected and entertaining. As explored in the previous chapter, it was ascribed to the late nineteenth-century ideal of the New Woman in the workforce. Circus fans consumed nearly as much news about the backyard of the lot, with circus women doing dishes and laundry, as they did the ticketed performances.[72]

Mabel Stark sits in the backyard with a young boy, bottle-feeding a tiger cub, circa 1926. Robert L. Parkinson Library and Research Center, Circus World, Baraboo, Wisconsin. Image CWi 10722.

The fascination with mothers on the circus lot, under the auspices of the New Woman ideal, provided women with an avenue to perform physical and emotional labor in ways that the general public related to and encouraged. Citing oft-quoted remarks about circus women while delivering a social club speech in Chicago, Al Priddy said that "circus women are among the finest in the world. The equestrienne is often a mother who has just kissed her baby good night in the dressing tent to go on for her act. They are among the finest needle women, making most of their own costumes during their spare time; and that these are done in exquisite taste, none knows better than the woman who patronizes the circus. The girl who nimbly scales a swinging ladder or climbs with easy grace to the highest swinging trapeze is often more skilled with the needle than many of her sisters who are watching her."[73] These ideal traits also became associated with how women nurtured animals. As one showman claimed, "women are more patient, and it is quite a mistaken idea to suppose that rough methods are necessary in training animals. . . . I think it is the mother instinct in women which enables them to command the obedience of animals."[74]

Circuses often tried to position themselves as sound animal caretakers, with knowledge about animal husbandry. In the case of the circus nursery, this did not always mean that mothers were simply displaced. John Meyers, the menagerie superintendent with Patterson's Trained Wild Animal Circus, noted that animal mothers in his circus behaved in ways that put their infant's life at risk, but that these behavioral abnormalities were directly tied to life in captivity. He reportedly attempted to remedy this not by removing the baby, but instead by using cardboard boxes to offer more privacy for the mother.[75] Although Meyers's sound solution targeted the root problem of motherhood in captivity, it was not practical for the capitalist nature of show business. Crowds sought baby animals in full, unobstructed view. More often, circuses dealt with the fallout of heavy interaction with infants. As the Barnum show noted during one of its seasons, "A female wolf and two young ones, born only last Friday, were also shown to reporters. There were three in the litter, but one the mother killed. The cage will be kept closed until the young are old enough to be fed, when they will be removed."[76]

Animal Mothers in the Decline of Tented Shows

Even as new entertainments emerged, the same narrative around animal motherhood remained. Animal collector Frank Buck, who pulled the highest salary from the Ringling show in the late 1930s, drew a wider audience into capture narratives through a foray into film, the 1932 *Bring 'Em Back Alive*. The advertisement for the film urged viewers to watch Buck "capture a baby elephant with bare hands! HEAR the infuriated tuskers trumpeting for their lost child!" The inclusion of these real images and sounds of mother displacement and animal capture speaks to the how these narratives brought in viewers and capital for the shows. The other advertised images in the film included fights to the death between big cats and footage of a "man eating cat entering a village."[77] Death and displacement underscored the entire film, which was set as behind-the-scenes footage for the public's favorite animal entertainments. The sight and sound of baby animals displaced from familial bonds were thus a widely consumed amusement not just on entertainment stages, but also in documentary film footage.

As the decades wore on, even with potentially better health-care systems for animal mothers and decades of knowledge that allowed spaces of captivity to keep animals alive longer, entertainment practices still created situations that inevitably required a constant influx of infants. A temporary absence of big cats under the big top in the 1920s (a response to public distaste and an emerging animal rights movement) preceded a new era of animal acts that once again projected dominion over animals. In the 1930s, Clyde Beatty, a former Ringling trainer (and husband to Harriet), started his own shows, featuring mixed cat acts. These novel acts were "tremendously dangerous considering that lions hate tigers, and tigers despise lions, and neither have much love for human beings." The nature of these acts made this statement obvious to circusgoers, who witnessed a new aesthetic that included Beatty with a pistol holstered to his hip and a chair and whip in hand. Both on- and offstage, the juxtaposition of tigers and lions in a single act remained dangerous. In his first ten years, eighteen tigers and lions died in what Beatty deemed expected fights between the two species. But, as Beatty noted, this is what the public wanted.[78]

With circus animals performing in death-defying situations, the need for more trainable animals remained high. The animal entertainment world still relied on infants to fill this role. But shifts in institutional guidelines surrounding animal capture, which inherently required the displacement of mothers, had begun in piecemeal policies across the entertainment industry. The Bronx Zoo took an early exit from the business in 1928, citing the increasingly taboo nature of the widespread practice. Manager William Blair of the New York Zoological Society, which ran the Bronx Zoo, exposed the well-known practice, admitting that all new gorilla arrivals to the zoo would have to be stripped from their family units in the wild, and that these families would need to be killed to get the infant. He went on to note that "the highest type of family devotion is to be found among the gorillas, and the mother and father and others in a tribe will put up a terrific battle before they let one of the little ones be taken."[79]

Although this policy shift acknowledged the inherent physical and emotional violence in securing infant primates, the same logic was not extended to other animals, particularly mothers who had garnered a reputation for killing their young to prevent human interaction. With decades of experience in breeding programs and animal nurseries behind them by the 1940s, circuses preemptively displaced mothers in service to the narrative that they were conservators of the species. In the first few weeks of the 1947 season, Ringling veterinarian J. Y. Henderson gladly detailed the plans for the circus's newborn leopards and jaguars.

> First, the leopards and jaguars had to be rescued from their respective mothers who, in captivity, eat their young. Next a substitute nursing mother had to be found. Susie, a beautiful white cat had given birth to four kittens about the time that two leopards were entering the world. But, then two baby jaguars were born prematurely and Susie became overworked, so "Spots," the mongrel mascot of the prop department who had just given birth to a litter, was recruited and now the faithful cur who thinks nothing of having a litter in the woodpile without benefit of sterility is being de-flead [*sic*] and cleaned to enter the sterile nursery. The last pair, born in New York, died soon after birth. These cubs are getting a break by being born in Florida where it is warm.[80]

Henderson's words reveal the shifts and continuities in the history of animal motherhood and circus nursery programs from the 1880s through the demise of the railroad shows in the 1950s. Throughout this long history, circuses displaced birth mothers in favor of caretaking practices they deemed better, healthier, or more profitable. This all came at the expense of the mother. As with other parts of the circus world, capitalism lurked over even small decisions in the breeding programs. The danger that mother leopards and jaguars posed to their own young was a direct product of captivity. Despite early wisdom that spaces of captivity could be altered, circuses still engaged in immediate removal to secure the infant for performance use. Fostering, whether by a human or nonhuman animal, placed an extra burden that remained unacknowledged by the shows. In the case of Susie and Spots, fostering meant giving up care for their own infants, thereby continuing a cycle of displacement for the good of more valued animals. The relatively undetailed reports of the infant deaths speak to the capitalist nature of the show. With thousands of human and animal workers laboring under grueling conditions in inherently dangerous jobs each day, death became a reality of circus life, particularly for vulnerable mother and infant animals. The death of the New York infants also points to the larger issues of maintaining breeding programs in mobile menageries. The Florida cubs might have had a few days of adjustment before joining the transient workforce, but the New York cubs were birthed on the road, demonstrating that pregnancy did not keep mother animals from taking their place in the menagerie tent for the performance.

• • •

Circus menageries, which held upward of one thousand animals each, dominated the entertainment industry and public imagination in the early twentieth century. The large animal workforce, which was treated as disposable and replaceable, meant that shows valued infant animals above all else. They required less training time and served multiple performance roles. This material value of baby animals led to an intrinsic valuing of mother animals and forced circuses to import and breed to keep their numbers up. But to have viable populations of baby animals, circuses removed mothers and acted as conservators and protectors. This flattened the complexity of motherhood on the circus lot into something that resembled scientific motherhood. This history of removing infants from birth mothers and creating viable reproductive populations set the stage for the caretaker narrative of zoos, which would begin to operate under much stricter and more standardized policies. Like the circuses that came before, zoos now boast of institutional caretaking of a species and motherly nurturing of individual infants. But mother and infant animals, both then and now, acted as more than simply part of an institutional plan to boost populations. Their experiences shed light on some of the most captive workers in the circus world.

5

Captive, Coerced, and Frontline Sideshow Workers

While circusgoers might see most women and animals in a variety of spaces on the circus lot, they expected sideshow workers to have less physical freedom. Their place on the lot was under a smaller tent that had a barker by the entrance convincing people to step inside. Sideshow workers were contracted because something made them innately different—whether that difference was an extraordinary talent, a well-thought-out con, or a physical difference that marked them as unique from most of the circusgoers who paid to see them. The categorical identities that existed among circus workers—children, animals, women, men, working-class people, and high-paid performers—existed in the sideshow as well. Yet the terms of their work usually varied greatly from those of their center-ring counterparts. They performed exhaustive schedules onstage, found themselves at the center of press attention, and could never escape the physical characteristics that made them sideshow workers. And yet, as with animal acts, sideshow workers came up against larger business shifts in the circus world that left them a dispensable part of the shows.

The thread of young workers (human and animal) at the circus is also interwoven into sideshows. Sideshows were often the spaces that housed the largest number of Black workers, including those in minstrel bands or on stages under the tent, as well as a significant number of children. George and Willie Muse, for example, entered the cultural imagination before either brother turned ten years old. The young boys had spent their lives sharecropping near Roanoke, Virginia. Neighbors and other community members knew of George and Willie as the boys who had albinism and a fiercely protective mother. This common knowledge proved dangerous as a sideshow manager came to town in 1899 to procure laborers to work as "freaks." Although the details of their abduction remain speculative, their disappearance from the small southern town loomed large in local histories.[1]

Their careers in the tented shows began immediately. Circusgoers came to know them as Eko and Iko, though they were billed under several different personas. In 1923, audiences were delighted by the "two wild and uncivilized men from the jungles."[2] Throughout their decades onstage, the public read about the "fungus-haired," "lion-headed," and "flaxen-haired" "white savages" who hailed from Zanzibar, Ecuador, or Mars. In the absence of a concrete description, newspapers referred to the brothers as "those strange people."[3] The brothers became most readily identified as Men from Mars, a distinction given by the Ringling Brothers Circus in 1932.

Although the 1932 season proudly advertised the Men from Mars as star sideshow attractions, the press created other categorizations and labels. *Time* magazine gave the opening stand a rave review and was especially impressed with the "subhuman animals," including Clicko the Bushman, the Ubangi women, the fat lady, and the Muse brothers.[4] Newspaper op-eds, entertainment recaps, and other articles in major publications casually spoke of sideshow performers as akin to the animals in the menagerie.[5] As Linda Frost and Benjamin Reiss have explored, the biographies that accompanied sideshow workers exacerbated public perceptions and further prompted readers to think that there was something inherently different about these workers.[6]

People also were drawn to the Muse brothers because of their albinism. Circus proprietors and audiences had a long history of fetishizing Black albinism. Billed in Barnum's American Museum in New York City as "white Negros," these early performers remained nameless and found themselves displayed next to family members who did not display the genetic trait. Along with the expected backstory of hunt and capture that accompanied circus animals, these early sideshow performances included ascribed histories and identities. For Barnum's early albino performers, their white skin and "decidedly Ethiopian" features were accentuated through the image and story of family members that were "distinctly African" in color.[7]

The falsified biographies of the Muse brothers were part of a larger practice in the circus. Workers in all circus sectors performed tropes. Manual laborers played the role of contented workers who preferred the lure of behind-the-scenes show business to paychecks; animals, who really did hail from the wild, often stood in front of name plaques that contained fictitious stories of capture; big top performers often pretended to be part of family units and circus dynasties; and sideshow performers stood onstage as something unnatural. The public draw to sideshow workers such as the Muse brothers, who obviously could not really be from Mars, was the seemingly magical lure of the sideshow. Circus proprietors openly advertised humbug—skillful deceptions—and circusgoers clamored to witness it. James W. Cook and Benjamin Reiss have explored these crafted cons and the lived experiences of those acting in the staged roles.[8] In the Wild West shows that traveled among and with circuses, a similar "artful deception" was at work, showing audiences a white-idealized version of the American West. Yet Louis S. Warren and Jacob Dorman have each set aside the binary question of whether a performer was authentic and instead explored the artistic expression of creating new and evolving identities. In this sort of work, the idea of a circus world becomes undeniably a space created by workers themselves as they offer up a version of the identities demanded by management.[9]

Most circus workers retained some control over their careers. Many workers negotiated contracts, held sway as celebrities, and had the power of mobility between circuses and across entertainment venues. The larger history of worker autonomy in the shows is part of what makes the experiences of the animal trainers and death-defying center-ring stars of chapters 2 and 7 so markedly different. But an inability to completely control public image defined life in the sideshow. For these workers, their celebrity status depended on their ability to perform degrading personas. Sideshow workers fought to gain control in alternative ways, although their autonomy as workers often looked different than others' and came up against deeply set stereotypes.

The circus had lots to offer audiences. They could catch glimpses of animals and people who were billed as foreign, and therefore exotic. They could see daring feats of strength and athleticism. And they could view child labor and coerced labor onstage. Child performers, like George and Willie, were especially vulnerable to unfair labor practices. This remained particularly true for young workers who came into the business without guardians. They joined the ranks of other child sideshow performers such as Charles Sherwood Stratton, who performed as General Tom Thumb; and Millie and Christine McKoy, the conjoined twins who performed under the single name Millie-Christine. While children performing under the big top or simply traveling with family had more protective management oversight, children in the sideshow were often contracted as workers more akin to adults.

The Muse brothers' battle over their careers played out in the courts in 1927, when they sued Ringling Brothers for decades of unpaid labor as Men from Mars and caged cannibals. By the 1940s, the Muses' lawsuit had filtered into their public personas. Newspapers reported on the "Ambassadors from Mars" with the caveat that they "were actually Albino Negros who had been stolen from their Negro Mammy when they were infants."[10] The way that the show capitalized on the lawsuit is indicative of the ways that the public expected the sideshow to contain exploited workers.

Their lifelong careers in entertainment, even after a legal settlement that resulted in decades of recouped wages, signal their roles beyond exploited people. Sideshow workers constructed careers, families, and identities through their work in circuses. During the circus's height, conversations about and by sideshow workers created a complicated narrative that reimagined them as both workers and performers.

The Muse brothers demonstrate the lack of autonomy that sideshow workers had over their image and bodies, yet the very real power they held as workers. Willie, George, and thousands of other sideshow workers fought for better working conditions, pay, and control. These workers were disproportionately exploited, relative to the rest of the circus workforce. This exploitation exemplifies the intersection of emotional, physical, and performance labor in the tented shows. The activism of sideshow workers reflected their demographics. They entered the sideshow at various ages, from different classes, and from various parts of the world. Put simply, workers had different lived experiences and different ideas of fair labor. And more than any other circus workers, sideshow performers stood on the front line and interacted with curious audiences.

The Circus Midway

The hours between big top performances belonged to the sideshow. As one newspaper claimed, "a circus without a midway is like an omelet without eggs."[11] Convincing "talkers" stood outside the sideshow tent and lured patrons in with promises of experiences they would not have under the big top. Talkers were good salesmen, but they were also culturally astute, often speaking several languages. Sneak peaks, called ballyhoos, were usually performed by "self-made freaks," like sword swallowers, who stood alongside the talker and gave customers incentive to spend just a few cents to see the sideshow.[12] If the talker's quickly spoken pitch did not convince curious audiences, then illustrated banners that made the sideshow performers appear larger than life often did the trick.[13]

To add to the festivities, a minstrel band played tunes outside the tent before the show. Unlike the big top band, which often played military classics and was lily white, minstrel bands outside the sideshow tents were made up of Black musicians. New England Conservatory of Music graduate P. G. Lowery, the most renowned circus minstrel band leader, played for decades in the shows, including more than ten years with the Ringling

Sideshow workers, the band, and a bear pose in front of a stage at the Welsh Brothers Circus, undated. Robert L. Parkinson Library and Research Center, Circus World, Baraboo, Wisconsin. Image CWi 1863.

Brothers show.[14] Sideshow bands offered a space where Black workers could experience moments of joy and perhaps leisure, even in their work. The sideshow bands were popular among all circusgoers, but especially African Americans, who gathered to hear the musicians.[15]

While the controlled audience environment of the big top maintained highly segregated spaces, the midway offered a space that was radically integrated by nineteenth- and twentieth-century Jim Crow standards. Historians Stuart Thayer and Gregory J. Renoff have contextualized this segregation around the big top audience space known as the pit, a standing-room-only section that was the only space available to Black circusgoers in some cases. As Renoff goes on to discuss, the midway couldn't operate under that level of control within a crowded lot. Even beyond the open-air midway, circusgoers rushed into sideshow and menagerie tents that lacked enforced segregation policies.[16]

Once inside the sideshow tent, circus patrons saw a version of what was advertised on the banners. Circuses regularly exhibited the same staple performers. Dog-faced boys, frog boys, half women, armless wonders, human pin cushions, and geeks often stood in for the true identities of people with undiagnosed medical conditions or unique physical abilities. The canvas tent, which was significantly smaller than its big top counterpart, usually had a strong musty odor and leaked anytime it rained. Performers stood on a stage a few feet above audience members. Although sideshows varied in size, the ten-in-one became the most recognizable format, where ten sideshow workers would perform, with an additional talker alongside providing introductions, until the final "blow-off," which cost patrons extra money to attend.[17] A photograph from the Barnum & Bailey European tour in 1899 shows a typical sideshow stage. It's lifted from the ground with signs in front of each performer, who is either seated or standing. A small ladder is perched against the stage, and audience members have fairly clear access to the performers, standing merely feet away.[18]

Freakshow formats became standardized in circuses. Even prior to this, sideshow performers had stepped into a profession that had been blossoming for decades in museums and other traveling shows. P. T. Barnum's early sideshow in the American Museum pressed a variety of workers into performance. Little people, missing links, bearded ladies, and other stereotyped workers were billed as "curiosities" and would continue to abound in sideshow performances through the mid-twentieth century.[19] These workers entertained audiences in several ways. They performed tasks that seemed impossible, such as armless men using their feet as hands. But they also gave personal accounts of their lives and interacted with audience members by answering questions and engaging in conversations.[20]

Life as a Captured and Contracted Performer

The European grab for Africa captured land, resources, and cultural imaginations. Sideshow exhibitors readily took advantage of the public interest in people from colonized places and began exporting them to sideshows around the world. Rather than acquire talent based on physical uniqueness, sideshows presented colonized people performing as an imagined identity of themselves. Barnum and other North American showmen understood that American audiences had an interest in seeing these performances, even if African colonization was a European endeavor.[21]

The appeal of sideshows and their long history extended far beyond US borders. American culture was exported throughout the world by the turn of the twentieth century. Entire circuses, individual performers, and state-sponsored artists frequented stages around the world.[22] Yet the display of humans as oddities was hardly an American phenomenon. Human zoos had dotted the European landscape, particularly in Germany and Paris, since the 1870s. A similar cast of performers stood in front of European audiences on stages and in reconstructed habitats.[23]

Like other global entertainers, individual sideshow performers entered a business that required constant travel. Workers who hailed from places outside of Europe and the United States performed exclusively in foreign countries. Despite this seemingly identical work environment of onstage labor, their working conditions differed from those of performers in other circuits. An entire business of procuring people emerged, particularly in Carl Hagenbeck's empire. Nubian exhibits were just one of many human displays across the globe. Hagenbeck, Barnum, and other human exhibitors saw financial value in contracting groups of people and offering something that white audiences would believe to be authentically tribal.[24] Behind-the-scenes deals and networks of so-called talent managers made the sideshow trade nearly seamless. An American-owned bar in London infamously attracted traders and procurers who did business dealings over British brandy and water.[25]

Along with his zoo and animal trading business, Hagenbeck made substantial profits and fame through his displays of people. His displays of "indigenous people," beginning with a group of Lapland families, piqued interest among European tourists. Hagenbeck, like his American circus counterparts, emphasized the cultural and scientific value of these displays, and deemphasized their exploitative nature. As Nigel Rothfels has discussed, this European display of people ultimately declined when the actors refused to act and instead openly engaged in Western behavior and dress.[26]

While spectacles such as "Cameroon shows" made their way across Europe, Barnum was also capitalizing on white interest in African performances with his Zulu performers. These sorts of African shows often presented offensively stereotypical performances of savagery. Shows in Europe required Eskimo performers to paddle canoes, Middle Eastern performers to be atop camels, and Native Americans to ride horses.[27] Barnum followed much the same model with the Zulu performers. Zulus found themselves performing on sideshow stages around the world to meet the demand of eager audiences. William Hunt began displaying Zulu women in London just a few months after the 1879 Battle of Isandlwana brought international attention to the Zulu nation. Hunt later teamed up with Barnum to bring the performance to an American audience. Dingando, Possoman, Maguibi, and Ousan crossed the Atlantic in the late nineteenth century and began their careers as the first Zulu performers in the United States.[28]

People expected and demanded savagery from the Zulu performers. Like with other circus workers, their performance extended well beyond the few hours per day they spent in front of paying customers. During a circus parade in 1892, a young boy claimed to have been bitten by a Zulu performer, who later reported to a judge under the name John T. Lucas. According to reports, Lucas, who was "nearly nude with his face painted to represent a bloodthirsty cannibal," attacked the child after enduring a horde of boys who cast jeers, fruits, and vegetables.[29]

The near riot was reported in several newspapers, as was Lucas's decision to break character and speak English when he was arraigned and charged with mayhem. Lucas reportedly attempted to stay in his Zulu persona in the first few moments of his arrest, but he "finally talked freely" to explain how the circusgoers had provoked him. In light of his revealed identity, papers began attaching other descriptors to Lucas that signaled to readers that although he was Black, he was not Zulu or even foreign. Still, his performance of savagery remained part of his intrinsic identity for audiences. Newspapers claimed that his response to the hecklers left him rightfully charged with practicing his "cannibalistic propensities."[30]

The decision to employ Lucas, a fraud by popular standards, was part of a larger trend in circuses following the sharp rise of Zulu popularity in the United States and Europe. Anthropologists, ethnographers, and the general public became fascinated with the people who had defeated the British during the Battle of Isandlwana. The Zulu identity became a popular performance, and individual Black men began taking employment with various sideshows as Zulus.[31] In addition to Lucas, other Zulu imposters found employment at circuses and performed similar cannibalistic personas in cages.[32]

The cannibal persona resonated with audiences, which sought firsthand experiences of colonized people around the world. Circus proprietors capitalized on their popularity and began employing a variety of workers who supposedly hailed from colonized places. Like animals in the menagerie, these workers performed under headlines that emphasized stories of capture and generalized identities. Images of cannibalism and savagery abounded in these performances. The Wild Man from Borneo displayed animalistic traits with surgically implanted horns and sharpened teeth. In actuality, Calvin Bird was a Georgia native. This began circulating in newspapers only after he slipped away from the show midseason.[33] Barnum's success with his Zulu performers offers just a small window into this business. He also hired workers from Fiji to perform as cannibals who supposedly had been taken as war captives, held ransom by the local king, and graciously rescued by Barnum for a mere $15,000. Their coming-to-America story, as told by Barnum in the program that was sold at the shows, exalted the circus as a benevolent protector that had rescued the men from certain death.[34]

While the Fiji workers provided the racialized performance that audiences sought, their travel mate, a supposedly reformed cannibal woman from Fiji, reinforced gender roles and ideas of white benevolence. She also performed for audiences, but rather than gnawing on bones, she read from a Bible in her native language. Her part in the performance reminded viewers of their assumed responsibility to civilize and Christianize. More importantly, it assured viewers that this sort of cultural imperialism could be a cure for cannibalism. But in meeting the expectations of viewers that colonized people were inherently different, shows continued to fabricate moments when they reverted to savagery. After the death of a Fiji performer, Barnum's circus related that the remaining Fiji performers cannibalized their dead comrade.[35] Though exposed as humbug, this story reinforces the idea that those performers could not escape the dehumanizing identities prescribed by the circus.[36]

Sideshow workers who came from colonized spaces often fell under the most coercive labor contracts, with their circus experience defined by an even deeper paternalism than encompassed other circus workers. A group of contracted performers, likely from the Belgian Congo, worked under the pseudonym of the Obongos. According to several newspaper reports, sideshow manager Claude Hamilton referred to his relationship with the performers as one of "ownership" and described buying them from a show in Key West.[37] Although this kind of interview was often fabricated or exaggerated, it still illuminates the public expectation of sideshow workers. The use of ownership to describe their relationship to the circus seemed normal, and perhaps even expected, for workers from areas where paternalistic policies were already in place.

Not all sideshow workers hailed from real or imaginary faraway places, or depended on otherness that hinged on their exoticness. Charles Stratton, who came to be known as General Tom Thumb, found his start in Bridgeport, Connecticut. P. T. Barnum, who had already attained some clout with his infamous Joice Heth and Feejee Mermaid frauds, contacted Stratton's parents in the hopes that he could sign a contract with the five-year-old boy. He was of small stature, standing just over two feet tall. Stratton's appeal did not come from an upbringing that seemed exotic. Neither did he perform a particularly impressive set of skills, although audiences seemed to delight in his song and dance numbers.[38] But like for the circus working class, whose everyday life and labor were part of the circus performance schedule, Stratton's public performance included more intimate details of his personal life, like his wedding and marriage.[39]

Most sideshow workers had to constantly contend with maintaining their persona beyond the staged performance. Any moment in the public eye, which constituted all hours between the train pulling into a town and leaving, required circus workers to be in character. But for sideshow workers, this emotional labor was most grueling, as they took jeers and stares in silence, maintaining their images as non-Westerners and non-English speakers. Spectators wanted one thing from their seemingly uncivilized spectacles: authentic savagery. This meant silence for sideshow workers, lest they appear too educated, too westernized, or too human. This also meant that their job required a constant performance, both on- and offstage. Obvious transgressions, like John Lucas's confrontation at the parade, came under the purview of circus owners and local law enforcement. These same performers also disrupted their public personas when they asserted their rights as workers.

Sideshow Workers on the Front Lines

At the start of the 1899 season, the Barnum & Bailey Circus readied for its European opening in London. The entire show had traveled across the Atlantic, including the forty sideshow performers. Just prior to the opening of the show, the sideshow performers announced a strike, stating their collective desire to change their known titles from freaks to something that better described their line of work. They refused to work until their demands were met. Media and public interest picked up on the strike immediately, and the sideshow workers settled on "prodigy" as an apt descriptor.[40] Circus management capitalized on the strike and set the press department to work to ensure that the story reached outside the circus world.[41] Within a few years, a union had formed among sideshow workers. They fought for bread-and-butter issues, sought increased freedom in their performances, and found ways to assert their collective rights. Dozens of sideshow performers across multiple outfits joined the union within a few years. Charles Tripp, billed as the Armless Wonder, served as an organizing member.[42] Tripp had some organizing experience prior to the official formation of the sideshow union. During the same season that the sideshow went on strike, Tripp also served on the inaugural board of directors for the Benevolent Order of American Tigers, an organization of circus workers.[43]

This unusual labor unrest, at least by the standards of folks outside the circus, signaled the overlooked identity of the sideshow performers as workers. The first public collective action among sideshow workers in London, called the "Revolt of the Freaks" by the press, as well as the sideshow strikes that punctuated later seasons, seemed at odds with the image that circuses projected about their performers. Like other circus workers, sideshow performers were acting out a unique persona and talent onstage, and they seemed content as the beneficiaries of paternalistic business practices offstage.[44] Newspapers surmised, for example, that the limbless Truncate Artist "seemed content with his lot" because he spoke casually with the audiences before the show.[45]

While newspapers praised shows for employing the otherwise unemployable sideshow cast, they also brought attention to the workers. As a result, sideshow workers found themselves in a brighter spotlight than some of their coworkers who performed short sets under the big top. In addition, sideshow workers were more accessible to audiences. Thousands of people filled the big top tent to view its several rings with multiple acts performing simultaneously. For audiences, the big top experience entailed the smell, sights, colors, and performances—but not close interactions with the performers themselves. For only a little extra money, circusgoers could get closer interactions in the sideshow tent as part of their circus experience.

With daily interactions between themselves and circusgoers on the circus lot, sideshow workers had significantly more opportunities to supplement their income. Their performances and life stories, whether fabricated or real, appealed to people. Circusgoers more readily spoke about stories of capture and the personal trials of sideshow performers than they did about the actual experience in the tent.[46] One of the most sought-after souvenirs on the circus lot was the sideshow cabinet card, measuring two and a half by four inches. This souvenir had a portrait of the performer on the front and some sort of identifying information on the back. The cards served as revenue-generating products, and an entire industry grew around sideshow performers. As with their career, however, the performers held very little autonomy over their portrayal. Sideshow performers frequented portrait studios, like the one set up by Charles Eisenmann in New York.[47] Their poses, backgrounds, and clothing would have been indistinguishable from what appeared in any other portrait in the late nineteenth century. But the financial value in the cards rested in the features that made the photographs different from ordinary postcards. Human skeletons modeled in skintight clothing, tattooed ladies bared their drawn-on arms and legs, and little people stood next to full-size furniture.[48]

Fedor Jeftichew, known to the public as Jo-Jo the Dog-Faced Boy, sat in several studios to capture portraits for the cabinet cards.[49] Jeftichew began his career at sixteen years old under the Barnum banner. In Eisenmann's studio, Jeftichew cocreated several portraits by offering his public persona alongside preselected backdrops and props. While Jeftichew's face remained nearly unchanged in each sitting, as he gazed off in the distance and rarely made eye contact with the camera, his attire and background appeared slightly different in each card. The public image of each sideshow worker was accentuated through the cards. People from tropical areas, for example, dressed as such with grass skirts and greenery surrounding them. But Jeftichew was born in Russia. For circusgoers, the hair covering his entire face may have closely associated him with animals, but his national identity as Russian dictated that his image steer away from the savage notions that surrounded some of his fellow sideshow workers. He always wore clothing that signaled loftier class identity, and sometimes even wore a Russian military uniform. Backgrounds sometimes harked back to Russia, with bearskin rugs, and nearly always referenced the natural world.[50]

Sideshow performers depended on being able to connect with circusgoers, even at a dangerous price. Without the larger weekly payouts that big top contracts offered, sideshow workers faced more dangers and less job security. When a woman identified as the Electric Girl performed on sideshow stages, audiences saw what appeared to be a person who could conduct and control electricity. Circusgoers excitedly reported receiving small shocks when they shook her hand. In reality, the women stood on a dampened mat with a nearby battery providing the electric shock.[51]

Like the Electric Girl, many sideshow workers performed dangerous stunts in order to maintain their identities. The circus world differentiated between "natural freaks" and "self-made freaks," although the latter category was much more likely to include what the press dubbed as "fake freaks," such as John Lucas and the Muse brothers.[52] These falsified performances by so-called self-made freaks hinged on a suspended sense of reality, where people could conduct electricity or swallow swords. Billy Wells worked sideshow circuits as a hardheaded man who allowed planks of wood and pieces of stone to be broken over his skull. He reportedly performed upward of six times a day since his feat was a guaranteed draw during the ballyhoo, when circusgoers usually made their decision to enter the sideshow tent.[53]

The diverse array of self-made and natural talents in the sideshow cast often worked in solidarity, as demonstrated by the Revolt of the Freaks. But they also lived in more insular communities than did their big top counterparts. This image of outsiders banding together resonated with the public, which consumed stories of the communities that sideshow workers built throughout the season and after their retirements. In Chicago, an otherwise unassuming boardinghouse on West Madison garnered the nickname the "freak boarding house." An array of sideshow workers who held contracts with the adjacent dime museum could often be seen eating together in the separate dining room. This image of sideshow worker solidarity seemed to fit within the larger paternalistic circus world identity.[54]

Despite the image of a united front, workers' experiences varied, depending on factors such as nationality, gender, race, and class. Transnational identity and experience could help workers with employment, particularly during the offseason. Before Ringling Brothers made a trip to Cuba at the end of the season, it downsized and disposed of all members of the sideshow except the snake charmer, who could speak Spanish.[55] Men and women in the sideshow often had markedly different experiences. While both were exoticized as the Other, women were also sexualized. Women were described as "beauties," and commentary often focused on their physical appearance.[56] The popular Ubangi performers, who worked over the course of several decades in the Barnum, Ringling, and Barnes shows, demonstrate that even though national identity dictated experiences, gender was also a marker in how sideshow workers labored. The Ubangis supposedly hailed from a part of French Equatorial Africa. Only later did a Ringling press agent admit that he culturally "resettled" the performers in the most exotic-sounding locale that he could find.[57] The men in the shows appeared unremarkable next to other circus performers from Africa. But the women wore distinct lip discs.[58]

The performance of the "duck-billed savages" included a fabled backstory that highlighted their degree of femininity. Similar to European billings of Sara Baartman as the Hottentot Venus, the Ubangi women were advertised as beauties.[59] The accompanying context claimed that the discs, despite serving as a symbol of beauty within their societies, actually deterred sexual advances on Ubangi women.[60] This description reinforced the exclusive connections between white Western womanhood and beauty that audiences sought out in entertainment.[61] It also reinforced women in the sideshow as different from their counterparts on other parts of the lot.

Ubangi women appeared to transgress gender norms in their staged performances, but their roles remained rigid. When the Ringling show began its 1930 tour at Madison Square Garden, audiences hurried into the basement of the stadium to view the sideshow. The Ubangi performers proved to be among the most popular. While the men did "little for the act," their female counterparts wore their now-iconic lip discs. Audiences may have hoped to catch a glimpse of their offstage personas, such as the women's pipe smoking or their diet of fish and rice, which newspapers detailed. Although audiences expected the Ubangi women to look and behave differently than themselves, they also expected a certain image of non-Western womanhood. These women may have been known to smoke pipes, but their staged personas also fell under the "ownership" of King Nebia, who accompanied them onstage.[62]

Media treatment of the Ubangi performers ran the gamut. Like other circus performers, they were subjected to outlandish humbug that played on people's underlying assumptions about non-Western people. The *New*

York Times reported that they appeared awestruck by the cityscape but could not bear the harsh weather outside the Congo. According to the article, the group had requested permission to kill the circus elephants so as to use their ears as drum heads. Their reported diet of fish, fruit, and rice stemmed from their belief that they were related to chickens and buffalo, although they had grown fond of North American cider. And their supposed polygamy only furthered the public belief that "society" should continue to be applied to the performers with a comedic gesture. The circus also applied typical advertising tactics, noting that this was the last generation of lip disc–wearing Ubangis, and that American audiences had to see it now before this cultural display was gone forever.[63]

Despite the varied reports of Ubangi activities and antics, "savage" was the one constant descriptor. While concepts of fashion, hunting, diets, and marriage norms played into this image, the workers' willingness to push against the benevolent paternalism of circus management also branded them as savages. In his 1960 memoir, Henry Ringling North noted that the women had not received pay for their work because they were simply rented from their home state, and the chief hoarded all the earnings. Throughout his recollections, North referred to the performers as "naughty children." He fondly recalled one woman who warmed up to him when he spoke "primitive French." He remembered instances when the workers became disgruntled before angrily shedding their clothes onstage but chalked it up to them being "mad" or "annoyed" for no specific reason.[64] In a similar vein, when the *Chicago Defender* reported that Ubangi workers had asserted their rights in the courts against their employer, the headline indicated that the Ringlings—self-proclaimed kings of the circus—were being sued by "savage troupers."[65]

Patrons often considered their visits to sideshows to be educational.[66] Even in the earliest days of Barnum's sideshow attractions at the American Museum, shows and displays claimed to educate as much as they did to entertain. The Ubangi performers stood onstage with a white man playing an equally fictitious professor role. He told audiences of their lives in Africa and spoke for them to reporters.[67] Route books offered a similar educational spin on the categorization of people in the sideshow. Following the 1936 season, general manager Sam Gumpertz penned a piece that systematically outlined various groups of people who had been contracted into the shows from Africa and Asia. He informed readers of marriage customs, laws, and family structures among groups of people in Bontoc, Somaliland, and Dahomey. But he also told stories that revealed the possible degree of labor exploitation that existed in these contracts. According to Gumpertz, the

Somali performers were at the mercy of their promoter, who, in this case, "speedily went broke," leaving the Somali performers "destitute."[68]

A distinct medical interest also informed the sideshows. Audiences marveled at people whom circuses claimed had medical deformities or were wonders. A mix of live workers and preserved remains became standard in sideshows. When a freak show set up at the Indiana State Fair, the ALL ALIVE! banner garnered significant attention.[69] Barnum's infamous Feejee Mermaid in the mid-nineteenth century stood as an early example of taxidermized entertainment. But even through the twentieth century, people found themselves face-to-face with a variety of preserved and faked remains. Pickled punks and bouncers, an insider term for preserved abnormal fetuses and their faked counterparts, abounded on the midway.[70] These displays became popular as natural history museums were seeking their own animal specimens for display.

When Eng and Chang, conjoined twins from Siam, died hours apart in their North Carolina home, newspapers reported on the likelihood that one could have survived the other, and the gruesome final moments before each twin died.[71] When Krao Farini, who spent decades in sideshows as a missing link (that is, the missing piece in Darwin's chain between humans and apes), passed away from influenza in 1926, she made the request to be cremated and avoid having her body on exhibition, as so many other sideshow performers experienced after death.[72]

As illuminated by Farini's request, most sideshow performers had little autonomy over their own bodies. Although live workers from non-Western places filled sideshows, their remains also became commodified on freak circuits, in museum cases, and on scientific research tables. The stories of exoticized people, such as Sara Baartman and Inughuaq (Inuk) Minik Wallace, demonstrate that circuses would continue to turn profits off sideshow bodies.[73]

• • •

The seemingly odd mix of authentically portrayed performances, outlandish counterfeits, people with extraordinary talents, people with disabilities, human remains, and animals fostered a contested workplace. Sideshow workers became among the first circus workers to organize when they formed their separate union following the 1899 European tour. Their own world under the sideshow tent remained an exclusive community within the larger circus world. Much to the amusement of the public, they banded together onstage and offstage.

But the public also complained and worried about the future of this particular circus tradition. The press lamented for decades that sideshow workers were becoming scarce. Crediting better health, papers worried that so-called natural freaks would soon cease to exist for their entertainment. But the sideshow's decline in popularity did not reflect a scarcity of sideshow performers. Although the Golden Age developed with the sideshow as a standard attraction, the circus had an uneven history with sideshow entertainment. The sideshow skirted in and out of favor with an increasingly "sophisticated public."[74] Newspapers in the 1920s claimed that the "heyday of freaks" was over and that the true stars like Zip the Pinhead and Jo-Jo the Dog-Faced Boy were a thing of the past. Sideshow fans blamed highbrow tastes and yearned for the unregulated display of people that had occurred regularly just a few years earlier.[75]

As the Golden Age of the circus began to wane, it became more difficult to obtain a living wage as a sideshow worker. For sideshows, the throngs of people that lingered on the circus lot from the arrival until the departure of the train were potential customers. They could be convinced by barkers to spend just a bit more money to see never-before-seen, last-of-its-kind, remarkably odd attractions. When parades became rarer and people began driving to the shows in cars, rather than spending entire days on the lot, the sideshow became a less-frequented attraction. While the change in audience behavior had less impact on big top performers, who still collected their weekly paycheck, sideshow workers suffered financially from the decline in daily interactions with circusgoers.[76] As with other parts of the circus world, the sideshow not only was shunned culturally for its exploitation but also could not afford changes in the labor landscape.

PART III

The Circus World from the Outside

The magic of circus day was perhaps best captured in the opening moments, hours before any billed performance started. It was in the early morning hours, when the train arrived, that circusgoers had their first physical interaction with the show in its entirety. The lead up, which started with the billing crew and intensified with newspaper reminders that the show would arrive soon, brought circusgoers to the train tracks to witness every moment of the day firsthand. The dozens of train cars owned by each outfit hauled the entire show, from people to animals to equipment. Seeing any part of the workforce emerge would have likely felt magical as the line between performer and worker was nonexistent in this space.

The photograph shown here, captured by Harry Atwell in the late 1920s, offers a view of the shows' biggest star, in both size and popularity, as well as some of its smallest fans. Though already massive, elephants must have seemed even more enormous on the lifted train car, looking down on the children. The train would have traveled through the night, so the open door of the elephant car might have also included smells that would be reminiscent of the menagerie that would soon be erected.

For this elephant, and the dozens that likely constituted the rest of the herd, the open door usually offered a breath of somewhat fresh air, often with cooler morning temperatures. While the train track noise would have subsided in this moment, the shrill sounds of excited children would be part of the soundscape for much of this elephant's day. Several children in the photo have their hands extended toward the elephant, likely offering some food. These treats given by excited

Children surround an elephant on the circus train, circa 1927. Robert L. Parkinson Library and Research Center, Circus World, Baraboo, Wisconsin. Image CWi 7124.

children would have also been part of the typical experience for circus animals. As the elephant saw the morning light, heard the stopping of the train and the murmur of circus crowds, and extended its trunk outside of the car, the promise of food was likely close behind. While the show had painstakingly secured food and water for its animal workers, it also knew that treats would be an informal part of the daily diet at each stop.

This scene happened hundreds of times each season, and the snapshot captured by Atwell offers a moment when several lines blurred in the circus world. In this moment everyone listed on the circus roster and featured in the program were both workers and celebrities for circusgoers. The elephant reaching toward the children would soon help pull wagons on the lot. But this moment when children gathered around the train car to feed the elephant also blurred the line between circus worker and audience member. People interacted with their entertainment on circus lots. They performed caretaking duties as they touched the animals and talked to the workers.

This image also provides a window into how race operated on circus day. As explored in previous chapters, Black workers had to navigate a different sort of circus world than their white counterparts did. Audiences, too, felt the impact of Jim Crow policies and practices, but the circus proved a tough event to segregate. As Gregory J. Renoff has explored in great detail and with astounding nuance in his study of the circus in Georgia, segregation came with ticketed shows, but not in the impromptu moments surrounding them.[1] Black and white southern audience members, and perhaps particularly children, had similar experiences during the unticketed performances as they came face-to-face with the workers.

Audiences deeply affected the form and function of the show, as the chapters in this part demonstrate. Their near-constant presence meant that they, too, became part of some of the most iconic circus images. Circus lots between performances transformed into worlds that included the audience and the owners during the peak decades, and then spaces that became largely absent of both as the Golden Age declined. The performative aspects of manual labor, as explored in the next three chapters, resemble what is found in studies by Eric Arnesen on New Orleans dockworkers and Dominic Pacyga on Chicago stockyards and slaughterhouses.[2] In a similar vein, circus spectators showed up to watch an array of skilled labor. Workers performed this labor publicly, with nearly every moment during the season either documented or watched. As this part demonstrates, the circus world may have been tightly knit for workers, but it was nearly always under the public eye.

6

The Circus as Big Business

Early circus magnates could honestly say that they were part of the shows. As the Ringling brothers claimed in their early career, they were competent in nearly every part of their tiny show.[1] But shows got bigger, work became more specialized and then mechanized, and owners had a multinational corporation on their hands. Slowly, the circus industry began seeing magnates as people who existed outside of the inner workings of the shows. This chapter explores the long history of the circus as a corporate entity that remained largely masked from workers and audiences. With its company town inner workings, incredibly transient nature, and overt paternalism by management, the circus fostered a high level of employee dependence. However, the circus world identity became more irrelevant in the twentieth century as the circus itself became a modern business, and employees began negotiating their role in the changing workplace.

Much of the change in the business side of the circus world is rooted in the larger landscape of twentieth-century industries, but at least some of it is the result of a single decision in 1929. At the end of the 1929 season, the last remaining Ringling brother, John, prepared to make his usual circus debut at Madison Square Garden in the spring of 1930. The thirty-day stand at the Garden was an annual tradition for New Yorkers. They saw new and exciting acts before the show hit the road on a two-hundred-day tour. For circus management, the opening grandstand was quite advantageous. The shows reaped substantial profits in the first thirty days by foregoing any tents and reducing the paychecks of workers. Ringling's show had retained the nickname "the big one" for a reason. The circus tycoon had quietly provided funding for the new arena (the old Garden was torn down and a new one built in 1925), and his substantial investments led *Fortune* magazine to declare him "the best millionaire alive." The title fit. Although the Garden was a coveted spot, Ringling seemed to always have dibs.[2]

But Ringling's reputation was usurped by competition both in and out of the circus world that year. Madison Square Garden had accommodated the Ringling show each season by accepting an offer that gave the show complete control of the venue, with prime show dates and times. But the rising international popularity of boxing suddenly came into direct competition with the tented shows. The Garden agreed to host the Ringling opening, but only as a limited engagement. The circus could not have its traditional Friday night show. Instead, New Yorkers would see Friday night prizefighting. The Garden regularly profited up to $8,000 from these fight nights. This decision to show Friday night boxing should have come as no surprise to the only remaining Ringling brother. Since its 1925 rebuild, the Garden had earned the nickname "The House That Tex Built," a nod to both the boxing-promoting genius behind the new arena, Tex Rickard, and the Garden's ever-popular baseball counterpart in New York City, Yankee Stadium (popularly known as "The House That Ruth Built" for its association with Babe Ruth). Without the Friday night shows, Ringling balked. He declared that "boxing and circuses do not mix." But Madison Square Garden management still wanted the arena to be the opening stand for a major circus, and there was never a short supply of circuses in the United States.[3]

With a void in the schedule at Madison Square Garden, and a rare opportunity to nearly double yearly profits, the American Circus Corporation (ACC) swooped in the next day to sign a contract at the venue with two of its shows, the Sells-Floto and Hagenbeck-Wallace Circuses. Formed in 1919 by smaller outfits as a means of protection against the more powerful Ringling Brothers, the ACC brought together five medium-sized shows to become a larger entity than its Ringling counterpart. The shows had spent the 1920s acting independently from one another on the road while sharing impressive winter quarters in Indiana. The conglomerate existed almost solely to stave off Ringling influence.[4]

With a bankroll dwarfed only by his ego, Ringling reacted swiftly to this slight by his competition. Talks moved swiftly as Ringling, a man described as "enormous, thick, and powerful," likely spoke quickly in his signature low register. He also had a fondness for cigars, which might have added to the ambiance of negotiations, as he was known for "removing the butt of the cigar between quick puffs of smoke." After a series of meetings with the ACC the following day, Ringling offered a generous buyout, adding an additional five thousand employees to the Ringling payroll and two thousand animals to the tented performance. Although Ringling was now the undisputed circus king, the Garden still refused to give up Friday nights to the circus. Moreover, the buyout of almost the entire circus industry was still beyond his means. To make the purchase, Ringling took out a loan for $1.7 million of the $2 million price tag. Brooklyn financier William Greve, who had his hand in real estate, horse shows, and railroads, suddenly became part owner of the Greatest Show on Earth. Now under the thumb of the Prudence Bond and Mortgage Company, the circus giant succumbed to its new status as debt-ridden corporation in September 1929.[5]

The devastating stock market crash just one month later upended the circus business. Ringling defaulted on his massive loan. Although proprietors, who had considered themselves part of the circus world, had bankrolled the shows up to this point, suddenly big banks owned the entertainment giant. When the loan went up for sale, Coney Island tycoon and Ringling family friend Sam Gumpertz jumped at the chance to claim a large chunk of the circus industry for a bargain price. Gumpertz's reputation at the time was shockingly similar to Barnum's legacy from decades prior; he unapologetically displayed "living curiosities" in his amusement park, Dreamland. The circus business, then, hardly seemed like a leap.[6]

Although Gumpertz made his name in show business, the circus was still new territory. His presence represented a shift away from traditional circus management. He enacted several lasting changes at the top, including a new open shop agreement with labor. But he also disrupted the image of the circus world. After a dispute with John Ringling a few years later, at Madison Square Garden, Gumpertz publicly ordered the last original circus tycoon off the lot of his former show.[7]

And yet, despite outward appearances, the circus's move out of its insular business model and into corporate America did not first happen with Gumpertz's takeover. When Ringling bought out nearly the entire circus field in 1929, critics called it a "chain store system" of running the circus, but this astute label could have been applied decades prior. The circus started as a burgeoning corporation in the nineteenth century. For Golden Age owners like Barnum and the Ringling brothers, the circus business was a unique game of mergers and acquisitions. Aside from Ringling Brothers, the last remaining nineteenth-century show to avoid a buyout or closure, hundreds of circuses in the Golden Age enjoyed only a short shelf life. Circus folks at the turn of the century noted the shows' "early tendencies to monopolize," and the transient workforce was accustomed to working under a new banner each year, whether through their own career move or a buyout.[8] Early circus proprietors ran their businesses in step with other American companies, and their unscrupulous tactics resembled those of other Gilded Age robber barons.[9] But this entertainment business, built on nostalgia, adopted labor and business practices that turned self-destructive by the mid-twentieth century. Although circuses had been acting as businesses from the start, they lifted the veil by the mid-twentieth century by adopting boardrooms, stockholders, and investors. The press assured the public that the near monopoly of the circus world under John Ringling would not affect the shows, but it did solidify the image of the circus as a modern corporation. That new image led to the decline of the circus.[10]

The Early Years of the Corporate Circus

In 1855, P. T. Barnum published his first of many autobiographies. The middle-aged showman had not yet entered the circus world, but he still had created a buzz around several other attractions that he deemed oddities or wonders. Joice Heth, supposedly the 161-year-old enslaved nurse of George Washington, toured throughout the Northeast with Barnum while audiences gaped at the blind elderly woman and openly refuted the legitimacy of the exhibit. Barnum relished the attention. Heth, on the other hand, faced many of the same workplace struggles that later sideshow workers would face.[11] Barnum also signed a performance contract—funded through a combination of personal loans and mortgaged properties—with Jenny Lind, the famed Swedish soprano. Unlike Heth, Lind performed to adoring American audiences in theaters across the country. Barnum reaped substantial profits with his presentation of the European performer. Lind's decision to perform in the United States was lucrative for the singer and increased her visibility.[12]

Barnum's autobiography also provided insight into the business side of his exploitative and lucrative ventures. He did not create the business of displaying people, performing under a big top tent, providing an exotic array of animals for the public, or taking shows on the road. He did, however, revolutionize these existing platforms to help usher in the Golden Age of the circus. Barnum credited the roots of this revolution to showmen who had come before him, such as Hachaliah Bailey. Barnum described Bailey as a "wealthy" and "self-willed" showman. Like Barnum, Bailey dabbled in varied investments such as property, steamboats, and menageries. But he more famously made a profitable business deal at a bar in the Bowery, New York, when he purchased and then exhibited Old Bet, who was rumored to be the first elephant in the United States. Building on his image as an elephant entrepreneur, Bailey built the Elephant Hotel in Somers, New York. Barnum later capitalized on the elephant's fame by exhibiting her bones after a farmer in Maine shot the animal. He also praised the hotel in Somers.[13]

But the three-story brick hotel with marble facade and a quaint statue of Old Bet at its entrance served an even more important role in early circuses. Savvy businessmen realized that they could turn a substantial profit by showing exotic animals. Bailey, too, did not end his dealings in the exotic animal business after the death of Old Bet. Instead, he acquired more elephants and partnered with several local investors. Ten years after the hotel's construction, Bailey, George Brunn, Isaac Purdy, Benjamin Lent, and more than one hundred other men from the Somers area met there to create a menagerie monopoly. Together they founded the Zoological Institute in 1835. They expanded their animal holdings with a supposed royal tiger and other imported animals. But it was their frequent meetings at the Elephant Hotel that solidified the sleepy farm town as the cradle of the American circus.[14]

Like Ringling, the Zoological Institute partners made New York City a unique stop for the circus. Rather than using the city as an opening stand, the early circus magnates used New York as a winter quarters. The Bowery was part of the city, but it was old farmland, with cattle and sheep still making regular appearances at the tavern. It became home to the more exotic assortment of animals in the winter months. To house the menagerie collection, the partners built the Bowery Amphitheatre. The theater continued to house exotic animals and host shows for the next two decades.[15]

As a capital stock company with dozens of animals, several different pieces of land, an impressive amount of equipment, and headquarters in the Bowery, the group of former farmers began priming the public for the Golden Age of the American circus. Their partnerships, holdings, and business dealings represented a predecessor to circus monopolies. While their previous careers included driving cattle across the state and trading workhorses, their new jobs brought them into the international markets of animal capture, trade, and performance. The owners quickly recouped start-up costs associated with the capture and shipment of the animals from Africa and Asia.[16] Each owner toured independently. Agreements between the men ensured that the shows' routes would not intersect and thus the shows would not come into direct competition with one another. By doing this, the Zoological Institute maximized both profit and visibility. In its first year, the group monopolized the entire field. Not a single menagerie show existed outside of the Zoological Institute. The organization also controlled the exotic animal trade. Audiences, then, could expect to see exotic animals under several different company banners, while behind the scenes the business acted as a single profit center.[17]

But the Zoological Institute succumbed to the Panic of 1837. On August 22 of that year, Somers residents witnessed a new sort of exotic animal show. The same leopards, tigers, and camels that had toured the country in the Zoological Institute shows suddenly sat on an auction block at the Elephant Hotel. Virginius and Siam, two elephants that had followed in the career footsteps of Old Bet, joined the other animals in the sale. At the same location where the group had been formed a mere two years earlier, the menagerie partners essentially liquidated their company. This sudden collapse and quick rebuilding into other trusts, monopolies, and partnerships became emblematic of the circus.[18]

Even though the Zoological Institute dissolved, the menagerie business continued. The legacies of menagerie men from Somers lived on as Barnum and other circus proprietors immediately filled the void in the traveling animal business. The members of the Flatfoot Party, the second generation of menagerie monopoly owners, acted similarly to their predecessors. With many of the same members, the Flatfoot Party constituted a syndicate of the most profitable menageries. Unlike the Zoological Institute, the Flatfoots faced slightly more competition in their field as upstart circuses successfully attempted to operate outside of the trust. Moreover, Flatfoot members began to migrate to the more profitable world of the burgeoning circus by the mid-nineteenth century, partnering with owners like James A. Bailey. Barnum first crossed paths with the syndicate when he worked as a freelance advertising writer for the Bowery Amphitheatre. But he became intertwined with the group when he joined forces with Bailey to form the Barnum & Bailey Circus.[19] Barnum's move to partner with James Hutchinson, and more famously with Bailey, was part of a forced relationship. In 1880, the circus owners met in Bridgeport, Connecticut. Operating as separate entities had cut drastically into their profits. The men split the potential earnings, with the more famous Barnum keeping half the profits from each season.[20]

Corporatization in the Golden Age

The explosion in circus popularity led to hundreds of separate shows that competed with one another. A bigger-is-better model emerged as showmen used bigger animals, more performers, and multiple rings to attract audiences.[21] Although the public knew of show closures and buyouts, the circus world image shielded the shows from a corporate image that included mergers. When rumors of a merger swirled in 1896, the press quickly quashed them, claiming that such a move would be a "humiliating confession" for shows that boasted of themselves as "peerless" and "unequaled."[22]

The key to gaining public acceptance, or simply ambivalence, for mergers was to maintain the circus world image. Shows had managed to do that through the end of the nineteenth century. Giant conglomerates often had a dominant presence or even complete control, as the Zoological Institute did in the early part of the century. But when Ringling Brothers, Barnum & Bailey, and Buffalo Bill's Wild West Show formed a trust, teaming up to coordinate routes and maximize profits, they disrupted the gratis performance owed to audiences. The three companies did not split profits or combine performances. Instead, they made informal agreements to rotate among US, British, and European tours. Together, the three also acted as a powerful decision-maker in the circus world and attempted to revamp traditions while maximizing profit.[23] The circus parade was becoming more expensive and less practical as shows began to expand their size. To offer the parades, shows had to haul equipment that served no other purpose. They devoted entire train cars to wagons that were unloaded just to roll down the main street. The newly formed trust deemed this too unprofitable.[24]

Public support for the newly formed corporate "octopus" waned when it cut into the circus experience. The proposed end to the parade made circus suddenly seem like a cold and "soulless" business rather than an all-inclusive source of entertainment. Newspapers encouraged readers to engage in "vigorous protest" of the monopoly, arguing that the parade was a necessity rather than a luxury. Audiences also seemed to fear potential ticket price hikes or more gratis performance reductions. The public became angry that entertainment suddenly looked like other workplaces.[25] These fears were not completely unfounded, although rumors abounded. The end of the circus parade also led audiences to believe that clowns would soon be cut from performances and that young boys would no longer have unrestricted access to help circus workers in exchange for free tickets. These ideas added to the public perception that the trust put profit ahead of performance.[26]

Merger rumors ran rampant, with varying amounts of truth. In 1906, a New Orleans news outlet reported that a complete circus merger was being secured that would bring all American circuses under the auspices of European animal trader and entertainer Carl Hagenbeck. The $5 million deal never came to fruition and likely was never even on the table, but the proposition seemed believable. Like the Hagenbeck rumors, the Sells Brothers Circus and the Royal Circus attracted short-lived attention for a possible merger. Even a motley crew merger of an investor, menagerie owner, and horse trainer was rumored, with the expectation that it would counter the circus trust.[27]

Circuses capitalized on public disapproval and began marketing themselves as "antitrust" shows. The Great Wallace Shows did this most often and loudly over the course of years. Advertisements not only presented the shows as "anti-Monopoly" and "not in the circus trust," but they also informed the reader that their moral compass made their performance superior.

While the Great Wallace Shows cited their antitrust status in newspaper advertisements, the John Robinson Circus, a slightly bigger show, gave a newspaper interview that demonized the trust owners as money-grubbers. The Hagenbeck-Wallace Combined Show separated itself from the trust shows by promoting the free parade. Even after the trust disbanded, the Sells Brothers Circus proudly announced that it had remained independent and fought off the trust despite the lost revenue. But by 1905, the power of the trust had seemingly disintegrated as newspapers announced that the "Circus Trust has decided to abandon their attempt to crush independent [shows]." Newspapers went on to report sparingly of any sort of monopolistic control for nearly a decade.[28]

Creating the Greatest Show on Earth

The two largest shows wrapped up successful seasons in 1907. In October, the Barnum & Bailey Circus ended its season in Dyersburg, Tennessee. The show had made a significant profit, suffered only one disaster (a tornado crossed its path in North Dakota), and traveled more than sixteen thousand miles. Just after midnight following the final performance, the roustabouts packed the circus into five trains, and the circus began its nearly weeklong journey back to Bridgeport, Connecticut. Although papers reported that the shows would immediately begin refitting for the next season, 1907 proved to be the final season for the show as an independent circus.[29] That same week, the Ringling Brothers show headed through Oklahoma. It would finish its season in Fulton, Kentucky, just a few weeks later. That circus also enjoyed record crowds, even during a cold spring opening in New England. Its six-month season included thirty-three states and had no major accidents.[30]

The Ringling Brothers and Barnum & Bailey shows had spent much of their existence prior to the trust avoiding crossed paths during the season while competing for performers during the offseason. When the Barnum show sailed for Europe in 1898 for a five-year run, Ringling dominated the American circus landscape, largely because of their unofficial deal. Both shows remained profitable when the Barnum show resumed its US tour in 1905. But the death of James A. Bailey in 1906 left the Barnum show in the hands of his widow. In the fall of 1907, she released it to Ringling Brothers for $500,000.[31]

Although the circus world had contained these sorts of mergers since its inception, and the Barnum and Ringling shows had unofficially dominated the circus market hand in hand for years, this deal felt different. In the thirty years since the Golden Age had begun, the circus market had been flooded with shows. Each time a show failed, its equipment, animals, and laborers were suddenly up for grabs. The public and people in the circus world became accustomed to seeing circuses quickly enlarge in conjunction with the failures of other shows. But Ringling Brothers had just purchased the largest, most renowned, and most successful show in the United States. The press began referring to the new show as a monopoly.[32]

But Ringling Brothers had not bought the entire circus world. It simply owned the most impressive parts of this world. Workers slowly became aware of the effects of this acquisition. In 1909, after several smaller circus mergers brought the circus field closer to its eventual monopoly, the clowns were among the first employees to recognize the loss of job security. They cited circus consolidation, which caused falling wages, in their attempt to unionize. Laborers, however, initially did not notice the changes at the top, since Ringling allowed the shows to run independently with their established names and acts.[33]

Even with the Ringling partnership, the Barnum show had stayed relevant in the United States through the smaller stateside shows that it had enveloped over two decades. The Adam Forepaugh Circus fell under the umbrella of the Barnum show following Forepaugh's death. Following circus tradition, the new ownership remained veiled, and the show toured under its original name for years. After the Barnum & Bailey merger, the show began to look different. The relatively small Wild West stock supplemented the larger Buffalo Bill show, and the Forepaugh show became a placeholder. But upon his return to the United States, Bailey realized a larger profit could be made by selling the formerly independent show, ironically to Ringling Brothers.[34]

Although Barnum and Ringling were household names in the nineteenth century, they were not alone. Nineteenth-century circuses often made unofficial regional claims. The Al G. Barnes show was relatively unremarkable, except for its acquisition of the famed elephant Tusko. It gladly accepted the nickname "the western wonder" for its dominance of the entire western United States and Canada.[35] Benjamin Wallace dominated the Midwest in the 1890s with his show the Great Wallace Circus, and he practiced similar business dealings as his larger counterparts. By doing this, and engaging in several buyouts to expand his show, Wallace fared well with a medium-sized show. His 1907 purchase of the Hagenbeck Circus for nearly $50,000 made Wallace a formidable competitor to the larger shows.[36]

Still, particular names resonated in the circus world. The fame of Barnum or Ringling could not be appropriated by smaller shows, but names like Sells or Robinson were regularly employed by upstart shows trying to make their shows appear long-standing. Often this practice went unchecked. But when show owner Frank Bostock began displaying his wild animals with the name Hagenbeck, he faced an injunction. The German animal trader and trainer had a very particular reputation to keep. With a seemingly endless supply of lions, tigers, elephants, and other wild animals, Hagenbeck had the distinct advantage of training and selling the most docile individuals of the species. This meant that animals in the industry with his name attached could often fetch higher market prices. When Bostock employed the famous name, he ignored a notice that Hagenbeck had released just months earlier, in anticipation of the latter's European and US tour. Claiming that he would "protect [his] name, fame, and reputation and business interest," Hagenbeck sent a clear warning shot, breaking with tradition and essentially trademarking his place in the circus world.[37]

Size, reputation, and name recognition did not always protect shows. Seemingly unsinkable circuses often went bankrupt. Wallace's Midwest powerhouse went under just ten years after he made the $50,000 purchase to expand his show. Selling for just over $36,000 to Bert Bowers and Jerry Mugivan, also circus owners, the show liquidated.[38] Wholesale-priced exchanges were not unusual, but this particular sale was an important precursor merger to what would soon become the American Circus Corporation (ACC).

The ACC, called the Corporation Shows among circus folks, was not an anomaly in the circus world. Formed in 1919 in response to the dominant presence of the Ringling shows, the ACC acted much like its larger counterpart. It bought up failing shows, like the Hagenbeck-Wallace Circus, and allowed them to run autonomously in name. The circus conglomerate had an edge on its Ringling counterpart, as its members had distinct regional identities. Although Ringling retained the title of "the big one," the ACC dominated much of the United States.[39]

Everything, it seemed, was bigger and better in the Corporation Shows. Residents of Peru, Indiana, delighted in the red, yellow, and blue wagons that made their winter home in the small Midwest town. But the excitement of the wagons did not compare with the thrill of seeing a herd of elephants taking their regular bath in the Wabash River or dozens of giraffes peering above the rural landscape. The outfit's nearly five thousand acres housed thousands of animals with the various Corporation Shows. Peru residents could visit the circus city zoo every Sunday during the winter season. The immobile winter quarters also brought a population influx of circus workers. At its height, the winter quarters in Peru employed five hundred employees who repainted wagons and tended to the animals from November until April. Although performers did not remain with the show in the winter, residents could still catch glimpses of manual labor performed during the offseason.[40]

The Corporation Shows consistently attracted an impressive cast of performers. Mickey King, the Flying Concellos, Emmett Kelly, and Clyde Beatty all started their career with the corporate band of shows.[41] In the 1920s, their popularity soared. The Ringling show continued to attract sold-out crowds, and the Corporation Shows remained collectively powerful. In addition to the near-constant changes and improvements made each season for the most popular shows, 1925 marked a watershed year in circus modernization as the Ringling show moved from its iconic three rings to five rings. Like any change that made the shows larger, this expansion garnered praise from the press, which deemed it the greatest change since the great Barnum and Ringling merger. Maneuvering around city ordinances that limited the size of the big top tent, the Ringling show elevated the two new rings above the regular three rings. Shows also bragged about upgrades designed to make them more appealing than their competitors. Even the purchase of new flat steel cars was newsworthy for the Al G. Barnes show.[42]

As the circus moved into the twentieth century, it modernized like any other company. But modernization meant the abandonment of some circus traditions. Tractors replaced manual laborers and literal horsepower. A show closure in Europe in 1907 gave Ringling Brothers the chance to buy new herds of horses and elephants. It seized the opportunity. With five elephant herds, 350 horses, and more than 800 performers, the show had reached a near peak. But this massive cast made the gratis parade impractical. Even with its increased size, the circus kept the same schedule. Now, with hundreds of additional animals and substantially more equipment, the shows still had to unload and set up the lot in just a few hours. Moreover, the show made room for the new animal acts by disposing of wagons that had been designated for the free parade. Newspapers predicted that the departure of the parade would be permanent.[43]

Behind the scenes, circuses started to resemble modern corporations. Although earlier shows netted huge untaxed profits, later circuses contended with the complexities of a large-scale business. For the Ringling monopoly, reporting income and paying taxes cut into its lucrative, formerly off-the-books profits. Despite new government mandates, the Greatest Show on Earth continued to operate like a circus world business. John Kelley began his career with the circus in 1905 when he defended Ringling Brothers against a lawsuit from a Missouri town. He cooked the books and engaged in creative accounting to keep the shows profitable. Kelley reportedly saved the Ringling dynasty upward of $200,000 with fraudulent claims of depreciation. Most famously, Kelley falsely reported losing the same rhinoceros for three straight years, claiming a $35,000 loss each time. Although Kelley had a long association with the circus world, he was a college-educated lawyer who championed the shows as a contracted employee. He was not fully familiar with the inner workings of the show. When he claimed that Ringling Brothers had a performance with sixty stallions, a subpoenaed employee swiftly corrected the lie, telling the court that trying to put sixty stallions in the same act would be the end of any circus.[44]

Behind-the-scenes changes in the circus world accelerated when John Ringling purchased the ACC, just ahead of the stock market crash. The circus attempted to stay afloat during the ensuing months and years of the Great Depression. Like with other businesses that grew by overextending their pockets, the Ringling fortune was not immune to the Great Depression. The Ringling Brothers Circus, as well as the rest of the circus industry, faced grim prospects in the 1930s. Floundering ticket sales created an investment disaster for the circus giant. At the end of the 1930 season, the John Robinson Circus, which dominated the southern circuit, permanently closed. The Sparks World Famous Show and Sells-Floto Circus quickly followed suit. In 1934, the barely successful Hagenbeck-Wallace show found a sudden surge in popularity. With so many closures, the circus business faced an influx of out-of-work circus stars and animals. By 1937, the Al G. Barnes show was the last circus standing from the buyout.[45]

The Great Depression had a tremendous impact on more than just the Ringling wealth. Even after the Ringling show controlled most of the circus industry, shows toured as if they were still autonomous. But as shows proved unable to recoup yearly expenses, Ringling quickly closed them. In 1937, the Great Al G. Barnes and Sells-Floto Combined Circus, still under Ringling control, attempted to outlast its fellow ACC shows by combining into a single touring entity. Although it could not claim a monopoly on the circus world, it boasted the largest assortments of both clowns and "ferocious jungle beasts."[46]

The circus world had operated on a series of mergers since its inception, but the 1929 buyout by Ringling elicited pushback from other owners. The Al G. Barnes show noted that the Ringling circus was historically incapable of running multiple shows.[47] Zack T. Miller and the Miller Brothers 101 Ranch Show filed a damages suit against the new circus kings, claiming that they had conspired to create a monopoly. The $1 million lawsuit critiqued long-standing circus business practices. The Miller show had toured since 1925 and featured Tom Mix, a western movie star. He remained a popular star and therefore a commodity in the circus world. Although the Ringling show was facing financial decline, it was still able to offer Mix a substantially higher paycheck and entice him away from the smaller show. Miller also accused the Ringling show of defacing its advertising and spreading malicious lies about the shows. Whether this accusation was true or not, these practices had occurred for decades in the circus world.[48]

Although monopolies were a fundamental part of the circus world, Ringling's 1929 merger opened the door to outside influences. This began with creditors and investors, and the new management of amusement tycoon Sam Gumpertz. John Ringling North, the son of Ida Ringling (the only sister to the Ringling brothers), still felt like an outsider to the circus world when he took out a substantial loan and purchased the Ringling dynasty from Gumpertz and the Allied Owners in 1937. And though he modernized the shows in much the same manner as his uncles had done, he did so at a quicker pace that mechanized traditional circus jobs out of existence.[49]

Although a series of labor strikes, detailed in chapter 8, permanently damaged the Ringling name, it did not substantially cut into profits for the 1938 season. With nearly two thousand employees laid off at the time, North could still make financial gains with the new surplus of acts and equipment. He sent these things to his other shows. Some shows added dozens of train cars, animals, and workers. Shows were even rerouted to ensure the most profitable season. The Barnes Sells-Floto show, which had dominated the Pacific Coast, immediately began its trek east to cover lost Ringling dates.[50]

To the unassuming eye, these changes appeared only to add top-billing performers to a smaller show. But workers with the Barnes Sells-Floto show felt much more substantial changes. Since Ringling performers, appropriately nicknamed Big Show performers, possessed the most fame and influence in the circus world, they replaced many of the Barnes Sells-Floto performers. The entire opening act in the last Barnes Sells-Floto show on the West Coast was replaced immediately before the circus headed east with Ringling. The head bandleader for Barnes Sells-Floto was demoted to the aftershow, and the more recognizable Merle Evans took over the top spot. Ringling managers, including the sideshow manager and general show manager, also usurped those spots with Floto. Even the cookhouse staff faced significant turnover.[51]

Although a few shows did not fall under the Ringling umbrella in 1938, they reacted accordingly to the troubles under Ringling's watch. Robbins Brothers, a small independent circus, capitalized on the midseason closing of the Cole Brothers Circus by acquiring several train cars, livestock, and performers. And that same season, the Barnes-Sells-Floto show, though now purportedly independent, rolled into town with Ringling-plastered equipment. In short, two large circuses (Cole Brothers and Ringling) closed midseason in 1938 and continued to reap profits by parsing out

Elephants with the Barnes Sells-Floto Circus pull newly acquired Ringling equipment, 1938. Special Collections at Milner Library, Illinois State University, Normal. Image BNP4306. Used with permission.

equipment, animals, and human labor to the other circuses under their respective banners.[52]

Over the next few years, the shows still turned profits and played to "straw houses," a term used to denote sold-out shows with spillover audience members standing on "hayloft luxury." Even though the total number of circuses traveling in 1941 had been reduced to just twenty-five, more than twelve thousand people turned out at the midseason Ringling shows. The Ringling show, with its five hundred animals and sixteen hundred employees, remained popular, and the well-planned big top performances still caught the public eye. But illicit glimpses of the circus remained more profitable. A *Life* magazine feature recalled the memorable unscripted moments when Gargantua the gorilla threw regurgitated food at the cameras, a trapeze artist lost some costume padding in midair, an elephant on the lot destroyed the food wagon, and two lions escaped and rolled around on the grass. At the most memorable gratis performance in Lexington, Kentucky, elephants had to rescue a fleet of tractors that had become stuck in the mud.[53]

Audiences still had a variety of gratis performances to enjoy during the years following the strikes, but the spectacle of elephants rescuing modern equipment signaled changes in the circus world. And even before North officially closed the curtain on the Golden Age of the circus, his route plans showed a clear indication that things were different. In 1950, he opted out of advance cars, a staple of early US circuses. These cars, detailed in chapter 1, were armed with dozens of employees and thousands of billposters to plaster towns with advertising days ahead of the circus's arrival. North's decision to abandon this tradition in favor of more cost-effective radio advertising signaled a new age for the circus.[54] Just one year earlier, North had attempted to recoup profits from a poor season by organizing a second route rather than staying in winter quarters. With his sights set on Havana, Cuba, North set sail with a substantially smaller show.[55]

North's modern vision continued beyond 1938. The next two decades included color-coordinated acts, fewer rings under the big top, prerecorded music, and a gratis performance led by Caterpillar tractors rather than horses and elephants. Even the identities of performers signaled a new era. An industry built on diverse worker identities began to strategically hire workers to avoid union wage scales. As a money-saving measure, North hired foreign performers, called continentals. Workers reported falling victim to "legal hocus pocus" that left them with low wages and little protection. With North paying their bonds to the Department of Immigration, workers reportedly sought to avoid being labeled "trouble-makers."[56]

With nearly the entire circus industry on his payroll, North single-handedly changed what circuses looked like in the United States. But even given these changes, it still came as a surprise to much of the circus world when North announced in 1956 that "the tented circus is a thing of the past," as he packed up the big top for the last time and began showing at indoor arenas and traveling by truck. In 1936, the press and the circus managers agreed that "a circus without a tent just isn't a circus," but by 1956 North saw things differently.[57]

· · ·

Although mergers in the first few decades of the Golden Age created stronger and more financially secure shows, later mergers destabilized the circus world. More stable shows bought out equipment from folded shows, allowing the buyers to stay afloat longer. Ringling's 1929 business deal, however, did not come at a wholesale price. Instead, he bought well above market value to retain his undisputed title in the circus world. As the show began to pass through the hands of various investors over the next several decades, each new owner made ardent attempts to revive the debt-ridden symbol of American culture.

Even though circus proprietors had sought efficiency in many parts of the business since the early years of the Golden Age, the work itself remained somewhat archaic, particularly during the gratis performance. But audiences embraced this lack of efficiency and tacitly required it. Modernization did not always trickle down from the larger shows to the smaller ones. The Al G. Kelly and Miller Brothers Circus remained small from its Depression-era opening through World War II. As a truck show, the Al G. Kelly and Miller Brothers Circus began with an inherent embrace of technology that disrupted the circus world. But the show continued to innovate by adding more modern touches each season, including enlisting an airplane for advertising.[58]

Early shows behaved like corporations well before their decline. Owners intentionally cornered markets and operated a series of insider agreements to stave off competition. The decline of the circus is linked not so much to the actual business of the mergers but to the increasingly public nature of behind-the-scenes circus activity, which struck a chord with audiences that were not accustomed to seeing the circus as a business. Although business deals constantly made headlines and shows touted their annual profits, they seemed, at worst, to be benevolent employers. Like with later twentieth-century corporations, their appeal depended on their noncorporate appearance. Circuses had to continually project an image of small-town, homegrown, family business.[59] When the circus's corporate nature briefly showed during its Golden Age, people responded accordingly. Audiences foreshadowed complaints about the later monopoly of tented shows when they grumbled, "it has come to a pretty state of affairs when a man can't go to a show without patronizing a trust."[60]

The Making of the Circus Celebrity

From the single circus day in Wichita Falls, Texas, in 1912 and across the nearly fifty years that followed, circus world management demonstrated that it knew how to attract an audience. The circus was a space where people could see the extraordinary. Opening specs offered people a chance to see nearly the entire workforce under one tent, as thousands of people and animals re-created a scene with stunning detail and in ornate costumes. These moments were created with as little left to chance as possible, as evidenced by the intricately planned itinerary that skilled routing agents drafted, the well-rehearsed performances in adjoining rings under the big top tent, and the efficiency of a workforce that could quickly create a circus lot out of a field. But workers, especially animals, could prove unpredictable, and the well-worn equipment could also prove faulty. This chapter explores these unscripted moments in the circus world and the ways that the working-class nature of the shows and visible manual labor it took to set up the lot also brought circusgoers, particularly working-class circusgoers, into the world. On the one hand, unscripted moments were part of what audiences craved. On the other hand, tragic accidents involving people that had been propelled to celebrity status brought renewed debate about whether the paternalistic shows could actually protect their workers.

As the circus entered the offseason in the winter of 1930, circus workers faced the inevitable decision of how to make money until the shows picked back up again around early March. Manual laborers often hoped to be kept on as a skeleton crew in the winter quarters, while midrange performers could transition to other performance stages. Some highly valued contracted workers, like Lillian Leitzel, took their acts to Europe for a few months to give nightly performances. Following the 1930 season with Ringling

Brothers, Leitzel did a long stint at several European theaters, including the Cirque d'Hiver in Paris and the Wintergarten Berlin.[1]

Leitzel's performances in the United States and Europe remained largely consistent and popular because her feats were extraordinary and daring. She attracted audiences by doing nearly a hundred aerial somersaults during each performance, without a net beneath her. She had decades of experience under her belt, after beginning her aerialist career at the age of twelve. The press noted that nonstop conditioning was "better protection to her than any net."[2] But just one week after that review was published, Leitzel fell while performing in Copenhagen. Crowds gasped as one of her rings broke and she plunged more than forty feet to the ground. Everyone appeared optimistic about what seemed to be her brush with death, especially Leitzel herself, who refused immediate assistance. Her husband even reportedly left her hospital bedside to return to the stage because her condition had improved.[3]

Yet days later Leitzel passed away from traumatic injuries brought on by her fall, prompting a flurry of public responses. Madison Square Garden offered up a darkened arena tribute to the circus star before the hockey game the night after her death.[4] Some circus fans understood it as a workplace accident, noting that "every day people die as they perform their tasks. That's what Lillian Leitzel was doing. It was her job." The circus world mourned openly, with media there to capture the emotional breakdown of her husband and images of circus workers comforting one another following her death.[5]

While the world mourned, Leitzel's death also perpetuated the long circus tradition of skills being passed between generations. Within weeks, the press invoked a common trope as it wondered whether she was perhaps a "fatalist" who "expected to die in the ring," given the level of danger that came with her performance. She had inherited her aerialist fame from her grandmother and mother, who had also performed daring acts in the ring. Upon her death, at least some of the public took solace in Leitzel's seven-year-old niece stepping into the family tradition and training to become an aerialist.[6]

The same month that the circus world reeled from the death of one of its most famous aerialists, it also came to grips with the hospitalization of Mabel Stark, who was famous for her big cat act. Rather than travel to Europe to perform during the offseason, Stark had stayed in the winter quarters, practicing her act for the Al G. Barnes show. In early February, she had spent about an hour running the routine with seventeen tigers in the ring, when one cat sprang from his pedestal and onto Stark, pinning her to the ground. The attack, as well as the ensuing rescue, characterized the danger of the job. Two men stayed outside the cage, jabbing the tiger with steel rods until it "abandoned the attack."[7] Stark projected control over the big cats, noting that "I don't merely pray that my tigers behave; I make them behave, if possible." Yet even as she spoke those words, her body bore more than eighteen scars from an attack three years earlier. She also played into the narrative that her workplace offered little protection, noting, "Of course, it is dangerous work and I expect these cats to finish me some day."[8]

Leitzel's death in the ring and Stark's series of near-death experiences captivated circus audiences and prompted a flurry of reactions that had tangible effects on the circus as a workplace. Protest against Leitzel's death was swift, representing as it did both a reaction to the immediate circumstances and also long-standing critiques of the circus as a dangerous job. This reaction was rooted in the audience's connection to the circus as more than simply a workplace. Although deaths under the big top often prompted major reforms, or at least calls to undertake them, near-death encounters were more generally accepted as worthwhile risks that made the shows exciting.[9] Circus work became synonymous with death-defying work, and circuses most often delivered on the promise to offer shows that met this expectation. But audiences also became enthralled with circus workers outside of the big top. The development of the circus celebrity—which included high-paid acts, low-paid working men, and thousands of animals—offers a fuller look into the lives of circus workers.[10] It humanized workers who were otherwise known for feats that seemed to defy reality. While much of their performance labor seemed unbelievable, their emotional and manual work made them relatable figures. Chapter 3 examined this phenomenon from a gendered perspective; this chapter, in contrast, explores the ways that this work was not always gendered. And while the autonomy of animal trainers is examined in the second chapter, this chapter instead looks at how their work created pushback against the tented shows. Circus workers conducted their personal lives between shows and had much of it documented for the press, as in the case of Leitzel's husband after her death. Circus workers embodied these contradictory identities in their celebrity images, from newspapers to advertisements to live-action encounters, while circuses embraced the press for their shows. But this also opened the door for wide-ranging critiques that undermined the longevity of the tented shows.

The Circus Spokesperson

When circus workers pulled into towns on the train, they immediately garnered public attention from audience members who may have been familiar with their body of work, life story, or simply their face. The latter became particularly true through the growing advertising industry and its use of the circus to sell a whole host of products and services. The range of products endorsed by the circus industry demonstrates the intimate ways that the circus interacted with audiences outside of the big top shows and the ways that circus workers were simultaneously seen as both extraordinary and relatable. Audiences encountered these advertisements in several mediums, including newspapers, mainstream magazines, and circus programs at the shows.

The push to view circus as family entertainment remained evident in its advertising partnership with Wheaties breakfast cereal. Like other aspects of the circus world, this association transcended any one particular outfit and instead was picked up by several different shows. The long-standing "Breakfast of Champions" tagline was featured, for example, alongside images of circus stars Antoinette Concello and Jennie Rooney performing aerial stunts, as well as blurbs about how their daily breakfast with the show included a bowl of Wheaties with "plenty of milk, sugar, and fruit." The Al G. Barnes show featured animal trainers in more than half of its Wheaties advertisements, with Terrell Jacobs noting that Wheaties was essential for his work because "being a lion-tamer is a hard, dangerous job. You have to be able to stand up and 'take it.'"[11]

Some advertisements targeted women by declaring that dressing room tents stocked products that were also available to everyday consumers. Lux soap ran multiple full-page advertisements for various ways the product could solve cleaning problems and declared itself the desired brand of "Circus, Hollywood Studios, and Broadway Musicals." With images of everyday women chatting and sipping tea juxtaposed against images of trapeze performers and women decked out in feathered costumes for the opening spectacle, Lux promised to keep both stockings and complexions safe and clear.[12] Advertisements for Lux in circus publications demonstrated the behind-the-scenes efficiency and professional nature of the circus, noting that the costumes, worth more than a quarter million dollars, were trusted to Lux. Again, the advertisement was tied to the domestic sphere: circus costumes, it said, were "kept fresh and new in just the same way most women in their homes keep their clothes fresh and new."[13]

Circus workers had to maintain a level of health that allowed them to do physical work and feats nearly every day of the season. Advertising targeted this reality, demonstrating to the public that ordinary people could consume the same wellness products that circus workers used. Tobacco was a major advertising campaign that made use of circus workers, particularly in the 1930s. Touted as something that was conducive to a healthy lifestyle, cigarettes seemed to fit with the necessities of circus work as a product that supposedly calmed nerves and eased digestion. Camel bought a full-page advertisement in the Al G. Barnes program, with equestrian trick rider Dorothy Herbert claiming to smoke during and after every meal to ensure a safe performance.[14] Sir Walter Raleigh Smoking Tobacco made a different pitch, claiming that the smell of other brands would surely upset the lions when circusgoers walked around the lot.[15] Beech-Nut Chewing Tobacco also advertised in programs, using a play on the Barnum slogan by calling itself "the greatest chew on earth" (alongside images of a circus parade).[16] Advertisements also alluded to the circus as a dangerous workplace, as with those for the Bauer & Black line of first-aid products.[17] Allcock Manufacturing Company created an array of products that targeted health and wellness. Circusgoers would have seen its advertisements for laxatives used by the general population of "circus folks," porous plasters used by "aerial stars with their death-defying feats," and corn plasters used by "the gymnasts, acrobats, and trapeze artists."[18]

Other advertisements catered to one of the circus's clear specializations: animal husbandry. The circus industry relied heavily on animal labor and depended on having animals healthy enough to make it through an entire season. The Capewell Horse Nail Company, headquartered not far from the Bridgeport, Connecticut, winter quarters, reminded consumers of its quality, its importance in the world of equine care, and its use by every horse in the Ringling Brothers and Barnum & Bailey shows, which were shoed with its nails.[19] Flit advertised itself as the "official insect-killer of the largest circus in the United States," and urged households to buy its products for their own mosquito and fly control.[20]

Local retailers also capitalized on the extra business brought on by circus day, with sales and advertisements that directly referenced the upcoming shows. In doing so, they normalized the association between their roles as consumers and spectators at the circus. Stores held "children's day" sales, knowing that there would be an influx of young people in town. They also gave away balloons or even circus tickets with a minimum purchase and encouraged shoppers to make purchases while waiting for the parade to start.[21]

While audiences felt connected to circus life through advertising, they also re-created the circus world with the niche hobby of model trains. Social clubs and periodicals spurred an entire industry where fans could re-create a day in the life of the circus world in painstaking detail. Train cars were built to scale, with hobbyists ensuring that every stripe of paint was correct, and every cage contained the right number of bars. Some model enthusiasts went beyond simply re-creating the train and instead built the entire circus world, often centering on the circus parade or the built lot. A plethora of articles and photographs, as well as personal memories of being on the lot, could ensure accuracy. Circus workers, including clown Emmett Kelly, publicly reminisced about the details of the circus lot, while other workers responded to personal correspondence that inquired about exact colors of wagons and tents, to the delight of model train enthusiasts.[22]

Creating the Circus Celebrity

Living and working in the circus world, where so much was idealized by the public, did not mean that circus workers were exempt from societal critique, especially regarding their profession. But these critiques reached beyond dangerous working conditions. Aerialist Mickey King began her career in 1923 when the Sells-Floto Show stopped near her Massachusetts home. King, an eighteen-year-old onlooker at the time, turned her big top infatuation into a legitimate center-ring career as the show made its way down the East Coast. King followed the career path of thousands before her by running away to join the circus.[23] Elephant trainer Lucia Zora took a similar career path as she embraced her "wandering instinct" when the circus stopped in New Orleans.[24] In interviews and autobiographies, women like King and Zora described a sense of liberation and independence. But their transgressions also attracted significant criticism.[25] Labor roles were gendered in the circus, but if a woman left home in search of a transient form of employment, she still countered gender norms. A performer's workday did not broach the level of grueling labor that working men faced in the shows, but it still required a near-constant work schedule. Practices, performances, and travel required a significant time commitment from circus workers. As a result, performers often took their families with them on the road. This solidified the image of the circus as a form of family entertainment, but it also opened up the worker's family life to criticism. Even with their families in tow, the image of these runaway circus women aroused critics. A cheeky cartoon published in *Lilliput* depicted a circus woman in an equestrian act with a befuddled man running behind her with a baby in his arms, screaming, "It's *you* he wants!" Similarly, a cartoon of a performing pair of acrobats flying through the air while discussing the need to have a more monotonous marriage highlighted the public and untraditional way of life for circus families.[26]

Fabricated family dynamics among circus workers helped cement a relatable celebrity image but also fed into the larger benevolent image of the industry. Many families performed together in the sideshow or under the big top. But in the interest of maintaining that image, circuses also promoted unrelated people as family acts. Unbeknown to audiences, sibling and parent-child acts were often hastily formed. Reaffirming the importance of image and everyday performance identity, these atypical units masqueraded as biological families. Anne Carroll, who rose to prominence in equestrian acts, debuted as the daughter of Professor "Pop" Carroll, whom she had really just met. When a trapeze artist fell to his death in 1891, the *Pittsburgh Daily Post* reported that it was one of the Hanlon brothers. The paper had to quickly retract the headline at the behest of the Hanlon family, however, reporting instead that the death was simply a pupil who had taken the family name.[27] Without standardized circus schools to train new workers, the image projected by these invented families supported the mentor-protégé relationships that existed in nearly every act.[28]

Shows made other deliberate attempts to promote themselves as safe spaces for audiences of all ages and served as a constant reminder of working-class presence on the lot. Behind the scenes, they enacted strict regulations that policed the behavior of their workers when in the public eye. A small pamphlet printed for Ringling Brothers employees spelled out both rules and "suggestions" for worker behavior. Made with the intention of showing the "town folks" that "circus folks [were] real men and women and ladies and gentlemen as well," this pamphlet made explicit demands of circus workers in public spaces. During the very well-attended parades, workers were forbidden from engaging in conversations or arguing with other employees, wearing unbuttoned coats, or smoking. Because performance spilled beyond the few hours in the big top and sideshow tents, shows felt compelled to police working men as well, particularly through a dress code.[29]

Animals also reached celebrity status, particularly through their accessibility beyond center-ring performances. Just as circus workers engaged in specific identity politics throughout their careers, they projected these same feelings of solidarity onto their animal costars. Trainers spoke of animals as "troupers" who enjoyed the nomadic life of riding trains each night and socializing with crowds of people each day.[30] Animals drew crowds, and circus proprietors were eager to display the "biggest" or "one of a kind" beasts for the public gaze. These early displays of exotic animals invoked a particular reaction from audiences. Even prior to P. T. Barnum's outlandish claims of mermaids, cannibals, and missing links, audiences had found themselves viewing the "first of its kind" in the United States.[31] This sort of advertising about the uniqueness of certain shows made animals an important and necessary draw. Audiences frequented parades, lot setups, and the menagerie tent to see glimpses of the animals outside of their center-ring performances. But audiences still valued center-ring performances, especially the dangerous wild cat acts. Dating back to Isaac Van Amburgh's

1883 decision to put his head in a lion's mouth, audiences expected to see trainers climb into the cat cages and demonstrate their dominance over the ferocious animals.[32] Trainer Lorraine Wallace engaged in "hand to claw" combat with her tiger Rajah during each show. Rather than encourage the audience to take the performance at face value, the Al G. Barnes show instead publicly offered $1,000 to any person that could prove the tiger had been made safer with dulled claws and teeth.[33]

Like with performances by humans, animal performances were sometimes created in haste, which offered dangerous working conditions to popular animal performers. Carl Hagenbeck, who supplied much of the circus world with animal workers, also created his own ticketed performances and shows. When Hagenbeck made his 1893 US debut at the World's Columbian Exposition in Chicago, he brought animals and trainers who showcased brand-new acts for the American public. Patrons were shocked at the "King of Beasts" act, a lion riding a horse. But the sudden death of the trained horse just after their arrival in Chicago also provided an intimate glimpse into the replaceability of animal workers. With more than fifteen years of experience, Ed Darling had become an expert in mixed animal acts. The trainer quickly found a local cart-pulling horse and broke him into the lion-carrying act.[34]

Circuses brought audience members face-to-face with the gruesome hazards of the show's workplace.[35] During the offseason, circus workers continued to have close encounters with danger at the winter quarters. Without a public meandering around the lot, these stories instead found their ways into newspapers, where the public could still hear about a worker bravely surviving treacherous work. Often, circus fans welcomed dangerous acts that risked the lives of animals and people. Although audiences protested big cat acts until they were finally disbanded in 1925, they encouraged dangerous acts that involved more domesticated animals. Horses abounded in both gratis and big top circus performances, and they also starred in Wild West shows and on the hippodrome track. Audiences delighted in "lofty hurdling" and "hazardous high-jumps."[36]

People, too, were encouraged by audience cheers to perform even more daring feats. Sometimes newspapers reported performers' deaths nonchalantly, as in the case of Ava Gilbert, a twenty-six-year-old flying ring performer who fell from thirty-five feet, breaking her neck and dying minutes later in front of the audience.[37] Charles Blondin, who traversed Niagara Falls on a tightrope, remained a crowd favorite in the nineteenth-century circus. His notorious daredevilry drew crowds. Only when he appeared above the audience with his infant daughter did the previously cheering crowd object.[38]

Critics blamed audiences for patronizing these daring stunts. Even as early as 1870, newspapers readily published pictures and descriptions of the gruesome deaths of both men and women in the ring.[39] After a series of deaths in 1908, including the first performance of the hoop-the-hoop (a quick performance that saw someone in an automobile on a track that made a complete upside-down loop), the *Charlotte News* compared these deaths in the ring to the barbarism of gladiator fights. It suggested that seeing the automobile as a mechanical success would be far more impressive. And if the car was the feature of the act, why should it be manned? The paper answered its own question: because people wanted to see something dangerous and deadly. Shows understood this audience desire and called the acts names such as "dip of death."[40]

The European press was more graphic and condemnatory of dangers to circus workers. French magazine *Radar* published a full-page illustration by famed artist Rino Ferrari depicting the death of lion tamer Nayara Swami in England. Swami, who performed in Ringland's Circus with three lions, took his bow after his lions had been escorted offstage. But an open cage door allowed Leo, the large male lion, access to the center ring. In front of thousands of circus fans, Leo mauled his trainer, leaving him for dead. A cartoon provided similar commentary, showing a cage full of lions and decapitated trainers. The caption read: "Whistle up another trainer: We must get this head-in-the-lion act just right by Tuesday."[41]

This remark about the disposability of animal trainers speaks to the informality of entering circus job markets, which meant that sometimes top-billing spots belonged to people who were more likely to get injured. Circus posts, including animal training, did not blossom under professional networks. Instead, trainers often stumbled their way into the jobs. The US circus boom in the 1870s meant that circuses had to quickly fill new labor openings. The impact was largest on animal trainers, as inexperienced people clamored to fill the role. High turnover rates, typical of seasonal laborers, which characterized the job, were much more common than long careers. Those who stayed and kept their animal training jobs over multiple seasons faced a constant barrage of stressors. Drunk animal handlers became a stereotype among circus folks.[42] Clyde Beatty, famed animal trainer, was remembered by his grandchildren as putting on a white robe and pouring up a highball at the end of each performance to "settle down and cool off."[43]

Some handlers worked their way into the high-profile job from more menial positions, which made their labor more relatable to the public. One of Hagenbeck's lead trainers went into the business after years as a schoolteacher, claiming that "it is much easier to teach animals than children." Eph Thompson was only fourteen when he joined the ranks of the Adam

Forepaugh Circus elephant department as an assistant. Some trainers, like elephant trainer Teddy Metcalfe, began much earlier as part of a circus family dynasty. Similarly, George Lockhart's first memories were in the circus while both of his parents were performers. He took up the elephant-training trade after spending time in an Indian circus. Without any sort of professionalization, animal training worked almost exclusively as an apprentice system. Tricks, trades, and styles developed within circuses and families.[44]

Within the circus workplace, trainers also possessed significant fame. Although no single trade journal was dedicated exclusively to animal training at the turn of the century, circus papers, magazines, and newspapers reported extensively on animals and their trainers. People were not just interested in seeing a tiger jump through a fiery hoop. They also wanted to know how the trick was learned and who taught it. As with other circus workers, the public was curious about trainers' personal lives outside the ring.[45]

As workers, animal trainers around the world had power over their careers because they often owned high-value animals and pulled in a substantial paycheck. In 1910, nearly one-third of equestrian performers with the Ringling Brothers show owned their own horses. While Ringling provided relatively strong job security (the strongest in the circus business), other circuses could hardly guarantee a full season. By owning their act, animal trainers were financially appealing to circuses if they ever found themselves between jobs. For a single salary, the circus could get a trainer, performer, and several animals. Once employed, these trainers often commanded some of the highest salaries.[46]

The public also took note of trainers' dangerous working conditions. Owners offered additional pay for especially dangerous acts, but workers faced constant fear of injury or death. Louise Montague demanded increased salary for her work with a particularly dangerous elephant and sued the circus after sustaining injuries.[47] William Philadelphia and Fraulein May Berg each suffered substantial injuries from big cats at the Chicago World's Fair in 1893. Papers reported on the horrific injuries and the determination of the trainers to get back into the ring as soon as possible.[48] Child labor, which proliferated throughout the circus world, brought more attention to the dangers of animal training. Martha Frazier, a twelve-year-old lion tamer, died during a 1911 performance in Mississippi. Although child labor laws existed in the United States, the entertainment industry was largely exempt. As death became a consistent reality for animal trainers, arguments over training methods, tricks, attire, safety, and performance pitted proprietors, handlers, and trainers against one another. The business of the circus meant that safety and profits often produced different performance visions. Injury and death occurred in the ring, to the shock and awe of audiences.

And although trainers faced significant risk during their performances, the low-paid handlers who fed and watered the animals were in much more danger on a daily basis and had even less employer protection.[49]

Circus workers who could do so used their celebrity to negotiate contracts. The tension between trainers and their employers often came to a head during negotiations. Worker contracts dictated more than just wages. Sought-after performers resisted noncompete clauses when they tried to navigate the circus world. Jack Joyce, a horse trainer with the Cole Brothers—Clyde Beatty Circus, found himself in court when he violated a stringent noncompete clause by providing services to the Hagenbeck-Wallace show.[50] Freelance performers often signed away full control over their animals outside of the scheduled performances. Circus proprietors, meanwhile, demanded or negotiated extra appearances. When Raymond Toole-Scott created his small English circus in 1936, he depended almost solely on these freelance performers. The ensuing contracts, which guaranteed almost no protections to the performers, included a mandatory clause stipulating that show animals were to be exhibited on the sideshow, with the performers charged for their upkeep. Performers who had acquired their own herd often refused to do their acts with any other animals.[51] This package deal sat well with circus owners. For Scott, this opportune situation allowed him to have top-billing animals performing both onstage and offstage, without purchasing them from expensive dealers like Hagenbeck.

But work looked different for trainers in the first few decades of the twentieth century as circuses had to contend with the more famous stars. While nineteenth-century tamers remained in the public eye for a short stage act during each performance, Mabel Stark and other animal trainers in the 1920s stayed in the cage with their animals for much longer. This meant that the public witnessed more animal attacks on trainers than in previous decades. Stark suffered from several attacks during her performances, as well as a horrifying mauling during a street parade, when the horse carrying the cage slipped and jostled the already disgruntled tiger. People inside and outside the circus world noted that Stark's body was a "network of scars" and "clawed."[52] At least partially because of these attacks, as well as increasing public pressure and instances of clear mismanagement of animals, the larger circuses ceased big cat acts for nearly a decade.[53]

Trainers in the United States continued to take substantial risks with their big cats in front of audiences, particularly after the acts returned to the Ringling Brothers Circus in the 1930s. Popular trainers also moved away from any semblance of kindness training in the ring. Instead, Clyde Beatty and other popular trainers of the 1940s exerted dominance over the cats with a holstered pistol, a whip, and a chair. Beatty famously changed

Cage wagon carrying lions and being pulled by horses, 1937. Special Collections at Milner Library, Illinois State University, Normal. Image BNP3523. Used with permission.

big cat performances by introducing mixed acts that included dozens of big cats, and sometimes hyenas and bears. As Beatty stood in a cage with up to forty male and female lions, tigers, and bears, his act signaled a quick departure from the Hagenbeck revolution of training.[54] The shows openly admitted the danger of these sorts of acts, telling audiences that these mixed acts contained big cat breeds that were "natural enemies."[55]

Circus performances and adjacent forms of entertainment ignored animal culture, such as the more solitary nature of tigers, by grouping animals together for performances and thereby raising the overall risk to performers. Cage sizes also increased over time, with more cats participating in each performance. As the circus began shifting its big cat performances, mixed-species acts became more popular, despite their danger. An early Coney Island act that included a lion, polar bear, and cinnamon bear ended in 1910 with a lion attack on both the smaller bear and the trainer.[56] Early acts also featured a series of horseback-riding animals, which often put horses in peril. While more benevolent performances placed small dogs on the backs of horses, larger shows used leopards, lions, and tigers.[57]

Although the performance persona of big cats was designed to illicit fear, circus workers understood other animals to be far more dangerous. In the case of bears, circus folks often regarded them as more capable killers. As one circus report noted, "You never ought to start beatin' a tiger around, because he'll kill you the first chance he'll get. . . . But when a bear's mean, he's a whole lot more dangerous than a cat because he can kill you quicker and in more ways. And, believe me, a lot of them are willing to try."[58] Bears, in particular, gained reputations for hurting trainers through the swipe of their paw. In 1907, trainer Millie Spellman had a black bear slap at her hand in front of audiences before crushing the hand in its jaws.[59]

For tigers, bears, and other predatory animals, their celebrity status rested on their ferociousness. For trainers, conversely, their celebrity status rested on their sense of bravery and their commitment to making sure that the show did in fact go on. In the case of Spellman, she wrapped her hand and continued performing, even when "blood began to spurt from the bear's jaws."[60] Trainers often used assistants in their performances, so when a leopard "tore the flesh from the trainer's left arm and shoulder" during a performance on a rolling globe, the assistant immediately stepped in to finish the performance.[61]

Elephants occupied a different entertainment sphere than big cats. They were thought to be wise and kind, as well as generally happy to perform tricks that accentuated these traits. But circus workers had real lived experiences and tall tales to remind them that sometimes elephants went rogue. Whether because of emotional or physical abuse, medical conditions, or personality, elephants infamously turned on their captors, usually at moments that appeared most opportune for them. Yet in the case of elephants like Big Charley of the Wallace Circus, who killed his trainer while bathing in a river at the winter quarters, the press and circus world portrayed him as inherently defective, an animal with an "ugly temper" and a man-killer instinct.[62]

In big top performances, among menagerie collections, and in the gratis performance, circuses pandered to audiences' wishes for animals. With an assortment of wild animals and sometimes very little knowledge of husbandry or behavior, the circus often backed itself into a corner when it came to handling the larger creatures. When elephants inevitably escaped, damaged buildings, injured other animals, or killed trainers, circuses had to explain away the behavior as an anomaly. Sometimes, shows blamed the behavior on circumstantial accidents, thereby pacifying the audience's curiosity about how seemingly gentle giants could revert to their wild instincts. But outside of the circus, nineteenth-century audiences also enjoyed watching punishments as a form of public entertainment. When elephants rebelled in public, killed multiple trainers, or simply brought a higher profit through death, the circus willingly killed the animals. Echoing the rituals of lynchings, shows offered public executions of "guilty" elephants to welcoming audiences.[63]

Despite the public executions, circuses also portrayed themselves as champions of animals rather than dealers and traffickers. Circus management tried to avoid abuse allegations by portraying the shows as part of the animal rights movement. In 1903, the Barnum & Bailey show noted in its brochure that James A. Bailey was an active member of the Society for the Prevention of Cruelty to Animals.[64] Circus workers in the United States and beyond fought hard against allegations of animal abuse and neglect. Joseph McCaddon, Frank Bostock, and August Kober were part of a "revolution in animal training" at the turn of the century that amounted to little more than increased advertising of kind and gentle methods.[65] Aside from portraying themselves as outstanding animal keepers, circuses also claimed dominion over their menagerie. Under the auspices of biblical imagery, the Sells-Floto Circus urged audiences to honor the "courage of men who go into jungles, into tropical heat, into freezing cold; who face disease and death to bring out for your edification the wild creatures over which man is given dominion by God."[66]

Even as circuses could get some sort of handle over the image of their animal workers by changing what acts looked like, they had a more difficult time changing the performances of aerialists to adhere to safety measures. Although newspapers gladly pointed to high-wire performers who preferred the chance of danger, real deaths in the center ring as circus celebrities fell to the ground were less appealing images to manage. The show-must-go-on motif appeared particularly out of touch in the ensuing decades. When the Flying Wallendas, a high-wire pyramid act that had been performing for nearly forty years for US audiences, performed in Detroit in 1962, a fatal mistake sent the troupe to the ground. The Flying Wallendas had notoriously resisted the use of safety gear. Despite the deaths of two of its members in the ring, the show went on for an additional hour with clowns and horses, and newspapers reported that "many in the crowd were crying when they left."[67] When patriarch Karl Wallenda died on live television in a high-wire stunt, the press coverage and replay of his death left audiences feeling like the circus had become out of touch. They insisted that "the death of a private figure should be treated with dignity and sensitivity."[68]

• • •

The circus offered up all its workers as celebrities who thoroughly enjoyed their job and employer. Part of the circus's appeal was creating connections between its public face and the people who patronized the shows. Through targeted advertising the shows were able to corner several cultural markets while pulling in receipts that made the shows highly profitable. But the appearance of center-ring stars on Wheaties advertisements also made them household names, which made their deaths in the center ring more personal.

In the case of animals and some people, pushback was reframed as proof that there should be a greater level of paternalism over certain segments of the circus population. This created the image of a circus worker who defied death and worked long hours for little pay but did so for the greater good of the circus community. When deaths did occur, the circus had to account for the conditions that led workers, particularly women and children under the big top, to die in front of thousands of audience members. Circus acts caved to public pressure, while abandoning their traditionalism and confronting the realities of a modern workplace. While more well-known pressures, like the animal rights movement, were part of the growing dissent against the circus world, public disapproval centered more squarely on issues of labor. The circus had to confront these issues immediately, offering shows that met public approval.

8

Organized Circus Labor and Working-Class Audiences

The circus proved that it knew how to create performances that generated audience approval. And as was the case with animal trainers, sideshow workers, or people doing dangerous stunts, it was willing to radically shift how a ticketed show looked to keep its relevancy. While the previous chapter engages with audience disapproval of big cat acts that endangered people, this chapter examines how audiences increasingly disapproved of acts that felt stale, socially irrelevant, or ethically wrong. But even as circuses were willing to adjust center-ring performances, they usually did not approach their working class in the same way. Despite the performative nature of the work, the circus working class was sometimes uncontracted, nearly always underpaid, and increasingly unnecessary as the circus industry brought in automated versions of their jobs. The circus industry demonstrated that it did not fully understand the appeal and necessity of its working class, or the identity of its audiences. While it is nearly impossible to know how the hundreds of thousands of people throughout the United States who saw the circus on any given day felt about it, certain interactions between audiences and the shows do provide insight into how audiences identified themselves in relation to their leisure. Moreover, many changes made to the circus highlight middle-class assumptions about working-class people. While previous chapters have explored the thin line between audiences and circus workers, this chapter demonstrates the evolution of circus audience participation throughout the Golden Age.

Like the 1929 circus world buyout, a series of worker strikes in 1938 set the stage for fractures among circus audiences. It was also a moment that raised the curtain of the circus world, revealing its identity as a workplace (chapter 6 explores management shifts around those labor disputes). John

Ringling North surely felt some anxiety as his circus headed into the second month of shows in the 1938 season. Distrust had abounded among employees and circus fans when North took over the family business just one year earlier. It had not abated. North's identity was a usurper, an Ivy League graduate, a distant relative to the Ringling success, and someone who did not understand the circus world.[1]

But North's anxiety revolved around more than just distrust. At the opening night of his second season, at Madison Square Garden before twenty thousand fans, circus employees—with help from the American Federation of Labor (AFL)—openly protested labor practices.[2] In the weeks that followed, they went on strike, sabotaged the lot setup, and demanded better pay. With still more than half of the season left, North shut down the show and headed to winter quarters, laying off most of the workers.[3] The disgruntled workforce had remained a manageable difficulty for North up to this point, but he now faced the stigma of being the first Ringling owner to end the season early because of labor strife. At first, it seemed that the entire circus fan base shifted the blame onto the workers who had protested. Fans used *White Tops* magazine as a platform and hastily formed the Save the Circus movement, aimed at bringing the show back at any cost.[4] English circus fans, too, threw their support behind the American movement and demanded that the circus return, even if that meant stigmatizing the striking workers.[5]

Relationships between the circus and its working-class audience worsened in 1940, as the AFL continued to try to organize in the tented shows. The Save the Circus movement fizzled out the next season, after the Ringling show hit the road with significant changes to the labor and structure of the shows. Labor organizers appealed to working-class circusgoers in unions by presenting the shows as unfriendly to organized labor. With the AFL sending letters to local unions days before the circus arrived, North suddenly faced the consequences of asking his working-class audience to cross organized labor. And the sly AFL tactic affected more than just ticket sales: it also affected circus workers and partnerships. Decades of horizontal business integration meant that North owned nearly the entire circus industry, but he was still dependent on contracted labor. In response to the AFL, North embarked on his own letter-writing campaign to dissuade laundromat and printing press unions from breaking ties with the circus.[6]

This shift in audience responses between 1938 and 1940 spoke to the diversity of circusgoers. Although historians have rightfully pegged the circus as a working-class form of entertainment, middle and leisure classes also frequented the big top shows during its entire history.[7] Circus day meant that factories closed, schools released students, and almost entire towns could be found on the circus lot during the performance.[8] Shows also counted on their ability to capitalize on whistle-stops and larger railroad networks to ensure sold-out crowds. While stops might have been largely in bigger towns like Norfolk, Virginia, special circus day trains brought people from hours away to the circus lot.[9]

Big top tickets were affordable and readily available to most people. Even if the low prices were still beyond a potential circusgoer's budget, the gratis performance offered a circus experience.[10] Sawdust rings, animal acts, and outdoor shows were more readily associated with working classes, but early circuses made ardent attempts to appeal to upper-class patrons with reserved seating and high-paid performers. As time wore on, management attempted to mold the shows into something that resembled even more legitimate theater, thereby alienating its larger working-class base. But throughout the circus's history, management depended on reaching each of these classes to maximize profits.

The labor strikes during the late 1930s forced audiences into action against either circus management or employees, solidifying and revealing the class divisions among audience members. For middle and upper classes, the three-ring circus represented a uniquely American form of entertainment that had cultural value. They saw the shows as a benevolently paternalistic employer for otherwise unemployable people. But for the working classes, the sudden presence of union activity in the late 1930s associated the shows with their own workplaces and frustrations.

The audiences in both 1938 and 1940 affected the shows with their responses. Although responses across the two years showed varying allegiances, they were uniformly devastating to the circus working class. The middle- and upper-class response, particularly through the Save the Circus movement in *White Tops* magazine, paid little attention to the working conditions or larger complaints of the workers who had joined the strike. Instead, it was focused on the detrimental cultural effect of losing the circus. Public sentiment followed suit; the AFL and the striking workers were demonized for disrupting the American cultural tradition. As this chapter will explore, however, the larger working-class response of 1940 signaled the decline of the circus and catalyzed modernization, which would significantly alter the role of its workers. This modernization also reduced the shows to a more ordinary form of entertainment that lost its cultural value.

The complicated relationships between the audience and the circus are deeply rooted in its intersections as a variety form of working-class entertainment, a pastime nearly everyone enjoyed, and a democratic form of amusement.[11] Because the performance itself was never simply relegated to the ring, audience members saw workers performing during lot setup.

Often, members of the audience pitched in, making the circus a "democratic amusement."[12] Early circus performances, as well as their predecessors, were considered one of many interactive amusements available to American audiences. Even though audience interaction with performers quickly declined on vaudeville and burlesque stages, the circus retained this blurred line well into the twentieth century.[13] Rather than remaining passive bystanders during the Golden Age of the circus and its decline, audience members directly affected the form and function of shows. Their direct and indirect participation reveals that circuses reflected audience tastes. Even though the shows exploited workers in various ways, working-class audiences spent decades patronizing the shows because the shows masked exploitation as benevolent paternalism. More importantly, circuses were workplaces with an ambiguous labor force of contracted employees and everyday townspeople that shaped their labor and business practices. Audiences sometimes advocated for the protection of certain workers in the circus world, like animals or children, but when labor organizing threatened the viability of the shows themselves, workers became their target.

Everyone Goes to the Circus

P. T. Barnum's American Museum, on the corner of Broadway and Ann Streets in New York City, attracted passersby of all classes in the mid-nineteenth century. Broadway had already established itself as a social and cultural capital for upper-class members of society. As elite patrons made their way to Barnum's museum, they passed longtime establishments such as Saint Paul's Chapel, as well as newer, upscale venues like the Astor House. Nearby, City Hall and its adjacent park hosted a constant flow of New Yorkers. But working-class patrons also had an impressive walk to Barnum's museum as they made their way down Ann Street. The oddly narrow and short cobblestone road served as a direct route for the working-class patrons that frequented the museum. Once they arrived, they were treated to a barrage of posters lining the white walls of the five-story building. Flags lined the roof, and a lighthouse beam flashed across Broadway.[14] Armed with entertainment news and advertisements from local attractions like Barnum's museum, patrons of all classes could plan their visits to view a constant rotation of performers, exhibitions, and plays.[15]

Barnum's museum attracted working-class patrons with both its exhibits and its prices. Although his twenty-five-cent admission was higher than at the typical dime museums, it remained within most people's financial means. The exhibits rotated, and audience members saw a variety of performers onstage—all, as Barnum noted in his guidebook, at no additional cost to museum patrons.[16] A flat-rate admission to the museum meant that working-class patrons could pay a relatively small fee to view a variety of performances and exhibits, foreshadowing much of the circus experience outside of the big top.

Although prices were conducive to working-class patronage, Barnum advertised a middle-class sense of respectability. The Lecture Room provided patrons with a space to watch staged performances of morality plays as well as "one of the most spacious and well-ventilated" rooms in New York City. Creature comforts aside, Barnum also guaranteed that patrons could enjoy the museum free of alcohol, profanity, and immorality.[17] But performances often imitated working-class forms of entertainment as minstrel shows frequented Barnum's stage.[18]

The museum advertised itself as a safe place of entertainment for women and families. Advertisements touted that women and children could enjoy entertainment at the museum without fretting about safety.[19] This appeal to families both set the circus apart from other spaces of entertainment and set the stage for the unique circus audience of the late nineteenth and early twentieth centuries. While burlesque served as a purely male working-class entertainment and vaudeville audiences became increasingly feminized, circus performances remained geared toward families.[20]

Through Barnum's museum and early circuses, audiences learned to interact with their entertainment. Circuses welcomed and cultivated this interaction under the big top with clowning, as audiences found themselves participating in the short comedic acts.[21] People not only cheered at amazing feats under the big top and gawked at sideshow performers, but also called out falsities and felt genuinely connected to their entertainment. This interaction created a long-lasting relationship between workers and audience members. Circus audiences were also uniquely part of the circus performance, often as laborers. Although early shows fit well within audience and performer relationship norms, the continued engagement by audience members became unique to the circus as it entered the twentieth century. Children earned free tickets when the show came to their town by helping with menial setup tasks. As the *Washington Times* noted, "Nobody ever wrote a circus story without a picture of impatient youngsters who hang around to alleviate the thirst of an elephant or to hold the stake as the guy with the hammer makes ready for spreading the big tent."[22] Young men often worked out similar deals with the circus as they provided extra grunt labor in exchange for a ticket to the show.[23]

Even if audience members did not act as sources of labor, they could still find themselves unintentionally interacting with the shows. With a dangerous and often undertrained group of animals in such proximity

Young boys climb onto a cage wagon belonging to Ringling Brothers to peek inside, undated. Robert L. Parkinson Library and Research Center, Circus World, Baraboo, Wisconsin. Image CWi 198.

to audiences, injuries were fairly common. Chains, cages, and tents often could not hold animals that weighed thousands of pounds. A small dog caused an elephant stampede in Edmonton, Canada, when it rushed the herd during lot setup.[24] In 1891, children in the audience found themselves pinned under an onslaught of runaway animals at the Prof. Williams and Company Circus when the tent gave way in a storm. Patrons at other shows faced horses who broke away during the performance and elephants who refused to follow the parade route.[25]

Accidental encounters with audience members also occurred. With the circus grounds open to the public during setup, adventurous circusgoers initiated their own animal encounters. This became particularly perilous with children, as evidenced by a young boy who scaled the bars of a leopard cage until the big cat swiped him back to the ground. Occasional runaway animals could prove unnerving for the small towns where a circus set up. Circus workers were on the front line during these escapes, but animals still made it off the lot.[26] When a leopard escaped from a circus in Crookston, Minnesota, a hunting party tried to pursue the big cat after it reportedly attempted to attack a child at a farmhouse. This mayhem became a common scene for circus audiences since the traveling circus cities were always on the move.[27] Mishaps like those at the Prof. Williams show generally did not affect either profits or attendance. If the animals were recaptured, the show could regroup and move on to the next town.

As Ringling Brothers employee Dexter Fellows stated, the danger in wild animal acts affected audiences more than trainers.[28] Animal handlers, often undertrained, were responsible for wheeling the cages into the ring for performances. A single slip or misplaced cage could result in the quick escape of a four-hundred-pound cat. In the nineteenth century, publicity of these sorts of accidents provided the circus with a welcome stream of headlines and attention. But audience safety became more important in the twentieth century. The thrill of a loose wild animal diminished, as people preferred viewing acts from a safe distance.

Amazingly, despite often leveling terms like "treacherous" against captive elephants and their behavior, circus folks continued to use them in performances, as manual laborers, and as interactive parts of the show.[29] Haia, considered a "pet" elephant who interacted with children regularly, burst out of the train car during the unloading in New Haven, Connecticut, in 1928. He barreled across vacant lots and roads until his capture with a team of eight horses, heavy-duty rope, and a gang of circus workers. Like rogue elephants before him, Haia was immediately executed.[30]

Unscripted performances outside of the big top, circus parades, and the rest of the gratis performance made the circus a form of entertainment that unabashedly pandered to the working class. The circus parade offered a transition from the candid nature of the circus's arrival and the lot setup to the planned performances of the ticketed shows. Despite the parade serving as a sneak peek with performers outfitted in their big top costumes, the trip down a town's main streets usually proved less controllable than the main event. Horse-drawn wagons on uneven streets lined with loud crowds often brought more anxiety to both the animals and people in the cages. This prompted occasional attacks, some of which proved deadly.[31]

As people read about performances under the big top, they also read about the audiences who attended the shows. Circuses regularly offered free tickets to children in precarious situations, like orphanages and hospitals, in exchange for free press.[32] In 1937, the Ringling show announced the usual Orphan Day matinee for May that year. Thirty-three years earlier, the show had noted that on Orphan Day, James A. Bailey himself stood at the main entrance to shake hands with the seven thousand children who attended.[33]

Circuses documented the audiences they encountered and the differences between regions as they traversed the country. In the South, circuses witnessed a different circus day culture than in other parts of the country. Black circusgoers in the South came from segregated spaces, where separate communities were formed and carefully cultivated. Circuses, which burst into a town at each stop, bore witness to these social realities and noted how they affected circus day. Snack stands became the most visible part of the southern Black circusgoer experience. These stands sold a variety of fried food, including fish. Historian Gregory J. Renoff has analyzed these snack stands as a "social space" for Black circusgoers, where socializing took priority over profits. Since they were located outside the lot, and outside the purview of circus management, they attracted a whole host of people who may not have actually bought a ticket but still wanted to socialize. Yet circus workers themselves looked forward to the cuisine and also patronized the stands.[34]

Circus day for Black audiences looked different than it did for their white counterparts. Black newspapers offer glimpses into how circus day looked for circus patrons and the ways that they interacted with the shows. Black papers noted in circus day reports across several years that the city was filled with people from out of town to see the show. Ringling Brothers relied on and provided reports about sharecroppers making the trek to the show. This was corroborated by the apparent influx of out-of-towners, particularly in Black spaces.[35] Black circusgoers also used social spaces, prompting Black businesses like barber shops to bring in extra help on circus day. Churches got involved and took the opportunity to reach folks by serving meals. During a 1912 show, a women's group with a First Baptist Church served dinner in a Black beauty parlor, which was a "financial success."[36]

The fuller circus experience outside the big top was so important that its disappearance, even for a night, drastically reduced the number of people willing to come to the shows. Rain could force attendance to dip nearly in half. While big top performances could easily go on, rainy weather prevented circusgoers from spending hours on the lot, enjoying the unticketed parts of the show.[37] Circus fans lamented changes as well, especially those that affected their interactions with the shows. The installation of fire hydrants warranted grumbles, like "the kid who used to get in for carrying water to the elephant can't understand the justice of putting a hydrant on the circus lot."[38]

An Activist Audience

As explored in chapters 2 and 7, animal acts have an uneven history in tented shows. Even as audiences gladly interacted with animals in various spaces on the lot, they wondered at times whether elephants and other animals were healthy and content. Handlers and trainers in the circus asserted dominance over the dangerous animals with recognizable tools that audiences had come to expect. But in conjunction with notions of evolution, prevalent by the nineteenth century, a new strain of animal activism emerged that decried the whips, chains, and elephant hooks. While dogs and horses could be trained behind the scenes with these tools (later performing without them), elephants and wild cats required a constant air of authority, according to trainers. People began seeing animals as genetically more connected to humans, and rights movements surfaced as a result.[39]

Criticism against the presence and treatment of animals in the entertainment field was not relegated to the United States. In London in 1921, witnesses, interest groups, and politicians took turns discussing the matter in front of the newly formed Select Committee of the Royal Commission on Performing Animals. With pamphlets directed to the public that included a series of eyewitness accounts of abuse, as well as legal backing, European activists made compelling cases.[40] These critiques moved beyond training methods. Simply owning the animals and "divorc[ing] [them] from their natural habitat" brought significant unrest from English audiences. Britons organized the Jack London Club, the Performing Animals' Defence League, and the Royal Society for the Prevention of Cruelty to Animals. This European activism was more comprehensive than its American counterpart, seeking to curb abuse outside the ring as well. Legislation regulated the transportation of circus animals and their accommodations.[41] This meant that shows had a vested interest in maintaining an offstage performance to appease their harshest critics.

European zoo mogul Carl Hagenbeck ran into issues with animal activism when he partnered with American circus owners. Trying the traveling shows, quite unsuccessfully, in the United States and Europe, Hagenbeck slowly slipped out of the circus world. Behind the scenes, he lacked any enthusiasm, reportedly calling the shows "rabble" and the workers untrustworthy "gypsies." But he continued to train wild animals and got ahead of abuse scandals by becoming a proponent of kindness training. Unlike circuses in the United States, which had a limited selection of animals to display, Hagenbeck could choose the most docile animals to train.[42]

Activists viewed animals as innocents under the care of negligent workers. But circuses did not consistently bill animals as simpleminded or innocent. In 1923, the Al G. Barnes Circus, self-billed as the world's greatest wild animal show, spoke about its animals in seemingly contradictory ways. Although it admitted a "lavish display of animal beasts" and touted their "savagery," it also referred to them as "animal actors." The Barnes show more famously presented mixed cat shows, which forced multiple

A hippo with the Mills Brothers Circus exits the big top, 1957. Special Collections at Milner Library, Illinois State University, Normal. Image BNP8199v1. Used with permission.

cat species into a single performance. In billing, the show referred to these cats as "educated." Likewise, Lotus the hippopotamus was described as both "subjugated" and "educated." Perhaps as a way to counter the intensified animal activism of the 1920s, Barnes and other shows described their animals in terms that invoked volunteer work.[43] Ringling representatives echoed these sentiments, claiming that the lions who snarled furiously at the trainers holding whips were simply "good actors." Similarly, the Great Carmo Circus in England assured audiences that its lion performances showed that "when humanely and kindly treated, [circus animals] respond to anyone who understands them in the same way as does any domestic animal."[44]

Criticism against the conditions under which animals worked peaked in the 1920s in both the United States and Europe. Ringling, the largest US circus at the time, ditched its big cat acts after years of audience pushback. The show cited new refined audience preferences for dispensing with the formerly popular acts, noting that "wild animal trainers were never swamped with fan letters anyway."[45] In Europe, government committees and legislation resulted in the same sort of changes.[46] Yet these similar trajectories show the larger divides between circuses in the United States and abroad.

The move to abandon big cat acts in the United States was not a matter of evolution in keeping with the times, as suggested by Ringling Brothers, but instead was an abandonment of circus traditions. The show both caved to "refined" audience demands and alienated a larger, working-class audience base that was pegged as less cultured. While the US circus self-regulated its shows and quickly evolved to meet the demands of upper-class patrons, European shows changed with government-imposed regulations.

The circus industry suffered when the press joined the ranks of animal activists. The circus depended on the press for marketing. When Ringling dumped the big cat acts, reporters praised the show for allowing "cold hard business sense to gallantly come to the aid of sentimentalists." The Hagenbeck-Wallace Circus, another large show, responded to public sentiment by emphasizing cruelty-free training methods.[47] In England, the press rallied around circus protesters and demonized the use of animals in the shows. When a 1921 sea lion performance in London claimed to demonstrate animals' intellectual superiority over that of women, a local newspaper admonished the absurd suggestion. Instead, it echoed popular sentiments among activists by calling the learned tricks and humanlike behavior "violations of natural instincts."[48]

Criticism against the circus world was not isolated to its treatment of animals. The American Humane Association, an organization associated with curbing animal abuse, also investigated more than fifty thousand cases of child abuse throughout the United States in 1887. As other critics also noted, the circus used children as both manual laborers and big top performers.[49] Even prior to his circus debut, Barnum enlisted children, like five-year-old Tom Thumb, to appear on his sideshow stage in the American Museum. During US tours in the late nineteenth and early twentieth centuries, circuses did not face legal objections to this sort of labor. Workers often described their childhood entry into the circus world by recalling the familiar trope of running away to join the show. Felix Adler, water boy turned acrobat turned clown, joined the circus world part-time at the age of twelve with his father's blessing.[50]

The air of benevolent paternalism in US shows often masked the circus as a real site of child labor. Although these children worked in the public eye, their performance seemed less like a job than the work undertaken by their counterparts in mills and factories. General audiences rarely spoke out against the clear labor abuses by the shows. But circuses in the United States and abroad sought out children as performers, often exploiting their youth and inexperience as workers. By 1910, a peak year in the Golden Age, industries collectively employed nearly two million adolescents.[51]

Critics argued that with little autonomy over their own lives, young workers must be performing under coercive circumstances. Exposés accused shows of forcing children to smile and thereby perform some sort of emotional labor to keep audiences unaware of unsavory conditions. Larger protests against child labor—efforts that drew substantial membership and attention in urban centers such as New York City—made great strides in regulating the general workforce. An 1876 law in New York criminalized dangerous work for children under the age of sixteen. But legal challenges came from factory workers rather than circus workers. Even when circuses heard allegations of child abuse, they faced few, if any, repercussions. Because legislation remained at the state level, circuses could evade the laws by avoiding those particular states. Moreover, as a place associated with leisure rather than labor, the circus was largely overlooked by these reformers.[52]

Despite being a US entity that often found ways to skirt local, state, and national laws, the circus also engaged in international tours, which put it into direct conflict with tighter European regulations. Even as the Golden Age began to flourish in the United States, child labor in European circuses was suddenly circumscribed. Progressive reformers wrote muckraking pieces for readers, detailing the horrors of a transient lifestyle and the dangers of the job.[53] Famed English feminist Millicent Garrett Fawcett and social reformer Ellen Barlee campaigned against the use of child performers in places such as the circus ring or sideshow stage, citing immoral workplaces, unpaid labor, and sexual exploitation.[54] Exposés from spectators also revealed the circus to be an unsafe workplace for children. An 1885 letter to a London newspaper described behind-the-scenes practices that included incessant whipping of exhausted young acrobats.[55] England passed the Children's Dangerous Performances Act in 1879, banning circus workers under the age of fourteen from engaging in acts deemed especially treacherous. England continued to strengthen its child labor laws, particularly in entertainment and performance workplaces, making parents or guardians responsible under a summary conviction for a child that performed in a banned act. Employers faced assault charges if children were injured.[56] When the Barnum & Bailey show entered Belgium on its 1901 European tour, it faced child labor laws that affected its workforce. Belgian law set age limits for working children. To continue many of its acts on the Belgian leg of the tour, the show produced a document demonstrating that child circus workers were either accompanied by their parents or engaged in nondangerous work.[57]

Audiences and Labor Activism

Despite outcries against labor exploitation of children and animals, audiences rarely addressed the plight of underpaid workers and their role as circus employees. But it is this space that usually demonstrated fault lines among audience classes. By the time labor strikes intensified in 1938, shows already had a long history of dealing with unrest among their working-class employees. Strikes and union formation by clowns, sideshow workers, big top performers, and animal trainers happened with little audience fanfare. Newspapers often reported the stories as a sort of novelty. As explored in chapter 5, real union formation in the sideshow was brushed off by newspapers as comical "freaks unions."[58] When workers, including those in the sideshow tent, explicitly said that paternalism did not offer suitable workplace protections and benefits, the public treated the complaint like humbug.

Strikes and union formation remained constant throughout the Golden Age, but rarely disrupted the shows. Audiences, then, hardly acknowledged working-class complaints. Like with the general absence of child labor critiques, audiences praised the benevolence of circus paternalism and failed to see the shows as sites of unfair working conditions. But when circus workers collectively organized with the AFL in 1938, audiences could no longer ignore growing tensions. As circus fans entered Madison Square Garden on April 12, 1938, they expected the self-proclaimed Greatest Show on Earth to live up to its illustrious name. With nearly two thousand employees, a whole host of exotic animals, a star-studded cast of performers, and more than fifty years of experience, the Ringling Brothers and Barnum & Bailey Circus had become the most exciting show in the world. But circusgoers instead witnessed picket lines containing animal handlers and other inadequately paid laborers, while elephants and lions remained caged behind the stage. The strike by nearly the entire workforce burdened audiences into choosing sides.

Throughout the circus's Golden Age, audiences had witnessed a seemingly complacent workforce that was fortunate enough to have free food and housing. The circus, it seemed, was a generous employer for people who were hard pressed to find alternative employment. The circus perpetuated this idea by cultivating a circus world identity that felt inclusive and tight knit to employees. When audiences came to the circus lot they generally saw a well-run city with little to no internal strife.[59] Upon entering the big top tent, circusgoers could peruse their programs, which previewed the show, provided performer biographies, and detailed the day-to-day and offseason lives of workers. Audiences also knew of the circus world through nearly constant reporting in newspapers.[60]

When the 1938 strikes hit, audiences reacted based on their class identity.[61] Middle-class circusgoers felt betrayed by the circus's working class and blamed the outrageous wage increase for the early closure. Although they did not fill most of the seats under the big top tent, this loud minority still had influence. The Save the Circus movement, led by Frank Magin, drew a substantial following in more than six hundred cities and reached a large fan base through *White Tops* magazine. But it also reached the general public, with significant support from advertising firms and the press, which saw the decline of the circus as a more immediate danger than an underpaid working class.[62]

The movement attracted substantial attention and shifted the conversation away from worker rights. In her syndicated newspaper column, First Lady Eleanor Roosevelt lauded the efforts of middle-class circusgoers to maintain the "healthy interest" of the circus.[63] Although Roosevelt more famously supported the labor movement and working-class unions, she saw the battle in the Ringling Brothers show as a threat to a more important form of entertainment.[64]

Circus fans stayed connected to their favorite pastime through regularly held events. The Save the Circus activists began co-opting these events to increase awareness about the perils of losing the shows. When the Circus Fans Association held its annual meeting in 1938, activists took the opportunity to increase their membership and reach out to already avid, albeit less politically active, fans. For the middle-class activists, the circus was in immediate and grave danger. They promoted their cause as an attempt to save something that was distinctly American. But they also understood the changing landscape of American entertainment and urged people to band together to save the circus, lest it share the same fate as "the small-town opera house and vaudeville too."[65]

As the movement intensified in the winter of 1938, these activists sought to mobilize a large swath of circusgoers beyond the movement's middle-class origins. In an effort to ensure that the shows would go on the road the following spring, activists reached out to anyone who could possibly put pressure on the shows. In the tiny town of Marengo, Illinois, school-age children welcomed activists who showed a movie, presented pictures of circuses getting ready to start their tours, and encouraged students to write letters to the shows and sign a petition to President Roosevelt to make sure that the Golden Age did not end due to labor disputes. They worked hurriedly through the winter months, staging "Circus Fans' Night" for families at armories and sending representatives to schools across the country.[66]

The movement applauded its success as the Ringling show returned for the 1939 season.[67] But as the 1940 season opened, circusgoers and newspapers wondered what the new show would bring. North brought a renewed excitement to the shows. He reintroduced big cat acts, having made a massive purchase of leopards and jaguars upon viewing an impressive display of these cats in Europe. With this deviation from the typical lion and tiger acts, North successfully promoted the new cats as a "never before seen" and "world's first" performance. This return to big cat acts brought new wonder and danger for the shows. Audiences and press wondered aloud: Would Indo the Siberian leopard attack his fellow big cat performers like he had just done days earlier? Would he again attack his trainer?[68]

In another ardent attempt to organize the circus world, labor organizer Ralph Whitehead and the AFL protested again outside of Madison Square Garden. Working-class members of the audiences responded to this wave of AFL-led labor disputes. Whitehead targeted union members, who heavily patronized the shows, and portrayed the circus as unfriendly to organized labor. Boycotts from local unions began as Ringling Brothers pulled into each town. Although the boycotts did not have the same national draw or organization as the Save the Circus movement, they still presented a constant headache for the shows and had the ability to inspire circus workers to join the picket line again.[69]

The shows had to constantly negotiate their place as a working-class source of entertainment that inevitably pushed back hard against the rights of their own workers. Circuses depended heavily on outside industries that were largely unionized to offer services and to patronize the shows. When several shows used printing services from a nonunion lithographic company, local unionized printers boycotted the shows and voted to fine members who attended. But unions also served as an incredible fan base for circuses. An early season show for the Ringling Brothers in 1910 doubled as a near "national convention for the Farmers' Union," which helped fill the circus seats.[70]

The circus struck back at the AFL in self-destructive ways. The resulting backlash led directly to its decline. Rather than cater to the disgruntled fan base, the Greatest Show on Earth attempted to dump its working-class appeal. In highly publicized moves, North tried to make the shows more appealing to upper-class patrons. He hired Charles LeMaire as a design consultant, color-coordinated all the acts, swapped the white top tent for dark blue canvas for better lighting control, and added box seats. North preemptively praised his own decision, telling the public that "with all due respect to my uncles, the circus could not expect to go on forever in the same old way and be successful."[71] Audiences noticed big and small changes, noting that even the smell of the circus had changed as air-conditioned tents regulated temperatures. For audiences of all classes, these sensory shifts indicated that the shows had lost their impromptu magic.[72]

• • •

As circusgoers used their rights as a democratic audience to critique or lament certain features, they shaped how circuses looked. While elephants were a necessary staple of early shows and late nineteenth-century menageries seemed incomplete without a spectrum of exotic animals, post–Golden Age circuses increasingly disassociated themselves from animal acts. New circuses, like Cirque du Soleil (founded in 1984), did not resemble their Golden Age counterparts at all, while old favorites like the Al G. Kelly and Miller Brothers Circus ditched the animal acts, citing higher insurance premiums. When circuses invoked the same sort of language that Barnum used in the nineteenth century, like the image of happy families of caged animals, audiences disdained the blatant propaganda.[73]

Even though child laborers had fewer advocates than their animal counterparts did, persistent outcry against their exploitation also changed the nature of the circus. By the 1950s, new child labor legislation had become much more specific and affected how the circus could utilize its labor force. In 1953, new child labor provisions in the Federal Fair Labor Standards Act further circumscribed the circus workforce by prohibiting youth from operating motor vehicles. As modernization had taken hold in circuses and literal horsepower had been replaced with mechanized vehicles, shows were vulnerable to this new protective legislation. And with this new national legislation, circuses could no longer evade state protective laws by rerouting their season. Moreover, the circus now faced direct and pointed warnings from the US Department of Labor. With stricter enforcement, circuses experienced loss of labor throughout the season as shows were found guilty of engaging in child labor and immediately lost these child workers.[74]

Audience praise or distaste for certain acts also had tremendous impact on the shows. Audiences had the biggest effect in the day-to-day lives of workers through their overwhelming support for or condemnation of certain acts. Circus owners kept their ears to the ground and responded when acts appeared to become stale. Although particular acts could have short shelf lives, workers simply revamped their performance. In an attempt to appeal to audiences and therefore stay relevant, performers constantly competed for poster headlines and center-ring performance spots. While dangerous acts were circus staples in the nineteenth century, they had fallen out of favor by the twentieth century. High-wire walker Harold Alzana ended his successful career because, according to the star, the shows were unwilling to pay him enough for high-risk acts that audiences no longer demanded. Circus publications seconded this notion, asking whether perhaps circuses were cruel to human performers and calling for increased safety. The sideshow, too, declined due to increased audience disapproval. By the mid-twentieth century, grotesque displays that had once garnered significant income for circuses had become stale. As one circus owner put it, that sort of sideshow attraction was a better fit for "carnivals and lower-class patrons."[75]

The audience's understanding of working-class labor in the shows proved to be the most influential factor in the decline of the circus. Employer paternalism, which promulgated the myth of a benevolent circus world, allowed working-class audiences to support the shows, despite their long history of underpaying and overworking employees during the circus's Golden Age. Despite the money and business sense that North brought to the shows, circus workers and devout fans realized that he did not even pretend to be part of the circus world. He stayed in boardrooms rather than joining his employees on the lot. For the first time, audiences realized that the circus world had unspoken class divisions.[76]

Conclusion
Circus Afterlives

When William F. O'Hara passed away in his Bridgeport, Connecticut, home in 1947, the local newspaper noted that the seventy-nine-year-old man had been a valued member of the community where P. T. Barnum had begun his circus career nearly a century prior. O'Hara was a local business owner who ran a movie theater and restaurant. He had also spent twenty-five years in the big top shows. He began his career at the age of fourteen, working "an assortment of jobs" in the Barnum show before taking a paycheck as an elephant trainer. Like other circus workers, O'Hara navigated various positions within several shows throughout his career, including working with the Adam Forepaugh Circus. But his greatest legacy in the circus world was not the work that provided him a paycheck. Instead, it was O'Hara's role as a founding member of the Benevolent Order of the American Tigers, which made him a voice for circus workers.[1]

Jacob Posey, the founder and first president of the Tigers, acknowledged the impact of a mobile workplace in the organization's 1898 formation. During the first year of the Barnum & Bailey's European tour, Posey supposedly conceived of the benevolent organization after repeatedly thinking about the phrase "One touch of Nature makes the whole world kin." These famous words from Shakespeare resonated with Posey while the circus was quartered at Stoke-on-Trent, England. They struck at a circus world identity of kinship, care, and family.[2] Despite how the Tigers implicitly critiqued gaps in the circus world's paternalism, they also brought with them a distinct circus world organizing tradition that drew in management as members. Their first organized roster included circus owner James A. Bailey as an honorary member. By the end of the European tour, the Tigers had fared well, with more than $10,000 in dues, donations, and sales in the last year before returning to the United States.[3]

Workers proudly noted the organization's quick popularity and well-attended events. The Tigers' annual dinner in 1901, held at the Continental Hotel in London, was a glamorous event. As members walked into the hotel dining room around midnight after a Thursday evening show, they found tables pushed together to form a T shape. Flags from the home countries of the members, including the United States, Austria, England, and Germany, brightened the tables and demonstrated the diverse membership that the organization attracted.[4]

But the Tigers did more than throw lavish parties. Founded in the aftermath of an accident on the circus lot that left one roustabout physically disabled and financially strapped, the Tigers served as a fraternal society and proto-union for circus workers across all departments and shows.[5] Leadership included well-known performers and lesser-known workers. Buffalo Bill regularly attended meetings. Charles Tripp, the Armless Wonder, served as a high-ranking member.[6] Upon the circus's return to the United States, three circus workers filed a charter with the state of Connecticut. They aimed to "support the social and material welfare of [their] members." The organization defrayed funeral and disability costs for members. For circus workers, this meant that the newly formed organization would fill gaps in benefits that their otherwise paternalistic employer provided.[7]

The Tigers also acted as a cohesive organization within the circus world, and membership in the Tigers reflected the cosmopolitan workforce that labored on the circus lot. Workers could jump between circus outfits within a single season and still retain membership in the circus world through the Tigers. Sideshow workers joined en masse, particularly prior to the organization of their own union. Within a few years of the organization's formation and after much debate, the Tigers opened membership to women.[8]

After leaving their careers within the circus world, workers faced the challenge of integrating into society. To reinforce their small-town appeal to audiences, circuses emphatically claimed that their performers preferred life outside of bustling cities.[9] They spun tales of former circus stars spending their fortunes and remaining days on ranches. This played into another popular claim, the idea that "nine out of ten are filled with the desire to own a farm." But urban settings were also appealing. The *Chicago Tribune* boasted of Chicago's sideshow population and claimed that the city was an urban mecca for these workers. According to the newspaper, these "industrious" people were especially desirable citizens because they had grown accustomed to the highly regulated and disciplined circus life. Berlin was another retirement destination for sideshow performers, who frequented a local beer saloon owned by a former circus worker.[10]

William O'Hara's life demonstrates how circus workers remained connected not necessarily to their former employer, but to a larger circus world identity. In a workplace that brought increased celebrity, and yet also allowed people to exist in historical anonymity with falsified identities or uncontracted work, the Tigers offer a window into how everyday circus workers navigated the circus world. Well-known workers in high-profile jobs, like trainers or tamers, are easily trackable in census records and other travel documents. The circus working class, however, is sometimes more difficult to track and most often found by searching job categories rather than individual names.

While the Tigers served early twentieth-century workers in important ways, folks who left the circus world following the Golden Age were perhaps better served by an organization that connected a larger swath of workers from various outdoor entertainments in a space that resembled the winter quarters of the tented shows. The International Independent Showmen's Association set up shop in Gibsonton, Florida, just outside of Tampa, in 1966.[11] Gibsonton was an ideal space for the burgeoning organization, since it had a long association with circus workers. Tented shows had thrived on whistle-stops to fill big tops throughout the Golden Age, and Gibsonton had served as just such a place: a whistle-stop away from the circus world's industry headquarters, in Sarasota, Florida.[12]

When the major circuses still showed under a big top tent and traveled the rails, Gibsonton's population would ebb and flow, growing substantially during each offseason. Circus people encountered familiar faces as they worked on circus equipment, stopped for breakfast at the local diner, or dropped by the post office. But it was not just the faces that seemed so welcoming. Counters at public spaces were low enough to accommodate the population of little people. Restaurant chairs varied in size to cater to the "world's tallest man" or "world's fattest lady."[13] And the town did more than simply serve former circus workers. It was also a space where circus workers took ownership and created community. Giant's Fish Camp, owned by former sideshow workers Jeanie and Al Tomaini, provided meals and tackle equipment to Gibsonton residents until 1999. Other circus workers went into public service, worked for the city, and ran businesses frequented by both locals and out-of-towners.[14]

Gibsonton also appealed to workers for much more practical reasons. The town held the distinction of being the only city in the United States that had a "residential show business" classification. In practical terms, this meant that like with life on the circus lot, there seemed to be no distinction between home and work. Animal trainers kept their tigers and elephants just feet away from their doorstep. Concession stands and circus wagons were just as likely to be seen in front yards as were vehicles.[15]

Despite the uniqueness of Gibsonton, the town was only one example of how the circus changed the American vista throughout the Golden Age. During the decades that circuses dominated the cultural landscape, shows spent the offseason in winter quarters. These few months each year in Baraboo, Bridgeport, Peru, or Sarasota gave a skeleton crew of workers a stationary, yet temporary, home, while contracted performers made ends meet on vaudeville and theater circuits. A passerby might see an elephant plowing a field in Bridgeport, Connecticut, or a herd of giraffes peeking above a fence in Peru, Indiana. But by the 1950s, circus attendance had declined, workers had unionized, and insurance premiums had cut into circus performance and profits. Gibsonton created a world for circus workers that resembled the close-knit kinship formed over decades in the tented shows. By protecting their community roots in the small Florida enclave, circus workers remained part of the circus world, even as the shows declined.

While some human and animal workers continued to find community together after the industry declined, other animal workers faced a dimmer outlook. Carl Hagenbeck's late nineteenth-century advertisements had sought to lure circus owners to his seemingly endless supply of animals from colonized spaces. By the end of the Golden Age, advertisements instead tried to lure buyers into purchasing "freak animals" and animal "specialty acts."[16] Circus animals found their final resting spaces in other spectacle industries, including zoos, where they had previously been born or temporarily housed. Like human workers, some animals found rest in their own retirement homes and sanctuaries.[17] The exotic licenses in Gibsonton meant that big cats and elephants might continue sleeping mere feet from a human bed, just as they had in the tented shows. But retirement communities that demonstrated a similar re-creation of circus life also cropped up elsewhere. At a farm called Rancho Glades outside of Los Angeles, circus worker Jim Evans welcomed a herd of retired circus horses.[18]

• • •

The history of the circus industry is the story of industrialism, transnational workplaces, technological innovations, and cosmopolitan workforces. The circus's fall from cultural relevance by the mid-twentieth century is intrinsically linked to the rise of other forms of entertainment. Circus, vaudeville, and other live entertainments took a backseat to television. Yet despite these obvious changes in front of the curtain, it was the behind-the-scenes business practices, labor, and modernization that chipped away at the status of the circus. People in the circus world often interpreted these changes as indications that the shows were slipping. Even in 1907, "old-timers" were lamenting about the circus of old; they complained that the canvas used to be whiter, or that the show used to fit under a single tent.[19] But each time that the circus updated itself, it lost part of its appeal. When tractors replaced roustabouts, part of the circus mystique disappeared.

In the early twentieth century, the circus operated through colonial-backed networks that ensured cheap animal and human labor. Traders were experts in animal shipping, and keepers had personal relationships with their animals. A voyage to the United States took weeks and often took a toll on the animals. Successful traders knew which animals would survive the trip and bring profits in the United States based on their age and origins. This knowledge served as a necessary job skill. By the 1960s, the animal trade business was unrecognizable. Lutz Ruhe, a German immigrant who emerged from a nineteenth-century canary-trading family, spoke to this change in a 1975 interview. The Ruhe family began importing larger exotic animals around 1900; it had a corner on the market through the first half of the twentieth century. But when shipping methods changed from boats to jet planes, the family's skills and knowledge were no longer necessary to their success.[20]

Changes in labor and regulations in the United States also facilitated the decline of the tented shows. The careers of workers like Frank Bostock represented the type of labor-driven migration that declined with changes within the circus and pressure from the outside. Acts such as Clyde Beatty's big cats provided a thrill that was unseen in earlier decades. But increased pressure to protect employees' lives from dangerous stunts, and to protect their own business from lawsuits, left smaller shows with the inability to afford insurance premiums.[21] Animal acts, which had seemed so indispensable at the turn of the century, were abandoned as archaic relics of the old tented shows. The uncontrollable nature of animal spectacle led to inevitable interactions between circus animals and audiences throughout the history of the circus. The range of reactions from audience members, however, changed after the mid-twentieth century. Especially after the folding of the big top, when animal encounters seemed inevitable, so too did lawsuits. When a leopard at the Dwight Brothers Circus broke free and clawed a six-year-old child, her parents immediately responded with a $10,000 lawsuit.[22] Smaller outfits, like Dwight Brothers, could not sustain themselves in the face of this sort of litigation.

Even shows that chose to keep animal acts faced a smaller market to offer their shows, particularly overseas. European legislation continued to circumscribe the shows after the decline of the big top, providing even fewer markets where the shows could operate. In 1959, Sweden tightened its animal show regulations, banning most circus animals from performing and requiring an outside veterinarian to inspect all animal quarters prior to showing.[23] As the circus modernized animals out of the role of general laborers, some of the inherent risk on the circus lot vanished. Tractors, wagons, and mechanized equipment still brought job hazards to workers on the lot, but the autonomy of animal workers had vanished from those roles. Rogue elephants may have still posed a risk to trainers, but they were no longer in a position to conduct work stoppages outside of the performance.

As the circus boasted of never-before-seen performances, people, and animals, it also promoted itself as a glimpse into the past. In attempts to capture bygone eras, the circus remained economically vested in old-fashioned ways of looking at the world. Pawnee Bill's Wild West Show purchased a herd of bison in 1901 that were reported to be among the last.[24] As much as tented shows offered first glimpses of exotic otherness, they also used marketing ploys that promised last-of-its-kind animals and people. Circusgoers flocked to see the "last" hippopotamus, giraffe, or reenacted buffalo hunt.[25]

These contradictions played out most prominently in the sideshow. By the 1960s, state laws had begun addressing the ethical implications of sideshows, particularly their use of child labor. North Carolina legislated the issue in 1969 by banning the display of children in sideshows. The law, dubbed an "antifreak bill," created a misdemeanor offense for displaying children who had evident disabilities.[26]

Circus workers and traditionalist circusgoers dubbed the new law a "repressive measure" that took direct aim at circuses themselves. These critics pointed to the trend that was expected to follow: increased legislation across multiple states that forced circuses to phase out their sideshows, rather than simply reroute their shows to avoid the laws. *Amusement Business*, a highly circulated magazine among circus folks, claimed that the "Save the Freak Shows" column had attracted a greater outpouring of letters than any other feature. Sideshow workers sought partnerships with several unions and civil liberties organizations as the legislation mounted against their careers.[27]

The language of these bills, as well as the counterarguments, laid bare some underlying assumptions about the role and purpose of circus workers. Sideshow performers had claimed some degree of autonomy over their own careers, particularly during decades of peak popularity, when their roles were highly visible. As a workplace, the sideshow had the most enmeshed variety of manual, performance, and emotional labor that the circus had to offer. When laws began to address exploitation, they undercut much of the activism that sideshow workers had started as legitimate performers asserting their own humanity. While the counterargument acknowledged the role of these performers as workers collecting paychecks, it ignored the low or absent pay that had plagued the sideshow tent.

The circus business lifted up the voices of sideshow performers who had made a substantial living in the tented shows, arguing that they proved that such displays were humane. The debate mirrored larger changes in American culture, especially with regard to people with disabilities. Discussions of the welfare state and the disability rights movement proliferated on both sides. During the Revolt of the Freaks in London, sideshow performers had leveraged their rights as workers, much to the amazement and dismay of outsiders. But when the circus business faced lost profits with the sudden end of sideshows, the so-called freaks were suddenly cast as workers, not performers. As sideshow operator Harvey Boswell claimed, the law was "attempting to put hundreds of people out of work." In the same vein, performer Mary Blackmon called the new laws a form of discrimination.[28]

By the late twentieth century, many circuses were nearly unrecognizable, in comparison to their nineteenth-century counterparts. West Brothers Circus provided several signposts of these changes. In a 1950 *Billboard* advertisement for workers, the circus described itself as "indoor." It also sought only acrobats for the upcoming season. No longer did circuses put a dizzying amount of effort into the menagerie and animal performers.[29] As the circus began to decline, its privileges did as well. By 1950, shows could no longer assume full rights to a town and expect schools and businesses to shut down. Instead, as the Ringling show found on its tour, red tape prevented circuses from even using circus staples like the calliope wagon without a police permit.[30]

The circus world did not go down without a fight when the big top folded in 1956. Prompted by the seemingly unending love of the circus in American culture, stockholders sued the North brothers for mismanagement of funds. John Ringling North asserted that the big top days were forever doomed because of labor costs. But the lawsuit also alleged particular forms of mismanagement that demonstrated how the circus world had shifted. North reportedly charged lavish hotel bills to the Ringling show, running up significant expenses.[31]

Even though the big top tents folded in 1956 and the sight of the circus pulling up on an early morning train would be forever gone, the circus continued to tour without missing a beat. Aside from no longer being able to honestly claim the title of being a big top or rail show, the circus also looked substantially different in other ways. The 1957 season included only fifteen outfits, all of which moved across the country on trucks. Of these fifteen circuses, only one show was entering its first season, but it was considered an "unorthodox" offering: an auto thrill show with some circus acts attached. Pulling back from the never-before-seen and bigger-is-better mantras, Mills Brothers Circus cut its elephant herd to five and declined to add any new wagons for the 1957 season. The form of these shows was a sharp departure from the height of the Golden Age, when hundreds of circuses had operated across the nation.[32]

Not only had circus labor shifted substantially by the second half of the twentieth century, but so had the ways that the public interacted with the tented shows. Clowns, who unionized early in the circus world, remained a fairly cohesive unit that was often situated counter to the circus world identity. Like the Puff Club of the early twentieth century, the Shriners had their own clown union that dominated the industry by the late 1960s and "put the professional clown out of business."[33] While billposters had performed their labor for circusgoers as they pasted posters over entire walls on downtown buildings through the mid-twentieth century, by the 1960s these posters were increasingly confined to store windows. When the ten-person billing team with the Cole Brothers–Clyde Beatty Circus arrived in Sandusky, Ohio, in 1962, there was nobody there to watch them unload from the advance car on the rails. Instead, the billers had discreetly pulled up in pickup trucks. As they entered the town looking for an ideal spot—often a large building that could be covered in posters—businesses denied their request. But the physical landscape had also changed, and many small towns had newly built architecture that increasingly left broad brick walls behind.[34] This shift in circus advertising reflected the changes to the manual and performative labor of the tented shows in the weeks leading up to the performance. Without weeks of constant reminders and hype, the circus began to exist in a town without being the place where most people would be spending their day.

The demise of the gratis performance was the most important signal that the Golden Age had ended. Even as the circus responded to labor unrest by mechanizing its workers out of a job, circusgoers still clung to the appeal of the gratis performance, or at least what was left of it. When the circus industry momentarily dropped its popular circus parade in the early twentieth century, it sold the idea that those savings would be invested in the shows and that performers would get more time to rest before showtime.[35] By midcentury, it was clear that parades were no longer viable parts of the show. Addressing "New York City youngsters" just days before the 1938 season opener, a Pennsylvania paper emphasized the part of the show that "doesn't cost a pretty penny."[36] By the time the big top folded in 1956, the gratis performance was minimal and unrecognizable. Men driving tent stakes into the ground, elephants hauling equipment into place, or even a parade taking over a town's main street proved to be absolutely necessary for the circus to remain a central part of American culture.[37]

Shifting postwar labor and business practices were not limited to US circuses. In Germany, the annual meeting of the Internationale Arbeitsgemeinschaft Fuhrender Circuseigentumer (International Association of Leading Circus Owners) in 1950 was devoted to discussion of several seemingly troublesome trends. Like their US counterparts, German circuses had experienced a substantial increase in the entertainment tax. They also encountered similar fights against unions and worker autonomy, as their insurance payout to employees for accidents doubled. In response, circus magnates leveled complaints against these changes by sending resolutions to the German government and the organizing body of circus musicians.[38]

Insurance costs, protective legislation, labor organizing, and freedom movements all penetrated the walls of the circus world. As an enterprise dependent on cheap unregulated labor, the circus could not survive or stay in step with modern industrial relations. Now families could no longer be contracted under a single income, circuses had to account for workers trampled by elephants, and circusgoers began to champion human rights over the desire to stare at Frog Girl and Lobster Boy. Cheap labor became expensive labor.

Although the circus also resembled other businesses of postwar corporate America, it retained remnants of its uniquely transnational and global workforce. In the early years, the relatively few shows in a season and fewer miles traveled had meant that shows performed largely for audiences on the Northeast coast.[39] But shows themselves had always contained workers and animals from around the world. Even in the nineteenth century, the circus business had to contend with borders in ways that other corporations had not yet encountered. By the 1970s, however, circuses were "up against some of the same mundane realities that other American businesses and institutions face[d]." As freedom movements overturned colonial governments and the legal animal trade slowed, circuses lost access to what had been an easy market to tap into. Simply put, animal workers were no longer as replaceable. The ones that did appear in the tented shows were no longer from faraway places, but instead hailed from the exotic breeding farms that had cropped up around the United States. Endangered species lists and wildlife conservation movements in these spaces exacerbated the issue for shows with menageries. When tigers, lions, and elephants began appearing on endangered lists, their appeal in the center ring diminished. Bull hooks, whips, and even holstered guns in the ring were not conducive to new narratives about rescuing species from extinction events created by humans.[40]

As circus management transferred to the Feld brothers, the circus became an almost indistinguishable part of the fabric of corporate America. John Ringling North's 1956 decision to move to indoor arenas had reportedly been made on the recommendation of Irvin Feld, a promotion savant, who promised a savings of thousands of dollars each week of the season. Irvin and Israel Feld and Roy Hofheinz (this last most readily associated with the construction of Houston's Astrodome) made a substantial $8 million offer to North's debt-ridden show in 1967. Given the waning popularity of the shows, North could not resist. Although the Feld brothers had been working closely with the circus since the 1950s, their ownership role resembled that of Sam Gumpertz, who had taken brief ownership of the shows without full immersion into the circus world. Following the precedent set by John Ringling in 1929, the new owners sought financial backers, investors, and creditors to complete the sale.[41]

Within two years, the official ownership changed hands from a family to an actual company, as the Mattel Corporation offered $49 million for the Greatest Show on Earth. Like North, the Feld brothers could not resist. More famous for its Barbie dolls than live entertainment, Mattel changed the circus world from the inside out. The company went public in 1968, and investors bought stock in the traveling shows. But Mattel also changed how the circus functioned on a day-to-day basis. While previous shows had operated under the bigger-is-better model, Mattel split the Ringling show into two touring units. Although this move increased profits by making two circuses out of one, the tactic made the shows even less culturally relevant. Mattel tried to tap larger cities to attract a segment of the population. But the Golden Age had prospered under different terms: one larger-than-life show had dominated small towns across America, even when it was accompanied by countless smaller shows.[42]

However, nothing felt more out of step with the circus world than when Mattel announced its own Florida-based theme park. Appropriately called Circus World, the new Mattel entity was expected to outperform Disney World, which was just twenty miles away. The newly minted circus conglomerate could not have been more wrong. Attendance was staggeringly low at the $100 million stationary circus. It floundered for years and did not draw even half as many visitors as nearby SeaWorld. Even after a $20 million revamp, the park could not turn a profit. It moved through several hands before closing permanently in 1986.[43]

Circus World, the amusement park, was a financial and cultural failure in the years after the circus industry declined. It attempted to capture the magic that existed in the imaginations of people all over the country. But Americans had no nostalgia for a modern amusement park built outside of a Florida swamp. The shows had been traveling cities that delivered an imagined culture to people's doorsteps during annual circus day holidays. The most memorable parts of the circus were free and unscripted. Circus World could not re-create the alluring free performance of manual laborers setting up tents, big top performers making their way to the cook tent for a quick breakfast, or elephants walking linked tail-to-truck in their procession across the circus lot. As the saga of Circus World demonstrates, the Golden Age of the circus could not be recaptured.

Yet the circus world created by workers in Gibsonton remains intact, with many people stepping in the center ring for an annual charity show. Perhaps Gibsonton, a home to so many circus workers, is not simply a vestige of the circus world. While the industry could not recapture what it meant to create a tented town and attract thousands of one-day visitors, circus workers could still re-create what it meant to work and live among themselves. As one resident noted, "you'll never hear of a local carnie going on welfare. We take care of our own."[44] The sentiment tapped into something real: from Matthew Scott to William O'Hara, circus workers often found ways to take care of their own after their time with the circus ended. Even within their working world, they understood how to take care of their own, or at least those that they included in the circus world identity; they had been doing so since at least the creation of the Tigers. That camaraderie certainly privileged certain workers (through workers' exclusionary ways and acceptance of paternalism), but it also ushered in change, sometimes at the expense of the larger industry. While Barnum, the Ringlings, and hundreds of other owners created circuses, workers created the circus world.

Notes

Introduction. The Circus World in the Golden Age

1. Newspapers on both sides of the Atlantic extensively covered the circus's first trip to England. For coverage in the United States, see: "Noah's Ark in 1889," *Evening World* (New York), October 17, 1889, 1; "A Circus Cargo," *Brooklyn Daily Eagle*, October 18, 1899, 6; "She Is a Modern Ark," *Brooklyn Daily Eagle*, October 20, 1889, 2; "Barnum's Show Safe Home," *Evening World* (New York), March 5, 1890. For coverage in England, see: *Times* (London), November 12, 1889; "Barnum's Embarkation," *Local Government Gazette* (London), February 20, 1890, 12.

2. "Tent City to Be Built This Morning: How the Work Is Done," *Washington Times*, May 10, 1903, 5 (qtd.); Janet Davis, *The Circus Age: Culture and Society under the American Big Top* (Chapel Hill: University of North Carolina Press, 2002). Davis also provides extensive analysis of the working men and their "spectacular labor."

3. "Barnum's Embarkation," *Harper's Weekly*, November 2, 1899, reprinted in *Circus Scrap Book* 1, no. 1 (January 1929): 11–13.

4. Charles Theodore Murray, "At Sea with the Circus," *McClure's Magazine* 11 (October 1898): 77; "Big Circus at Sea: Barnum's Show Animals Go across the Atlantic," *Chicago Daily Tribune*, November 28, 1897, 10.

5. "Will Sail the Seas," *Inter Ocean* (Chicago), October 24, 1897, 18; Murray, "At Sea with the Circus."

6. Murray, "At Sea with the Circus"; "Big Circus at Sea," *Chicago Daily Tribune*. In 1921, employees with Howe's Great London Circus and Van Amburg's Trained Wild Animals found their four lions dead when they checked on them to offer food, two days after departure. *Official Route Season 1921: Howe's Great London Circus and Van Amburg's Trained Wild Animals* (n.p., 1921), 44, Circus Route Books, John and Mable Ringling Museum of Art, Sarasota, FL.

7. Murray, "At Sea with the Circus"; "Big Circus at Sea," *Chicago Daily Tribune*; *The Circus Annual: A Route Book of Ringling Brothers World's Greatest Shows Season 1902* (n.p., 1902), 22, Circus Route Books, Special Collections, Milner Library, Illinois State University, Normal.

8. Murray, "At Sea with the Circus"; "Big Circus at Sea," *Chicago Daily Tribune*.

9. In 1898, successful captive breeding programs were still rare, and most animals had been caught in the wild. See "How Bailey Beat Barnum," *Central Record* (Lancaster, KY), January 21, 1898, 4.

10. "Suggestions and Rules: Employees: Ringling Brothers," series 1, box 29, Raymond Toole-Scott Circus Collection, University of California–Santa Barbara Library.

11. Michael Daly, *Topsy: The Startling Story of the Crooked-Tailed Elephant, P. T. Barnum, and the American Wizard, Thomas Edison* (New York: Atlantic Monthly Press, 2013); Fred D. Pfening Jr., "Circus Baseball Teams," *Bandwagon* 11, no. 5 (September–October 1967): 10–11; "The Backyard Is the Social Center of the World's Largest Circus," *Ringling Brothers and Barnum & Bailey Magazine and Daily Review* (1935), Circus and Buffalo Bill Collection, Long Island University Archives and Special Collections, NY; "Home Life of Circus Freaks: Many of the Human Prodigies Own Their Own Homes and Make Good Citizens," *Washington Post*, April 19, 1908, 7.

12. "Elephants Did Not Bathe," *Kansas City Times*, August 21, 1899, 8.

13. "Impressions of the 101," *Reno Gazette*, May 3, 1912, 3.

14. Mary Rawls, interview by Juliana Nykolaisyn and Tanya Finchum, June 13, 2011, 13, 16, 25–26, *The "Big Top" Show Goes On: An Oral History of Occupations inside and outside of the Canvas Circus Tent*, Oklahoma Oral History Research Program, Oklahoma State University.

15. This work intervenes in the scholarship of mobile workplaces and migrant laborers. Historians have most recently analyzed maritime workforces, the labor of hoboes, and migrants within the Black Atlantic; see Leon Fink, *Sweatshops at Sea: Merchant Seamen in the World's First Globalized Industry, from 1812 to the Present* (Chapel Hill: University of North Carolina Press, 2014), 148; Frank Tobias Higbie, *Indispensable Outcasts: Hobo Workers and Community in the American Midwest, 1880–1930* (Urbana: University of Illinois Press, 2003), 108–9; Marcus Rediker and Peter Linebaugh, *The Many-Headed Hydra: Sailors, Slaves, Commoners, and the Hidden History of the Revolutionary Atlantic* (New York: Verso, 2012), 14. Julie Greene examines a similar workforce and its relationship to capitalism, and Cindy Hahamovitch provides an analysis of Jamaican guest worker protest and migration. See Julie Greene, *The Canal Builders: Making America's Empire at the Panama Canal* (New York: Penguin Books, 2010); Cindy Hahamovitch, *No Man's Land: Jamaican Guestworkers in America and the Global History of Deportable Labor* (Princeton, NJ: Princeton University Press, 2013). W. Jeffrey Bolster provides another important history of the mobility and transnationality

of maritime workforces; see his *Black Jacks: African American Seaman in the Age of Sail* (Cambridge, MA: Harvard University Press, 1998).

16. Historians have examined emotional labor, particularly in the postwar service economy of the United States. Amy Tyson's work, for example, considers museum workers; see her *The Wages of History: Emotional Labor on Public History's Front Lines* (Amherst: University of Massachusetts Press, 2013). A deeper breadth of scholarship has examined Black workers in service jobs in the nineteenth and twentieth centuries; see Louwanda Evans, *Cabin Pressure: African American Pilots, Flight Attendants, and Emotional Labor* (Lanham, MD: Rowman and Littlefield, 2013); Zachary Schwartz-Weinstein, "The Limits of Work and the Subject of Labor History," in *Rethinking U.S. Labor History: Essays on the Working-Class Experience, 1756–2009*, ed. Donna T. Haverty-Stacke and Daniel J. Walkowitz (New York: Continuum, 2010), 289–306; Rawls, interview by Nykolaisyn and Finchum, June 13, 2011, 24.

17. Eric Arnesen, *Waterfront Workers of New Orleans: Race, Class, and Politics, 1863–1923* (Urbana: University of Illinois Press, 1994), vii.

18. Isaac Marcosson, "Saw Dust and Gold Dust: The Earnings of Circus People," *Bookman*, June 1910, reprinted in *Circus Scrap Book* 1, no. 2 (April 1929): 10.

19. David Brody, "Labor History, Industrial Relations, and the Crisis of American Labor," *IRL Review* 43, no. 1 (1989): 7–18; David Brody, "Reconciling the Old Labor History and the New," *Pacific Historical Review* 62, no. 1 (1993): 1–18.

20. See Kendra Coulter, *Animals, Work, and the Promise of Interspecies Solidarity* (London: Palgrave Macmillan, 2016); Sharon Sharp, "Interspecies Labor in Early Cinema: Making Animal Pictures at David Horsley's Bostock Jungle and Film Company," *Film History: An International Journal* 33, no. 2 (Summer 2021): 34–59; Peta Tait, *Wild and Dangerous Performances: Animals, Emotions, Circus* (London: Palgrave Macmillan, 2011), 12–37. Scholarship on interspecies labor in factories and other worksites that have been less associated with spectacle industries include: Jeremy Zallen, *American Lucifers: The Dark History of Artificial Light, 1750–1865* (Chapel Hill: University of North Carolina Press, 2019); James L. Hevia, *Animal Labor and Colonial Warfare* (Chicago: University of Chicago Press, 2018); Alex Blanchette, *Porkopolis: American Animality, Standardized Life, and the Factory Farm* (Durham, NC: Duke University Press, 2020).

21. "1000-Animal Menagerie Feature of Big Circus," *Buffalo (NY) Times*, August 15, 1925, 2.

22. "Sells-Floto Circus Here 3 Days Beginning Friday," *St. Louis Star and Times*, June 25, 1922, 4.

23. Quoted in Fred Dahlinger Jr. and Stuart Thayer, *Badger State Showmen: A History of Wisconsin's Circus Heritage* (Baraboo, WI: Circus World Museum, 1998), 73.

24. Davis, *The Circus Age*, 7; Charles H. Day, "An Early Tendency to Monopolize," *Washington Post*, January 27, 1907, 10.

25. Neil Harris, *Humbug: The Art of P. T. Barnum* (Chicago: University of Chicago Press, 1981), 254.

26. Tom Ogden, *Two Hundred Years of the American Circus: From Aba-Daba to the Zoppe-Zavatta Troupe* (New York: Facts on File, 1993), 3.

27. John Springhall, *The Genesis of Mass Culture: Show Business Live in America, 1840 to 1940* (New York: Palgrave Macmillan, 2008), 2–5.

28. "When the Circus Comes to Town—A Marvel in Organization," *Baltimore Sun*, May 5, 1912, 24; Nigel Rothfels, *Savages and Beasts: The Birth of the Modern Zoo* (Baltimore, MD: Johns Hopkins University Press, 2012), 177–78.

29. The global nature of the shows intersects with larger historiographical trends that have begun to explore international and transnational labor histories. Global perspectives have been a cornerstone of new labor history, as led by Marcel van der Linden; see his articles "The 'Globalization' of Labor and Working-Class History," *International Labor and Working-Class History*, no. 65 (2004): 136–56; "Transnationalizing American Labor History," *Journal of American History* 86, no. 3 (1999): 1078–92; "The Promise and Challenge of Global Labor History," *International Labor and Working-Class History*, no. 82 (2012): 57–76. See also Sjaak van der Velden, "Strikes in Global Labor History: The Dutch Case," *Review (Fernand Braudel Center* 26 (2003): 381–405; Peter Winn, "Global Labor History: The Future of the Field?," *International Labor and Working-Class History*, no. 82 (2012): 85–91.

30. "Amusements: Foreign Acts," *Burlington Daily News*, August 25, 1922, 7; "Big Foreign Acts Feature Circus," *Yazoo (MS) Herald*, October 19, 1934, 2; "Get Ready, Kids, the Circus Is Here Today, and Papa Will Have to Take You to the Big Tent City," *Star Tribune* (Minneapolis, MN), July 19, 1914, 8.

31. The idea of a diverse workforce forming a collective circus world that often informed workers' politics relies on Benedict Anderson's concept of imagined community and Elijah Anderson's cosmopolitan canopy. See Benedict Anderson, *Imagined Communities: Reflections on the Origin and Spread of Nationalism* (London: Verso, 1991); Elijah Anderson, *The Cosmopolitan Canopy: Race and Civility in Everyday Life* (New York: W. W. Norton, 2011).

32. US Census, 1880, 4th Ward, Precinct 41, St. Louis, St. Louis County, Missouri, National Archives Film T9-0727, p. 565A; US Census, 1880, 9th Ward, Precinct 93, St. Louis, St. Louis County, Missouri, National Archives Film T9-0729, p. 632A.

33. Susan Nance, *Entertaining Elephants: Animal Agency and the Business of the American Circus* (Baltimore, MD: Johns Hopkins University Press, 2013), 119. This popularization of manual laborers was not unique to the circus. As Nance shows, the advertising industry in the late nineteenth and early twentieth centuries often depicted labor and the consumption of that labor within the same picture. Laborers, then, became nameless parts of advertising.

34. Leon Fink, *In Search of the Working Class: Essays in American Labor and Political Culture* (Urbana: University of Illinois Press, 1994), 33–50; Crandall Shifflett, *Coal Towns: Life, Work, and Culture in Company Towns of Southern*

Appalachia, 1880–1960 (Knoxville: University of Tennessee Press, 1991); Robert Maxwell, *Sawdust Empire: The Texas Lumber Industry, 1830–1940* (College Station: Texas A&M University Press, 1993); Marcelo Borges and Susana Torres, *Company Towns: Labor, Space, and Power Relations across Time and Continents* (New York: Palgrave McMillan, 2012).

35. Rawls, interview by Nykolaisyn and Finchum, June 13, 2011, 11.

36. See Michael H. Frisch and Daniel J. Walkowitz, eds., *Working-Class America: Essays on Labor, Community, and American Society* (Urbana: University of Illinois Press, 1983). This study fits within larger frameworks set forth in this collection of essays. Along with implementing vertical and horizontal analyses of labor history, this study also considers working-class history alongside the development of capitalism. This scholarship intersects with the history of capitalism, which considers labor and business history together. See Bethany Moreton, *To Serve God and Wal-Mart* (Cambridge, MA: Harvard University Press, 2009); Joshua Clark Davis, *From Head Shops to Whole Foods: The Rise and Fall of Activist Entrepreneurs* (New York: Columbia University Press, 2017); Sven Beckert and Christine Desan, eds., *American Capitalism: New Histories* (New York: Columbia University Press, 2018).

37. *Report of the Select Committee on Immigration and Naturalization; and Testimony Taken by the Committee on Immigration of the Senate and the Select Committee on Immigration and Naturalization of the House of Representatives under Concurrent Resolution of March 12, 1890* (Washington, DC: Government Printing Office, 1891), 190.

38. Hahamovitch, *No Man's Land*, 9; George Teeger, "John Ringling North: The Lowdown on the Big Top," *Confidential*, August 4, 1953, Billy Rose Theatre Division Scrapbooks, New York Public Library for the Performing Arts.

39. See Hahamovitch, *No Man's Land*. Mae Ngai's examination of "illegal alien" as a raced category provides the groundwork for illegal immigration scholarship; see her *Impossible Subjects: Illegal Aliens and the Making of Modern America* (Princeton, NJ: Princeton University Press, 2004). Recent immigration scholarship has taken its nose to the ground with borderland studies and has thought deeper about movement and globalization than was done in earlier decades; see Jeremy Adelman and Stephen Aron, "From Borderlands to Borders: Empires, Nation-States and the Peoples in Between in North American History," *American Historical Review* 104, no. 3 (1999): 814–41; Alden T. Vaughan, *Transatlantic Encounters: American Indians in Britain, 1500–1776* (Cambridge: Cambridge University Press, 2006). For a more contemporary look at the implications of global movements across borders, see Philip Martin, Manolo Abella, and Christiane Kuptsch, *Managing Labor Migration in the Twenty-First Century* (New Haven, CT: Yale University Press, 2006).

40. Hahamovitch, *No Man's Land*, 7. In her examination of guest workers, Hahamovitch shows that twentieth-century Caribbean migration operated in markets that favored businesses that took illegal measures to work around government programs and protections.

41. Industrial relations, as a subfield of labor history, has evolved through the Wisconsin School, the Oxford School, cornerstone work by Philip S. Foner, and new critiques of top-down analysis. This work situates itself in new labor historiography while still answering Dave Lyddon's call to use the theoretical framework set forth by industrial relations scholars; see his "Industrial-Relations Theory and Labor History," *International Labor and Working-Class History*, no. 46 (1994): 122–41; see also Philip S. Foner, *History of the Labor Movement in the United States*, 10 vols. (New York: International, 1947–94).

42. See Jocelyne Porcher, *The Ethics of Animal Labor: A Collaborative Utopia* (Cham: Palgrave Macmillan, 2017), 9.

43. "If You Would Join the Big Circus You Must Be Prepared to Sign a Cast-Iron Contract," *Daily Continent*, April 19, 1891, Scrapbook 8, Barnum & Bailey, Information and Address Book, box 24, McCaddon Collection of the Barnum and Bailey Circus, Princeton University Library, NJ.

44. See Philip A. Loring, "The Most Resilient Show on Earth: The Circus as a Model for Viewing Identity, Change, and Chaos," *Ecology and Society* 12, no. 1 (2007): article 9. Loring, an anthropologist, describes the circus world identity as a tribe.

45. Rawls, interview by Nykolaisyn and Finchum, June 13, 2011, 12.

46. Beverly Kelley, "The Wonder City That Moves by Night," *National Geographic Magazine*, March 1948, 294, box 20, folder 13, Heiser-Alban Collection of Circus Historical Materials, Houston Metropolitan Research Center (qtd.); "With the Ladies of the Circus," *New York Times*, April 1, 1906, SM3.

47. "Notes from Indian Bill's Wild West," *New York Clipper*, July 11, 1903, 465; "Pan American Show Notes," *New York Clipper*, March 29, 1903, 123; "From the No. 1 Advertising Car of the Buffalo Bill Wild West," *New York Clipper*, July 12, 1902, 433; "Roster of Advertising Car No. 1, Ringling Bros.'s World's Greatest Shows," *New York Clipper*, May 10, 1902, 240.

48. "The Barnum & Bailey's Greatest Show on Earth Route Inspector's Report," c. 1905–46, Circus / Vaudeville / Minstrel Collection, University of California–Santa Barbara Library.

49. *1924 Souvenir of John Robinson's One Hundred and First Annual Tour* (n.p., 1924), 15, Route Book Collection, Milner Library, Illinois State University, Normal.

50. Davis, *The Circus Age*, 71. Janet Davis, a historian, briefly addresses these racial discrepancies in circuses, noting that the Walter L. Main Circus paid Black laborers one dollar less per week than their white counterparts in the 1890s.

51. *Variety*, July 6, 1907, 8.

52. Alfred T. Ringling, *Seasons of 1895 and 1896 with the Circus: A Route Book of Ringling Bros. World's Greatest Shows* (St. Louis, MO: Great Western Printing, 1896), 77, 85, Circus Route Books, Circus World Museum, Baraboo, WI.

53. Drawing from labor and immigration histories, Krystyn Moon explores broader union exclusion in an article on artists' unions; see her "On a Temporary Basis: Immigration, Labor Unions, and the American Entertainment Industry, 1880s-1930s," *Journal of American History* 99, no. 3 (December 2012): 783.

54. Kerry Segrave, *Actors Organize: A History of Union Formation Efforts in America, 1880–1919* (Jefferson, NC: McFarland, 2007), 178.

55. Springhall, *The Genesis of Mass Culture*, 8.

56. Rawls, interview by Nykolaisyn and Finchum, June 13, 2011, 6.

57. Quoted in "The Animal Man," *Weekly Kansas City Star*, August 16, 1933, 14.

58. "How the Circus Dodges the Railroad Blockade," *Literary Digest* 56 (March 16, 1918): 87.

59. Sharon L. Smith and Stephen T. Fletcher, *Life in a Three-Ring Circus: Posters and Interviews* (Indianapolis: Indiana Historical Society, 2001), 6.

60. *Variety*, March 21, 1908, 13.

61. "A Word with the Mayor," *Algona Upper Des Moines*, April 18, 1894, 1; Diana J. Kleiner, "Bailey, Mollie Arline Kirkland," *Handbook of Texas Online*, Texas State Historical Association, updated January 2, 2019, https://www.tshaonline.org/handbook/.

62. Eric Ames, *Carl Hagenbeck's Empire of Entertainments* (Seattle: University of Washington Press, 2009), 223–24, 228–29.

63. "Circus Headquarters at Peru Is Fascinating with Preparations Under Way to End Winter Hibernation within a Few Short Weeks," *Indianapolis Star*, February 26, 1922, 8; E. P. Wiley, "My Toughest Season as a Circus Agent," *Circus Scrap Book*, July 1931, 43–48.

64. "Germans with Circus Are Watched," *New York Clipper*, April 24, 1918, 4.

65. "War Hits Circus Man," *New York Clipper*, April 24, 1918, 7.

66. "Ringling Circus Arrives Here to Stay for Winter," *Bridgeport (CT) Telegram*, October 15, 1918, 1.

67. "1,000 Orphans See WPA Circus," *Brooklyn Daily Eagle*, December 29, 1938, 18.

68. "WPA Circus Elephant Stays on U.S. Relief," *Spokesman Review* (Spokane, WA), December 2, 1937, 16; "Bread and Circuses and Other Things: $9,000,000,000 in Work Relief," *LIFE*, February 29, 1928, 41.

69. "Performers under Wing of New Deal," *Mount Carmel (PA) Item*, October 21, 1935, 6; "Old Stars Rehearse WPA Circus to Be Held at Armory This Month," *Brooklyn Daily Eagle*, October 6, 1935, 12.

70. "'Bigger and Better' WPA Circus Arrives; 1,000 Enjoy Thrills," *Brooklyn Citizen*, April 17, 1936, 3.

71. "Performers under Wing of New Deal," *Mount Carmel (PA) Item*.

72. "Old Stars Rehearse WPA Circus to Be Held at Armory This Month," *Brooklyn Daily Eagle*.

73. "WPA Circus: Official Route Book," 1937–38, 6, 19, box 3, folder 24, Midwest American Circus Collection, Newberry Library, Chicago, IL.

74. Laura B. Haddock, "All Is Calm behind the Scenes at the Circus," *Christian Science Monitor*, May 15, 1942, 3.

75. Roland Butler, "The Circus of '43," in *Ringling Bros and Barnum & Bailey Combined Shows Route, Personnel and Statistics for the Season of 1943 Together*

with *Complete Itineraries from 1919 to 1943 Inclusive, Covering Every Exhibition Date since the Famous Ringling Bros and Barnum & Bailey Circuses Were United* (Sarasota, FL: J. C. Johnson, 1943), n.p., Circus Route Books, Special Collections, Milner Library, Illinois State University, Normal.

76. "Ringling Chooses Fairgrounds as Local Show Site," *Janesville (WI) Daily Gazette*, August 17, 1954, 11; "Moose Bringing Greatest Show Here in October," *Daily News Leader* (Staunton, VA), August 18, 1952, 6.

77. "Artist's Independent Contractor Agreement between Henry Bedow and the Ringling Brothers," October 25, 1935, Ringling Brothers Corporate Collection, Circus World Museum, Baraboo, WI. Bedow's contract lays out typical regulations for the work he would perform during the season as an independent contractor. It also cites the possibility of work outside of circuses: "It is also agreed that if the artist is re-engaged for the following season he shall not appear at any other circus, theater or Wild West show in the United States without the written consent of the show."

78. Gary Nash first asserted this idea in his 1979 work on early American seamen; see his *The Urban Crucible: Social Change, Political Consciousness, and the Origins of the American Revolution* (Cambridge: Harvard University Press, 1979), 16. Historian Marcus Rediker expands on this idea in his study of men working in the Atlantic world; see his *Between the Devil and the Deep Blue Sea: Merchant Seamen, Pirates and the Anglo-American Maritime World, 1770–1750* (New York: Cambridge University Press, 1987), 5.

79. Robert Rydell, *All the World's a Fair* (Chicago: University of Chicago Press, 1984); Robert Rydell and Rob Kroes, *Buffalo Bill in Bologna: The Americanization of the World, 1869–1922* (Chicago: University of Chicago Press, 2005).

80. Matthew Wittmann, *Circus and the City: New York, 1793–2010* (New York: Bard Graduate Center, 2012); Dahlinger and Thayer, *Badger State Showmen*; Gregory J. Renoff, *The Big Tent: The Traveling Circus in Georgia, 1820–1930* (Athens: University of Georgia Press, 2008).

Part I. The Circus Migrant

1. "Official Route, Season 1929, Sells Floto Circus," 1929, Circus Historical Society, Online Archive.

2. "State of Weather," *Chicago Tribune*, April 1–30, 1929.

3. "The Lady or the Tiger?," *Chicago Tribune*, March 24, 1929, 63.

4. Mabel Stark with Gertrude Orr, *Hold That Tiger!* (Caldwell, ID: Caxton Printers, 1938), 206.

5. "Daring Animal Trainer of John Robinson's Circus," *News and Observer* (Raleigh, NC), August 30, 1928, 16.

6. Stark with Orr, *Hold That Tiger!*, 190–206.

7. Stark with Orr, 95, 196.

8. "Prince, Lincoln Park's Big Tiger, Is Ill; Goes on Diet," *Chicago Tribune*, May 7, 1929, 16.

9. Daniel Bender, *The Animal Game: Searching for Wildness at the American Zoo* (Cambridge, MA: Harvard University Press, 2016).

10. Jay Kirk, *Kingdom under Glass: A Tale of Obsession, Adventure, and One Man's Quest to Preserve the World's Great Animals* (New York: Henry Holt, 2010); Rachel Poliquin, *The Breathless Zoo: Taxidermy and the Cultures of Longing* (University Park: Pennsylvania State University Press, 2012).

Chapter 1. Making Circus Day

1. "How Circus Men Do Things," *Landmark* (White River Junction, VT), June 16, 1921, 9; "Barnum and Bailey's Billing Crew Here," *Wichita (KS) Daily Times*, September 24, 1912, 4.

2. Ruby Haag Brown, interview by Sharon L. Smith, John Fugate, and Tom Dunwoody, March 22, 2000, in *Life in a Three-Ring Circus: Posters and Interviews*, by Sharon L. Smith and Stephen T. Fletcher (Indianapolis: Indiana Historical Society, 2001), 67.

3. *Billboard*, July 2, 1921, 100. For a report of contract men, see "Circus Men Were Here," *Junction City (KS) Daily Union*, August 14, 1919, 1.

4. "Barnum and Bailey's Billing Crew Here," *Wichita (KS) Daily Times*, September 24, 1912, 4 (qtd.); Don Wilson, "Circus Employees Get Big Pay; Nearly Every Trade Represented," *Washington Herald*, May 26, 1912, 28.

5. "When the Circus Comes to Town—A Marvel in Organization," *Baltimore Sun*, May 5, 1912, 27; "Circus Brings Many New Attractions This Year," *Arizona Daily Star*, September 22, 1912, 5; "Barnum and Bailey's Billing Crew Here," *Wichita Daily Times*, September 24, 1912, 4; "Circus Parade Today," *Baltimore Sun*, May 8, 1912, 16.

6. "When the Circus Comes to Town," *Baltimore Sun*.

7. "The Circus Looked at as a Business Proposition," *Morning Post* (Camden, NJ), April 9, 1912, 8.

8. Fred Dahlinger Jr. and Stuart Thayer, *Badger State Showmen: A History of Wisconsin's Circus Heritage* (Baraboo, WI: Circus World Museum, 1998), 77.

9. Alfred T. Ringling, *Seasons of 1895 and 1896 with the Circus: A Route Book of Ringling Bros. World's Greatest Shows* (St. Louis, MO: Great Western Printing, 1896), 110, Circus Route Books, Circus World Museum, Baraboo, WI.

10. Gregory J. Renoff, *The Big Tent: The Traveling Circus in Georgia, 1820–1930* (Athens: University of Georgia Press, 2008), 98–99.

11. J. Y. Henderson and Richard Taplinger, "Circus Doctor," *Argosy*, June 1951, series 1, box 27, Raymond Toole-Scott Circus Collection, University of California–Santa Barbara Library.

12. *Billboard*, November 18, 1911, 27; *Billboard*, December 2, 1911, 23; *Billboard*, June 29, 1912, 38.

13. J. Louis Sampson, "A Real Old Time Circus Man," *Bandwagon*, December 1955, 8; Statement by William Fraser, *Ringling Bros. Barnum & Bailey Combined Shows Inc. v. American Federation of Actors*, July 12, 1938, MSS 131, box 28,

folder 1, Union Strike Papers, Robert L. Parkinson Library and Research Center, Baraboo, WI (qtd.).

14. Mary Rawls, interview by Juliana Nykolaisyn and Tanya Finchum, June 13, 2011, 11, *The "Big Top" Show Goes On: An Oral History of Occupations inside and outside of the Canvas Circus Tent*, Oklahoma Oral History Research Program, Oklahoma State University.

15. Joyce Ferguson and Homer Ferguson, interview by Sharon L. Smith, February 23, 2000, in Smith and Fletcher, *Life in a Three-Ring Circus*, 43.

16. See, e.g., Robert Hunt to Al, February 4, 1943, series 4, box 36, folder 8, George Eells Papers, Arizona State University Libraries, Special Collections, Tempe.

17. "Circus Acts Shown in Court," *Inter Ocean* (Chicago), June 10, 1900, 3; Janet Davis, *The Circus Age: Culture and Society under the American Big Top* (Chapel Hill: University of North Carolina Press, 2002), 80.

18. "Moving Day for the Circus," *New York Times*, March 11, 1912, 13; "When the Circus Comes to Town," *Baltimore Sun*, May 5, 1912, 24.

19. "The Circus—Barnum's—Here!," *Sun* (New York), March 20, 1911, 5.

20. "Barnum and Bailey Have Found Something New in Circus Life; Old Program Entirely Upset," *Topeka (KS) Daily Capital*, March 24, 1912, 23; Winnifred Harper Cooley, "New York Folks Interest Themselves in Jiu Jitsu; Circus in Madison Square Garden Not Like Country Show," *Star Tribune* (Minneapolis, MN), April 28, 1912, 47; "How Circus Women Live," *Baltimore Sun*, June 29, 1912, 12.

21. Cooley, "New York Folks Interest Themselves in Jiu Jitsu."

22. "A Polyglot Crowd," *Buffalo (NY) Express and Illustrated Buffalo Express*, May 12, 1912, 26.

23. "Four Train Loads," *Butte (MT) Miner*, August 20, 1900, 5 (qtd.); Rawls, interview by Nykolaisyn and Finchum, June 13, 2011, 12.

24. "Speak 32 Languages," *Reno Gazette Journal*, August 26, 1912, 8; "Barnum and Bailey's Wonderful Pageant," *Vancouver Daily World*, August 17, 1912, 34.

25. "Smells and Roars Lure," *Los Angeles Times*, March 4, 1912, 24; "Peanuts," *Courier-Journal* (Louisville, KY), September 2, 1912, 3.

26. "Barnum and Bailey's Parade 3 Miles Long," *Wichita (KS) Daily Times*, October 1, 1912, 3.

27. "Baseball Stars with Barnum & Bailey," *Wichita (KS) Daily Times*, October 10, 1912, 8.

28. "Circus Parade Today," *Baltimore Sun*, May 8, 1912, 16.

29. "Barnum and Bailey's Parade 3 Miles Long," *Wichita (KS) Daily Times*.

30. "Circus Attractions," *Butte (MT) Minor*, June 28, 1912, 17.

31. "Need Train Mile Long to Transport Circus," *Pittsburgh Daily Post*, May 9, 1912, 4.

32. "Throng Greets Great Circus," *Greenwood (MS) Commonwealth*, November 7, 1934, 1.

33. The commuter train was a common occurrence at many stops during the Golden Age, thus ensuring that circuses could fill stadiums in otherwise sleepy communities.

34. "Barnum & Bailey's World's Greatest Show," *Wichita (KS) Daily Times*, October 15, 1912, 2; "Thousands View Forenoon Parade," *Dispatch* (Moline, IL), July 27, 1912, 5; "About Circuses," *Morning Herald* (Uniontown, PA), March 27, 1942, 26; "Yes, It Is All So," *Topeka (KS) Daily Herald*, September 21, 1904, 7.

35. "Sells-Floto Circus in the City for Two Performances and Parade," *Great Falls (MT) Tribune*, July 1, 1912, 7.

36. *The Circus Annual: A Route Book of Ringling Brothers World's Greatest Shows Season 1902* (n.p., 1902), 24, Circus Route Books, Special Collections, Milner Library, Illinois State University, Normal.

37. "Thousands View Forenoon Parade," *Dispatch* (Moline, IL), July 27, 1912, 5.

38. "Circus Parade Today," *Baltimore Sun*, May 8, 1912, 16; "Circus Day Comes Around Once More," *Arizona Republic*, September 23, 1912, 1 (qtd.); "Loading Circus Train Was Complex," *Waukesha (WI) Daily Freeman*, July 10, 1965, 16; "Circus Beautiful Is Coming Back Sept. 21," *Wichita (KS) Beacon*, September 7, 1912, 10.

39. "Oh, You Circus Parade!," *Asbury Park (NJ) Press*, June 29, 1912, 4; "Show to Be Novel," *Evening Star* (Washington, DC), May 5, 1912, 34; "Barnum and Bailey Parade Is the Best Ever," *Butte (MT) Daily*, August 9, 1912, 7; "Must the Circus Parade Go?," *Reading (PA) Times*, May 17, 1905, 4; "Circus Here with Parade and Crowds," *Evening Journal* (Wilmington, DE), May 10, 1912, 1; "Barnum and Bailey's Great Show Here Today," *Butte (MT) Miner*, August 9, 1912, 10; *Billboard*, January 7, 1911, 21.

40. "700 Women Appear in Biggest Show," *San Francisco Examiner*, September 1, 1912, 1.

41. "Barnum & Bailey Circus Coming," *Buffalo (NY) Commercial*, May 14, 1912, 14; "All the Kiddies Keep Tab on Date," *Courier-Gazette* (McKinney, TX), October 14, 1912, 5; "Barnum & Bailey Big Shows Are Here Today," *Altoona (PA) Tribune*, May 5, 1913, 5 (qtd.).

42. "Thousands View Forenoon Parade," *Dispatch* (Moline, IL), July 27, 1912, 5; "Peanuts," *Courier-Journal* (Louisville, KY), September 2, 1912, 3; "How They Set Up the Big Top Circus Tent," *San Francisco Examiner*, June 15, 1919; "Big Show Arrives; Small Boys Rejoice," *Brooklyn Daily Eagle*, April 21, 1912, 8; "When the Circus Comes to Town—A Marvel of Organization," *Baltimore Sun*, May 5, 1912, 24; "A Polyglot Crowd," *Buffalo (NY) Morning Express and Illustrated Buffalo Express*, May 12, 1912, 26 (qtd.).

43. "Good Grafts and Easy Those of the Old Circus," *Macon (GA) Telegraph*, February 9, 1913, 6.

44. "Circus Detectives Have Many Duties," *York (PA) Gazette*, June 1, 1918, 5; "One-Man Circus Police Force Long Nemesis of Pickpockets," *New York Times*,

April 21, 1943, 27; *Ringling Bros and Barnum & Bailey Combined Shows Route, Personnel and Statistics for the Season of 1943 Together with Complete Itineraries from 1919 to 1943 Inclusive, Covering Every Exhibition Date since the Famous Ringling Bros and Barnum & Bailey Circuses Were United* (Sarasota, FL: J. C. Johnson, 1943), n.p., Circus Route Books, Special Collections, Milner Library, Illinois State University, Normal.

45. "Circus Research," series 4, box 36, folder 3, George Eells Papers, Arizona State University Libraries, Special Collections, Tempe.

46. "Circus Day around the Clock," *Ringling Bros. and Barnum & Bailey Magazine Program 1946*, 11, K. Barr Circus Collection, series 1, box 4, folder 8, University of California–Santa Barbara Library.

47. "1901, Strictly Personal and Confidential," Scrapbook 24: Barnum & Bailey, Information and Address Book, box 40, McCaddon Collection of the Barnum and Bailey Circus, Princeton University Library, NJ.

48. Diamond Jim Parker, "A Real Clown's Circus Layout," *0-Gauge Rail-Roading*, Run 123 (June 1992): 44.

49. Advertisement, *Hutchinson (KS) Gazette*, December 24, 1912, 3.

50. "Clown Studies," *Tennessean*, October 24, 1948, 104.

51. "Acres of Clown Alley," *Evening Star* (Washington, DC), May 18, 1930, 84.

52. "Greatest Company of Clowns," *Spokesman-Review* (Spokane, WA), August 3, 1912, 8.

53. "Barnum and Bailey's Great Show Here Today," *Butte (MT) Miner*, August 9, 1912, 10; "City Sees the Circus," *Baltimore Sun*, May 9, 1912, 16 (qtd.).

54. "Rose of the Ring Changes Her Costume Thirteen Times a Day," *San Francisco Chronicle*, September 8, 1912, 43; "700 Women Appear in Biggest Show," *San Francisco Examiner*, September 1, 1912, 48.

55. "Julia Murdock Writes of Private Lives of Circus People," *Washington Times*, May 4, 1912, 8.

56. Philip A. Loring, "The Most Resilient Show on Earth: The Circus as a Model for Viewing Identity, Change, and Chaos," *Ecology and Society* 12, no. 1 (2007): article 9.

57. Rawls, interview by Nykolaisyn and Finchum, June 13, 2011, 10–11.

58. Gilbert Taylor, interview by Sharon L. Smith, March 29, 2000, in Smith and Fletcher, *Life in a Three-Ring Circus*, 31. Taylor's job as a sideshow band member was one of the most common positions held by circus workers. Route books from 1912 in various circuses indicate their own minstrel bands as well. See "Official Route, Season 1912, Sells-Floto Shows," 9, Circus Route Books, John and Mable Ringling Museum of Art, Sarasota, FL.

59. *Official Route Book of Robert Hunting's New Enormous R. R. Shows Circus, Museum and Menageries for the Tenting Season of 1894* (Suffern, NY: Chas. E. Griffin, 1894), 20, Circus Route Books, Circus World Museum, Baraboo, WI.

60. "How Circus Women Live," *Sun* (New York), June 29, 1912, 12.

61. "George Geffert Hurt at Circus: Fight between Roustabouts and Mishawaka Young Men," *South Bend (IN) Tribune*, August 8, 1913, 12; "Wild Buffalo

in Streets: Circus Animal Escapes Its Keeper and Alarms Many Citizens," *Passaic (NJ) Daily Herald*, May 7, 1902, 1.

62. "Negroes Start Riot on a Circus Train," *Courier-Journal* (Louisville, KY), October 3, 1910, 2.

63. "Almost a Lynching at M.S.U.: Students Demanded That a Negro Circus Employee Be Given Up," *Iola (KS) Daily Record*, May 13, 1903.

64. "Duluth's Orgy of Blood Concluded," *Barre (VT) Daily Times*, June 16, 1920, 1.

65. *Official Route Book of the Adam Forepaugh and Sells Bros Combined Circuses Season of 1898* (Columbus, OH: Landon Printing, 1898), 87, Circus Route Books, Circus World Museum, Baraboo, WI; Alfred T. Ringling, *The Circus Annual Season 1901: A Route Book of Ringling Bros. Worlds Greatest Shows* (Chicago: Central Printing and Engraving, 1901), 94, Circus Route Books, Special Collections, Milner Library, Illinois State University, Normal.

66. "Shot at Patrolman," *Montgomery (AL) Advertiser*, November 23, 1905, 7.

67. "Duluth Mob Murders Three Men Suspected of Revolting Crime," *Monitor* (Omaha, NE), June 24, 1920, 1.

68. Vanessa Toulmin, "Black Circus Performers in Victorian England," *Early Popular Visual Culture* 16, no. 3 (2016): 267–89.

69. "The Circus—Barnum's—Here!," *Sun* (New York), March 20, 1911, 5; "Circus Doctor Has an Important Job," *Fort Wayne (IN) Daily News*, July 15, 1915, 4 (qtd.); "Doctor of Circus," *Topeka (KS) State Journal*, July 22, 1916, 17; *Billboard*, August 3, 1912, 22.

70. "Doc Waddell," *Hobby Bandwagon* 5, no. 3 (April 1950): 3–4; "'Doc' Waddell Here with Circus," *Linton (IN) Daily Citizen*, June 7, 1948, 6.

71. "Show People Had Money," *Chanute (KS) Daily Tribune*, September 4, 1912, 1.

72. "Barnum & Bailey Circus Here in Its Grandeur," *Franklin Repository* (Chambersburg, PA), July 8, 1912, 5.

73. "World's Best Circus Coming," *Buffalo (NY) Enquirer*, May 13, 1912, 6.

74. "Menagerie Department of Barnum and Bailey Show," *Anaconda (MT) Standard*, August 7, 1912, 9; "Baby Giraffe Is Pet of Big Circus," *Oregon Daily Journal*, August 6, 1912, 3; "Baby Giraffe Thrives," *Evening Star* (Washington, DC), May 3, 1912, 3; "Barnum and Bailey's Great Show Here Today," *Butte (MT) Miner*, August 9, 1912, 10; "Barnum and Bailey Keeper Chats about Habit of Animals," *Butte (MT) Daily Post*, August 6, 1912, 5; "The Circus Has Its Own Zoo," *Tacoma (WA) Times*, August 19, 1912, 3; "Circus Animals' Welfare," *Buffalo (NY) Enquirer*, May 17, 1912, 10 (qtd.).

75. "The Circus Looked at as a Business Proposition," *Morning Post* (Camden, NJ), April 9, 1912, 8.

76. "About Circuses," *Morning Herald* (Uniontown, PA), March 27, 1942, 26.

77. "Barnum and Bailey's Great Show Here Today," *Butte (MT) Miner*, August 9, 1912, 10; "When the Circus Comes to Town—A Marvel of Organization," *Baltimore Sun*, May 5, 1912, 27.

78. "Many Going to Circus," *Norcatur (KS) Dispatch*, July 25, 1912, 1.

79. "Barnum & Bailey Circus Here in Its Grandeur," *Franklin Repository* (Chambersburg, PA), July 8, 1912, 5.

80. Lynn Abbott and Doug Seroff, *Ragged but Right: Black Traveling Shows, "Coon Songs," and the Dark Pathway to Blues and Jazz* (Jackson: University of Mississippi Press), 166.

81. Jacob Dorman, *The Princess and the Prophet: The Secret History of Magic, Race, and Moorish Muslims in America* (New York: Beacon Press, 2020), 9.

82. "Many Going to Circus," *Norcatur (KS) Dispatch*, July 25, 1912, 1; "Barnum and Bailey's World's Greatest Show," *Wichita (KS) Daily Times*, October 15, 1912, 2.

83. "A Wonderful Troupe," *Norcatur (KS) Dispatch*, July 25, 1912, 1; Janet Davis, *Circus Queen and Tinker Bell: The Memoir of Tiny Kline* (Urbana: University of Illinois Press, 2008), 144; "Wonders of Circus Beheld by 24,000," *Dispatch* (Moline, IL), July 28, 1912, 7.

84. Janet Davis and Louis S. Warren have each argued that mass entertainments, like the circus and Wild West shows, were windows into current events, reenacting current events with commentary that circusgoers would have likely been familiar with through newspaper coverage. See Davis, *The Circus Age*; Louis S. Warren, *Buffalo Bill's America: William Cody and the Wild West Show* (New York: Alfred A. Knopf, 2005).

85. "Barnum and Bailey Circus Will Show Here Tomorrow," *Santa Ana (CA) Register*, September 19, 1912, 3.

86. "You Going to the Circus?," *Buffalo (NY) Morning Express and Illustrated Buffalo Express*, June 29, 1908, 8.

87. "Baby Giraffe Is Pet of Big Circus," *Oregon Daily Journal*, August 6, 1912, 3; "Society Circus—At Last—Tonight," *Evening Sun* (Baltimore), May 21, 1912, 5; "Pink Lemonade, the Ally of Barnum," *Los Angeles Times*, September 19, 1912, 5; "Wine Flows at Funeral," *Los Angeles Times*, September 19, 1912, 5.

88. "Barnum and Bailey Peanuts and Lemonade," *Houston Post*, October 20, 1912, 13; Don Wilson, "Circus Employees Get Big Pay; Newly Every Trade Represented," *Washington Herald*, May 26, 1912, 28.

89. "A Good Circus This Year," *Hartford (CT) Courant*, June 26, 1912, 7.

90. "Untitled Notice," *Wilmington (NC) Star*, June 5, 1912, 4.

91. "When the Circus Comes to Town—A Marvel of Management," *Baltimore Sun*, May 5, 1912, 27.

92. "Circus Day around the Clock," *Ringling Bros. and Barnum & Bailey Magazine Program 1946*, 11, K. Barr Circus Collection, series 1, box 4, folder 8, University of California–Santa Barbara Library.

93. "The Circus Looked at as a Business," *Daily Arkansas Gazette*, April 7, 1912, 52.

Chapter 2. Human and Animal Circus Workers and Their Knowledge Networks

1. "Launch of the Steam Ship Assyrian Monarch: The Vessel Christened by Lady Brown," *Sheffield and Rotherham Independent*, August 11, 1880, 3 (qtd.); "Advertisement: Monarch Line," *Leeds Mercury*, February 14, 1882, 3.

2. "Jumbo Landed in Safely," *New York Times*, April 10, 1882, 1.

3. "Jumbo Landed in Safely."

4. "Jumbo Landed in Safely"; Matthew Scott, *Autobiography of Matthew Scott: Jumbo's Keeper* (Bridgeport, CT: Trow's Printing and Bookbinding, 1885).

5. For a longer history of the development of zoos, see David Hancocks, *A Different Nature: The Paradoxical World of Zoos and Their Uncertain Future* (Berkeley: University of California Press, 2001); Nigel Rothfels, *Savages and Beasts: The Birth of the Modern Zoo* (Baltimore, MD: Johns Hopkins University Press, 2008); Vicki Croke, *The Modern Ark: The Story of Zoos: Past, Present, and Future* (New York: Scribner, 1997).

6. "Jumbo Landed in Safely," *New York Times*.

7. This chapter explores how migration affected the lived experiences of animal trainers, while focusing on the intellectual threads of continuity in their training methods. Because their careers were inherently transnational and global, this chapter engages with scholarship that explores what constitutes intellectual history and its geographic boundaries. See Sudipta Kaviraj, "Global Intellectual History: Meanings and Methods," in *Global Intellectual History*, ed. Samuel Moyn and Andrew Satori (New York: Columbia University Press, 2013), 295–320; Edward Baring, "Ideas on the Move: Context in Transnational Intellectual History," *Journal of the History of Ideas* 77, no. 4 (October 2016): 567–87; Mia Bay et al., eds., *Toward an Intellectual History of Black Women* (Chapel Hill: University of North Carolina Press, 2015).

8. This chapter engages with several threads of migration historiography, within both the Atlantic world and the Black Atlantic. Circuses were a global phenomenon, operating well beyond the borders of the Atlantic world. This chapter examines trainers who largely operated within the physical boundaries of the Atlantic world while laboring in workplaces that were much more globalized. Ulbe Bosma explores the compartmentalization of labor markets, largely in connection to race and country of origin. He calls for new "historical markers" of time as a way to decenter the 1924 Quota Act and instead shift perspectives beyond US borders, while still connecting labor and race. This chapter engages with ideas of path dependency, particularly in thinking about how animal trainers carved out new paths to success while maintaining social and professional networks. See Ulbe Bosma, "Beyond the Atlantic: Connecting Migration and World History in the Age of Imperialism, 1840–1940," *International Review of Social History* 52, no. 1 (April 2007): 121.

9. Several scholars have explored the history of census taking in the United

States and its connection to racialized laws. See Paul Schor, *Counting Americans: How the US Census Classified the Nation*, trans. Lys Ann Weiss (New York: Oxford University Press, 2017); Joel Perlmann, *America Classifies the Immigrants: From Ellis Island to the 2020 Census* (Cambridge, MA: Harvard University Press, 2018); Melissa Nobles, *Shades of Citizenship: Race and the Census in Modern Politics* (Stanford, CA: Stanford University Press, 2000).

10. This history intersects with the histories of other seasonal labor in the nineteenth and early twentieth centuries, particularly that of hobo workers. See Frank Tobias Higbie, *Indispensable Outcasts: Hobo Workers and Community in the American Midwest, 1880–1930* (Urbana: University of Illinois Press, 2003); Jeff Ferrell, *Drift: Illicit Mobility and Uncertain Knowledge* (Oakland: University of California Press, 2018); Mark Wyman, *Hoboes: Bindlestiffs, Fruit Tramps, and the Harvesting of the West* (New York: Hill and Wang, 2010).

11. "When the Circus Chrysalis Becomes a Butterfly," *Oregon Daily Journal*, April 19, 1914, 58.

12. "It's a Near Heaven for Boys Where the Circus Sleeps," *Daily Herald* (Provo, UT), January 25, 1925, 12; "More Winter Circus Acts," *Kansas City Star*, February 2, 1902, 7.

13. Running away to join the circus became a familiar backstory within the circus world as workers dreamed of working their way up to pay and perhaps fame. "Rowan Ran Away to Join a Circus," *Times Union* (Brooklyn, NY), November 14, 1926, 30.

14. *Billboard*, August 4, 1900, 3.

15. This craze for international performers also occurred in European circuses. The talent scout for Tom Arnold's Circus in London claimed to be almost unwilling to look at certain acts, like high-wire performers, out of England. "All the World His Circus: He Searches the World for Stars of the Sawdust Ring," n.d., PA MSS 14, series 1, box 27, Raymond Toole-Scott Circus Collection, University of California–Santa Barbara Library.

16. *Billboard*, May 30, 1903, 9.

17. Earl Chapin May, "With the Circus Candy Butcher: Venders Are Keen Students of Human Nature and Help to Keep the White Top Moving," *Popular Mechanics*, August 1927, 275–76.

18. In 2012, Peter Winn called for a global push in labor history following Marcel van der Linden and Jan Lucassen's iconic 1999 pamphlet that established the subfield of global labor history. Since then, scholars have taken up the call, using global frameworks to understand the connections between labor and migration, particularly between the Global North and Global South. This work is situated within this subfield. It answers Winn's call to explore the complexities in spaces where formal and informal labor mingle in unmistakably globalized spaces. See Peter Winn, "Global Labor History: The Future of the Field?," *International Labor and Working-Class History*, no. 82 (2012): 90; Marcel van der Linden and Jan Lucassen, *Prolegomena for a Global Labour History* (Amsterdam: International Institute for Social History, 1999).

19. Catherine and Emil Pallenberg, bear trainers from Germany, settled down in Sarasota, Florida, while Matthew Scott lived out his life in Bridgeport, Connecticut. Sarasota, Florida, City Directory, 1960; Bridgeport, Connecticut, City Directory, 1913; Bridgeport, Connecticut, City Directory, 1914; all accessed through Ancestry.com., U.S. City Directories, 1822–1995.

20. Schor, *Counting Americans*, 137–39; Perlmann, *America Classifies the Immigrants*, 19.

21. Perlmann, *America Classifies the Immigrants*, 41–43.

22. "Hagenbeck-Wallace Circus: Over One Thousand People of Different Nationalities Are Carried," *Lancaster (PA) Examiner*, May 14, 1913, 8.

23. "Big Circus Comes to Make Us Young," *Salt Lake Herald Republican*, August 8, 1910, 4.

24. "Circus Troop in a Sea of Mud," *Lincoln (NE) Star*, September 23, 1910.

25. Harvey Watkins, *Four Years in Europe: The Barnum & Bailey Greatest Show on Earth in the Old World* (Paris: printed by the author, 1901), 65–66.

26. Janet Davis, *The Circus Age: Culture and Society under the American Big Top* (Chapel Hill: University of North Carolina Press, 2003), 260.

27. Davis, 80; Robert Hunt to Al, February 4, 1943, series 4, box 36, folder 8, George Eells Papers, Arizona State University Libraries, Special Collections, Tempe.

28. Albert J. Beveridge, "Child Labor Laws," *Journal of Education* 68, no. 12 (October 1908): 330–32.

29. "Hagenbeck-Wallace Circus: Over One Thousand People of Different Nationalities Are Carried," *Lancaster (PA) Examiner*, May 14, 1913, 8.

30. "Spring Heralds Coming Circus: Much Geography Actually Seen in Sawdust Ring," *Legal News*, May 5, 1933, 1.

31. Jumbomania had swept through England in the years prior to his migration to the United States. Just prior to his departure from England, one newspaper noted that the Jumbo craze meant "paper notes everywhere decorated with his image, and even a certain greyish cloth for dresses called Jumbo cloth in some of the shops." The same obsession with Jumbo's image continued in the United States with posters, toys, and paraphernalia. "The Ladies Column," *Nottingham Guardian*, March 31, 1882, 11.

32. *Times* (London), March 9, 1882, 2. Several animal husbandry theories have arisen to explain why male elephants turned on trainers. Sexual frustration due to hormonal changes during a period called musth could be a factor in some of these cases. Unnatural diets, like the candy and liquor that Jumbo consumed regularly, could have also led to dental issues. Skeletal analysis of Jumbo showed proof of impacted molars. See Hancocks, *A Different Nature*.

33. "With Saw-Dust in Veins, Local Circus Fans Await Old Friends," *Post Crescent* (Appleton, WI), September 8, 1954, 19; "Behind the Scenes of the Big Show," *Fond Du Lac (WI) Commonwealth Reporter*, May 31, 1913, 9.

34. C. J. Cornish, "The Moltke of Menagerie Owners," *English Illustrated Magazine*, October 1895, 81–88, PA MSS 14, series 1, box 27, Raymond Toole-Scott Circus Collection, University of California–Santa Barbara Library.

35. W. C. Thompson, *On the Road with a Circus* (New York: New Amsterdam Book, 1905).

36. John B. E. Gasmann, "Hagenbeck's Wild Animals and Their Trainers," *Sawdust Ring*, Winter 1938, PA MSS 14, series 1, box 19, Raymond Toole-Scott Circus Collection, University of California–Santa Barbara Library.

37. "Big United States Circus and New Great Eastern Menagerie: Nula Delavanti: Hindoo Serpent Charmer," poster (Strobridge Lithographing, 1886), Tibbals Circus Collection, John and Mable Ringling Museum of Art, Sarasota, FL; "Two Jet Black Camels; A Pair of White Sacred Camels," poster (Strobridge Lithographing, c. early 1880s), The Circus Poster Collection: Barnum in the late 1800s, Bridgeport Library, CT; "Pallenberg's Wonder Bears," *American Circus Posters in Full Colour*, ed. Charles Philip Fox (New York: Dover, 1978).

38. Scott, *Autobiography of Matthew Scott*, 76.

39. Benjamin Reiss, *The Showman and the Slave: Race, Death, and Memory in Barnum's America* (Cambridge, MA: Harvard University Press, 2009), 148. Barnum began his career with this practice, when he arranged a public autopsy of Joice Heth, a Black woman whom Barnum claimed was 161 years old.

40. P. T. Barnum to Henry A. Ward, October 9, 1883, box 24, folder 9, Henry Augustus Ward Papers, University of Rochester Special Collections, NY. Within the letter, Barnum told Ward, "I shall have my managers understand that if we lose Jumbo (which Heaven forbid!) you must be telegraphed to immediately, & hope you will lose no time in saving his skin & skeleton." See also "Condensed News," *Indianapolis News*, September 29, 1885, 1.

41. Henry Ward to Professor John P. "Doc" Marshall, 1885, box 24, folder 9, Henry Augustus Ward Papers, University of Rochester Special Collections, NY. For a look at this letter within the larger history of Jumbo's death, see Susan Wilson, "An Elephant's Tale," *Tufts Online Magazine*, Spring 2002, https://news.tufts.edu/magazine/spring2002/jumbo.html.

42. Jan Bondeson, *The Feejee Mermaid and Other Essays in Natural and Unnatural History* (Ithaca, NY: Cornell University Press, 1999), 96–130; *Appleton (WI) Crescent*, October 3, 1885, 1.

43. "Keeper Scott Pensioned," *Boston Weekly Globe*, September 22, 1885; "Jumbo's Old Chum: He Won't Return to England Because Jumbo's Carcass Is Here," *New York Times*, February 11, 1887, 8 (qtd.).

44. US Census, 1910, Bridgeport, Fairfield, CT, Roll T624_129, p. 4B, enumeration district 57, Family History Library (FHL) microfilm 1374142.

45. Bridgeport, Connecticut, City Directory, 1913; Bridgeport, Connecticut, City Directory, 1914; both accessed through Ancestry.com., U.S. City Directories, 1822–1995.

46. *New York Clipper*, November 26, 1910, 1027.

47. "Man Who Kept Jumbo Dies at Lakeview Home," *Bridgeport (CT) Times and Evening Farmer*, December 24, 1914, 1; "Circusmen Save Comrade from Potter's Field," *Bridgeport (CT) Times and Evening Farmer*, December 26, 1914;

"Veteran Circusmen at Obsequies of Trainer of 'Jumbo,'" *Bridgeport (CT) Times and Evening Farmer*, December 29, 1914.

48. US Census, 1870, Ypsilanti, Washtenaw, MI, Roll M593_708, p. 463B, FHL microfilm 552207.

49. "Wicked Elephants," *Independent-Journal* (Ottawa, KS), March 9, 1882, 4.

50. "Forepaugh Dissatisfied," *Philadelphia Inquirer*, February 22, 1883, 3.

51. *Route Book of the Great Forepaugh Show, Circus Hippodrome and Menagerie: Season 1883* (n.p., 1883), Circus Route Books, Circus World Museum, Baraboo, WI; *Circus Historical Society Note Sheet*, no. 6 (May 15, 1943): 2.

52. "Three Leopards Loose," *Watertown (WI) News*, September 7, 1906, 6; "Circus Elephant Captured and Town Is Relieved," *Salt Lake Tribune*, October 13, 1922, 1.

53. Vanessa Toulmin, "Black Circus Performers in Victorian Britain," *Early Popular Visual Culture* 16, no. 3 (2018): 267–89; Vanessa Toulmin, *What Is Circus Today? Explorations through 250 Years of British Circus, Black Circus Performers in the 19th Century* (Sheffield: Weston Park Museum, 2018), 14.

54. "Forepaugh's Fakes: The Ten Thousand Dollar Beauty in the White Elephant," *San Francisco Examiner*, September 23, 1888, 12.

55. Thompson, *On the Road with a Circus*, 190; "Treat in Store: Forepaugh & Sells Elephants to Swim," *Gazette* (Cedar Rapids, IA), July 9, 1898, 8; "Forepaugh's Innovations," *Leader-Telegram* (Eau Claire, WI), June 5, 1885, 3.

56. "Stars from Every Great Circus in the Old World," *Philadelphia Times*, April 12, 1885, 5.

57. "Announcements," *Chicago Tribune*, August 13, 1885, 4.

58. Eph Thompson, emergency passport application, 1892, National Archives and Records Administration (NARA), Washington, DC, roll 7, vol. 9, Chili to Haiti.

59. Eph Thompson, emergency passport application, 1895, NARA, Washington, DC, roll 12, vol. 19, Haiti to Russia.

60. *Variety*, June 20, 1908, 13.

61. "Eph Thompson's Four Elephants: Recognized as Leading Animal Actors in Existence," *Gazette* (Cedar Rapids, IA), September 29, 1906, 7; "Mr. E. Thompson," Tibbals Circus Collection, John and Mable Ringling Museum of Art, Sarasota, FL; "Palace—Eph Thompson's Performing Elephants," *Standard* (London), September 28, 1900; "Eph Thompson," *Era* (London), April 11, 1896.

62. Advertisement, *Daily Times* (New Philadelphia, OH), July 27, 1906, 4.

63. "Elephants at Polls Next Week," *Hartford (CT) Courant*, December 2, 1905, 7; "Orpheum: Always a Good Show," *Standard Union* (Brooklyn, NY), October 22, 1905, 19; "Orpheum Theatre," *Courier* (Harrisburg, PA), February 16, 1908, 11 (qtd.).

64. "Thompson's Elephants: Successful Trainer, Now at Orpheum, Tells Experiences," *Harrisburg (PA) Daily Independent*, February 19, 1908, 5.

65. "Kindness and Carrots, That's How the Orpheum's Elephants Were Trained," *Harrisburg (PA) Telegraph*, February 22, 1908, 8.

66. Susan Nance, *Entertaining Elephants: Animal Agency and the Business of the American Circus* (Baltimore, MD: Johns Hopkins University Press, 2013), 5.

67. "Outlaw Elephant 'Taken for Ride' by His Mates: 'Put on Spot' by Friends," *Corsicana (TX) Semi-Weekly Light*, October 18, 1929, 1; "Joe E. Claims Elephant Remembered for 30 Years," *Los Angeles Evening Post-Record*, August 22, 1934, 2.

68. Royal Society for the Prevention of Cruelty to Animals, open letter, September 1938, PA MSS 14, series 1, box 29, Raymond Toole-Scott Circus Collection, University of California–Santa Barbara Library; "Sweden to Bar Wild Animal Acts; Mistreatment Blamed and Denied," *Chattanooga (TN) Daily Times*, November 18, 1959, 29.

69. Frank Charles Bostock, *The Training of Wild Animals* (New York: Century, 1903), 3.

70. *Acts of the Legislature of West Virginia at Its Twenty-Fifth Regular Session* (Charleston, WV: Tribune, 1901), 601; "A New Trust," *Billboard*, June 16, 1900.

71. "Injunction Served on Show Manager," *Democrat and Chronicle* (Rochester, NY), August 25, 1900, 9.

72. "Pan-American Exposition: Few Words about Frank C. Bostock, the Animal King," *Buffalo (NY) Courier*, July 9, 1901.

73. Peta Tait, *Wild and Dangerous Performances: Animals, Emotions, Circus* (New York: Palgrave Macmillan, 2011), 21–25.

74. "Bostock's Dreamland: Animal Arena, Coney Island," *New York Times*, May 31, 1904, 14; A. W. Stencell, *Girl Show: Into the Canvas World of Bump and Grind* (Toronto: ECW Press, 1999), 7–9; "Amusement Notes," *Standard Union* (Brooklyn, NY), June 13, 1903, 120, 182.

75. Bostock, *The Training of Wild Animals*, 3.

76. *Census Returns of England and Wales*, 1891, National Archives of the UK, class RG12, piece 4207, folio 13, p. 19, GSU roll 6099317.

77. *Etruia* passenger list, 1893, arrival in New York, microfilm serial M237, 1820–1897, line 6, p. 11, National Archives of the UK, Board of Trade: Commercial and Statistical Department and successors, Inwards Passenger Lists, class BT26.

78. *Campania* passenger list, 1898, National Archives of the UK, Board of Trade: Commercial and Statistical Department and successors, Inwards Passenger Lists, class BT26, piece 125; Advertisement, *Era* (London), October 7, 1899, 25.

79. Elizabeth Hanson, *Animal Attractions: Nature on Display in American Zoos* (Princeton, NJ: Princeton University Press, 2002), 83; Advertisement, *Era* (London), October 27, 1999, 31; "Musical and Dramatic Notes," *Railway Official Gazette* (London), January 1908. It is unclear whether Bostock personally toured the United States and Mexico in 1900, or whether it was just his namesake traveling carnival that he established.

206   Notes to Chapter 2

80. "Music and the Stage," *New York Age*, November 19, 1908, 6; *Variety*, October 1908, 5.

81. "On the Pike in the World's Fair," *Garnett (KS) Journal Plaindealer*, July 1, 1904, 4; "The Fair at the Agricultural Hall," *Era* (London), December 31, 1881, 13; "Presentation to Martini Maccomo: The African Lion Tamer," *Liverpool Mercury*, February 8, 1866, 5.

Part II. The Circus Lot

1. "Jenny Wallenda Lived a Full Circus Life," *Herald-Tribune* (Sarasota, FL), April 5, 2015.

2. Jack Altshul, "Heads and Tails," *Newsday* (Hempstead, NY), April 14, 1965, 54.

3. Janet Davis, *The Circus World: Culture and Society under the American Big Top* (Chapel Hill: University of North Carolina Press, 2002), 10–11.

Chapter 3. Women's Work and Gendered Circus Labor in the Tented Shows

1. "With the White Tops," *Show World* (Chicago), August 24, 1907, 12; *New York Clipper*, April 13, 1878, 23; *New York Clipper*, February 23, 1884; "Josephine De Mott, Equestrian, Dies," *Billboard*, March 20, 1948, 54; Charles Eldridge Griffin, *Four Years in Europe with Buffalo Bill* (Albia, IA: Stage, 1908), xiv; William Schell, *Integral Outsiders: The American Colony in Mexico City, 1876–1911* (New York: Rowman and Littlefield, 1999), 40.

2. "Josie De Mott: Circus Rider Had a Romantic Career, Is Wealthy," *Harrisburg (PA) Telegraph*, April 24, 1907, 2; "Romance of a Circus Rider's Home," *Statesman Journal* (Salem, OR), August 1, 1911, 3; "Circus Romance Is Rival of Fiction," *Indianapolis Star*, May 5, 1907, 28; "Josie De Mott Quits Society for Her First Love: Circus Ring," *Star-Gazette* (Elmira, NY), August 11, 1906, 8 (qtd.); "Nearly Starved in Alaska: Mrs. Robinson Has Seen Excitement Outside of the Circus World," *Baltimore Sun*, May 18, 1906, 14; "Pretty Romance of a Circus Rider: The True Story of Josie De Mott's Brave Battle against Adversity," *Washington Times*, May 6, 1906, 9.

3. "Pretty Romance of a Circus Rider," *Washington Times* (qtd.); "Josie De Mott Quits Society for Her First Love," *Star-Gazette*.

4. "Youth Possible to Every Woman Who Really Wants It," *New York Times*, February 16, 1913, 44; "Josie De Mott Quits Society for Her First Love," *Star-Gazette*; "Nearly Starved in Alaska," *Baltimore Sun*.

5. Josie De Mott, "Artists' Forum," *Variety*, June 20, 1908, 9; Josie De Mott, "The Real Women of the Circus," *Washington Post*, May 13, 1906, EA6.

6. Bertha H. Smith, "Behind the Scenes at the Circus," *Modern Sanitation: Devoted to the Advancement of Sanitary Plumbing* 4, no. 5 (October 1907): 5,

series 1, box 1, folder 2, American Circus Collection, 1891–1939, Newberry Library, Chicago.

7. De Mott, "The Real Women of the Circus." The circus seconded this notion during these years by noting that circus folks were less prone to scandals, such as divorces. See "How Circus Women Live," *Baltimore Sun*, June 29, 1912, 12.

8. De Mott quoted from "The Real Women of the Circus," *Washington Post*, May 13, 1906, EA6. Ideas of race suicide gained traction and notoriety with President Theodore Roosevelt's 1905 speech "On American Motherhood." See Christopher N. Matthews, "Gilded Ages and Gilded Archaeologies of American Exceptionalism," *International Journal of Historical Archaeology* 16, no. 4 (December 2012): 717–44; Marlis Schweitzer, "The Salome Epidemic: Degeneracy, Disease, and Race Suicide," in *The Oxford Handbook of Dance and Theater*, ed. Nadine George-Graves (New York: Oxford University Press, 2015), 891; Ralph Bergengren, "Taking the Circus Seriously," *Atlantic Monthly*, May 1909.

9. Krystyn Moon, "On a Temporary Basis: Immigration, Labor Unions, and the American Entertainment Industry, 1880s-1930s," *Journal of American History* 99, no. 3 (2012): 771–92.

10. De Mott's emphasis on emotional strength tied to physical strength was a personified New Woman ideal. It offered a way to explain and justify the work that circus women engaged in both in the ring and behind the scenes. But her ideas of national belonging and identity pointed to the imperialist undertones of the shows. For a gendered reading of imperialist ideologies during these years, particularly around manliness, see Kristin L. Hoganson, *Fighting for American Manhood: How Gender Politics Provoked the Spanish-American and Philippine-American Wars* (New Haven, CT: Yale University Press, 1998).

11. "With the White Tops," *Show World* (Chicago), August 24, 1907, 12; Billy Rose, "Pitching Horseshoes," *Dunkirk (NY) Evening Observer*, March 29, 1948, 6; "Youth Possible to Every Woman Who Really Wants It," *New York Times*, February 16, 1913, 44; Josie De Mott, "Exercise as Rest for the Woman Who Gets Tired," *New York Times*, January 20, 1918, 60 (qtd.).

12. This chapter engages with historiographies of the intersection of women's history and labor. Historians have examined the lives and labors of women workers in industrialized settings like cigar shop floors. But the intersection of performance and labor, with forebears like Robert Allen and M. Alison Kibler, offers new examinations of how women understood their own labor and how they engaged in activism and advocacy for fellow women workers. See, e.g., Jayna Brown, *Babylon Girls: Black Women Performers and the Shaping of the Modern* (Durham, NC: Duke University Press, 2008); M. Alison Kibler, *Rank Ladies: Gender and Cultural Hierarchy in American Vaudeville* (Chapel Hill: University of North Carolina Press, 1999); Robert Allen, *Horrible Prettiness: Burlesque and American Culture* (Chapel Hill: University of North Carolina Press, 1991).

13. Katherine H. Adams and Michael L. Keene provide a sweeping overview of women in the circus. They also interrogate gendered depictions of the circus, particularly though novels and memoirs, to understand how these circus

women signified American women. See their *Women of the American Circus, 1890–1940* (Jefferson, NC: McFarland, 2012), 17. Janet Davis has written several astute analyses of gendered constructions in the circus; see, e.g., her "Spectacles of South Asia at the American Circus, 1890–1940," *Bandwagon*, May 2012, 40–47.

14. Historian Janet Davis also considers Wild West shows in her cultural history of the circus. As she notes, James A. Bailey's purchase of Buffalo Bill's Wild West Show makes it integral to the history of the circus. See Janet Davis, *The Circus Age: Culture and Society under the American Big Top* (Chapel Hill: University of North Carolina Press, 2002), 10.

15. L. G. Moses, *Wild West Shows and the Image of American Indians, 1883–1933* (Albuquerque: University of New Mexico Press, 1999), 107–11. For a digitized film of Ghost Dance performers who reportedly traveled with Buffalo Bill, see W. K.-L. Dickson and William Heise, *Sioux Ghost Dance* (Edison Manufacturing, 1894), film, 0:38, Library of Congress, https://www.loc.gov/item/00694139/. See also Griffin, *Four Years in Europe with Buffalo Bill*, xxi.

16. "Two Bumps at the Circus," *Anaconda (MT) Standard*, January 20, 1907, 26.

17. Sam A. Maddra, *Hostiles? The Lakota Ghost Dance and Buffalo Bill's Wild West* (Norman: University of Oklahoma Press, 2006), 147.

18. Louis S. Warren, *Buffalo Bill's America: William Cody and the Wild West Show* (New York: Alfred A. Knopf, 2005), 409.

19. "The Queen's Visit to the Wild West Show at West Brompton," *Graphic* (London), May 21, 1887, 544; Maddra, *Hostiles?*, 51.

20. "Robinson Circus Squaw's Death Is Bringing Trouble," *Circleville (OH) Herald*, July 21, 1928, 1.

21. Griffin, *Four Years in Europe with Buffalo Bill*, 133; Moses, *Wild West Shows and the Images of American Indians*, 190.

22. "Will Show Far West Life: Buffalo Bill's Exhibition Will Be Here," *Washington Post*, May 17, 1908, 11; George Bird Grinnell, *The Fighting Cheyennes* (New York: Charles Scribner's Sons, 1915), 299–304.

23. Griffin, *Four Years in Europe with Buffalo Bill*, 31.

24. "Elephant Makes Dash for Liberty," *Daily Review* (Decatur, IL), May 1, 1915, 3.

25. Moses, *Wild West Shows and the Images of American Indians*, 5, 112; Maddra, *Hostiles?*, 51.

26. Karen Bearor, "The *Illustrated American* and the Lakota Ghost Dance," *American Periodicals* 21, no. 1 (2011): 151.

27. Eric Willey mines facts from the myths surrounding Pawnee Bill by considering his interactions in his hometown; see Willey's "One of Our Own: Pawnee Bill's Life as Viewed by Bloomington Residents," *Bandwagon* 60, no. 4 (2016): 72–90.

28. Within a few years of Buffalo Bill's return to the United States, the two Wild West shows combined to form the "Two Bills Show" to stay afloat amid

waning interest in the Wild West. "Circus News," *Variety*, July 28, 1906, 6; Lou Sampson, "A Gala Day in Iowa Circus History," *Bandwagon* 7, no. 2 (1952): 3–4.

29. "Circus News," *Variety*; "A Woman's Experience as a Trainer of Mustangs," *New York Times*, June 10, 1906, X4.

30. "Pawnee Bill in Town with Wild West Show," *Plain Speaker* (Hazleton, PA), July 1, 1903, 1; Sampson, "A Gala Day in Iowa Circus History"; "200 Indians in War Paint Arrive Today for Pageant," *Washington Post*, March 3, 1929, M4; "Thrills by Pawnee Bill," *Washington Post*, August 26, 1906, 10.

31. Jay Grelen, "A Tale of Tragedy for Pawnee Bill," *Oklahoman*, October 24, 1999.

32. Adams and Keene, *Women of the American Circus*; Davis, *The Circus Age*.

33. "The Snake Charmer of the Wild West Show: Tells How the Most Deadly Snakes Can Be Safely Handled," *Tatler*, no. 164 (July 27, 1904): 150. See also Ottavio Canestrelli with Ottavio Gesmundo, *The Grand Gypsy* (Lexington, KY: Lulu, 2016).

34. "She Charms the Serpent," *Saint Paul (MN) Globe*, April 16, 1888, 4; "The Snake Charmer of the Wild West Show," *Tatler*.

35. "The Snake Charmer of the Wild West Show," *Tatler*.

36. "Suggestions and Rules: Employees: Ringling Brothers," series 1, box 29, Raymond Toole-Scott Circus Collection, University of California–Santa Barbara Library; "With the Ladies of the Circus: The Life behind the Scenes of the Young Women Who Risk Their Lives in Automobile Flights, Bareback Feats, and Gymnastic Stunts," *New York Times*, April 1, 1906, SM3 (qtd.); "How Circus Women Live," *Baltimore Sun*, June 29, 1912, 12.

37. "With the Ladies of the Circus," *New York Times*.

38. Adams and Keene, *Women of the American Circus*, 74.

39. Quoted in "Life of Circus Women," *Times-Democrat* (New Orleans), November 5, 1902, 11.

40. "Circus Women and Children Happy, Healthy, 'Homey' Gypsies," *Ogden (UT) Standard*, August 4, 1914, 4.

41. "Circus Women Interesting," *Star-Gazette* (Elmira, NY), July 7, 1913, 3.

42. "Circus Mother Enjoys Her Big Healthy Family in Tented City," *Allentown (PA) Leader*, May 1, 1917, 8.

43. "Hurrah! The Barnum and Bailey Circus Show Here Monday," *Sheboygan (WI) Press*, August 28, 1915, 8.

44. "Suggestions and Rules: Employees: Ringling Brothers," series 1, box 29, Raymond Toole-Scott Circus Collection, University of California–Santa Barbara Library; "How Circus Women Live," *Baltimore Sun*, June 29, 1912, 12; "Behind the Glitter in the Circus Tent," *Denison (IA) Review*, July 31, 1912, 3 (qtd.).

45. Howard Y. Bary, "Strange Customs and Weird Beliefs of the Padaung Giraffe-Necked Women," 1933, series 1, box 1, folder 3, American Circus Collection, 1891–1939, Newberry Library, Chicago.

46. W. C. Thompson, *On the Road with a Circus* (New York: New Amsterdam

Book, 1905), 13 (qtd.); Richard Lane, "She Stitches Elephants' Bloomers," *Lilliput*, January/February 1953, series 1, box 27, Raymond Toole-Scott Circus Collection, University of California–Santa Barbara Library; "Elephant's Gay Robe," *Washington Post*, April 9, 1905, F6; "Circus Wardrobe Enthralls Keeper," *New York Times*, April 8, 1936, 25; "All Is Calm behind Scenes at the Circus," *Christian Science Monitor*, May 15, 1942, 3.

47. "Small Army of Equestriennes with Barnum and Bailey Circus," *Montgomery (AL) Times*, November 4, 1912, 5 (qtd.); "All Is Calm behind Scenes at the Circus," *Christian Science Monitor*; "How Circus Women Live," *Baltimore Sun*, June 29, 1912, 12; "A Girl Falls from Trapeze," *Philadelphia Telegraph*, April 15, 1880, 9; "Woman Training Lion Is Killed as Children Look On," *Washington Post*, December 21, 1949, 1; "Circus Women: What Life in a Canvas Home Is Like," *Los Angeles Times*, July 25, 1897, 20.

48. "All Is Calm behind Scenes at the Circus," *Christian Science Monitor*; "How Circus Women Live," *Sun*; "A Girl Falls from Trapeze," *Philadelphia Telegraph*; "Woman Training Lion Is Killed as Children Look On," *Washington Post*; "Circus Women," *Los Angeles Times*.

49. Mary Rawls, interview by Juliana Nykolaisyn and Tanya Finchum, June 13, 2011, 15, 18, *The "Big Top" Show Goes On: An Oral History of Occupations inside and outside of the Canvas Circus Tent*, Oklahoma Oral History Research Program, Oklahoma State University.

50. Rawls, 15, 18; Ernestine Clarke, "Performer Comes of Circus Family," *Washington Post*, November 8, 1936, PY3.

51. Adams and Keene, *Women of the American Circus*, 14.

52. Jennifer Hargreaves, *Sport, Culture and Ideology* (Boston: Routledge, 1985), 40–46; Davis, *The Circus Age*, 82; Martha H. Patterson, *Beyond the Gibson Girl: Reimagining the American New Woman, 1895–1915* (Urbana: University of Illinois Press, 2005).

53. "The New Woman on Horseback," *Washington Post*, April 26, 1896, 12; "Change in the Circus, There Is, Really," *Cleveland (OH) World*, April 19, 1896; "Out to See the Circus," *Washington Post*, September 8, 1896, 2; "The 20th Century Girl," *Washington Post*, April 29, 1897, 12; Peta Tait, *Circus Bodies: Cultural Identity in Aerial Performance* (New York: Routledge, 2005), 63–65; Sally Ledger, *The New Woman: Fiction and Feminism at the fin de siècle* (Manchester: Manchester University Press, 1997); Fred Dahlinger Jr., "Barnum & Bailey in the Old World," *Bandwagon*, November 2010, 37–45.

54. Dahlinger, "Barnum & Bailey in the Old World."

55. Cecile Lindsay, "Bodybuilding: A Postmodern Freak Show," in *Freakery: Cultural Spectacles of the Extraordinary Body*, ed. Rosemary Garland Thompson (New York: New York University, 1996), 358; Jan Todd, "Center Ring: Katie Sandwina and the Construction of Celebrity," *Bandwagon* 56, no. 2 (March 2012): 28–35; John D. Fair, "Katie Sandwina: Hercules Can Be a Lady," *Bandwagon* 56, no. 2 (March 2012): 36–37.

56. "Barnum and Bailey's Circus Is One of the Greatest Beauty Shows on the

Road," *Reno Gazette-Journal*, August 30, 1912, 7; "The Barnum & Bailey Show Tuesday," *Houston Post*, October 27, 1912, 45; Todd, "Center Ring."

57. Historians have explored the movement's use of parades, particularly with the influence of Alice Paul beginning in the mid-1910s. See Linda J. Lumsden, "Beauty and the Beasts: Significance of Press Coverage of the 1913 National Suffrage Parade," *Journalism and Mass Communication Quarterly* 77, no. 3 (Autumn 2000): 593.

58. The suffrage movement in California succeeded weeks later. Historian Gayle Gullett has pointed out that the movement itself, which she analyzes in relation to its failed counterpart of 1896, constructed an identity of a woman citizen that emphasized women in both public and private work. The women of the circus, then, fit within the larger scope of the woman citizen for these California activists. See Gayle Gullett, "Constructing the Woman Citizen and Struggling for the Vote in California, 1896–1911," *Pacific Historical Review* 69, no. 4 (2000): 573–93; Rosanne Barker, "Small Town Progressivism: Pearl Chase and Female Activism in Santa Barbara, California, 1911–1918," *Southern California Quarterly* 79, no. 1 (1997): 47–100; Holly J. McCammon and Karen E. Campbell, "Winning the Vote in the West: The Political Successes of the Women's Suffrage Movements, 1866–1919," *Gender and Society* 15, no. 1 (2001): 55–82.

59. "Jennie Puts Down Her Foot for Suffragettes," *Los Angeles Daily Times*, September 18, 1911, 2E. Although the circus goes unnamed, suffrage activist Florence Luscomb described the same events in a personal letter. See Ellen Cantarow with Susan Gushee O'Malley and Sharon Hartman Strom, *Moving the Mountain: Women Working for Social Change* (New York: Feminist Press, 1980), 17.

60. "Circus Women Suffragettes," *Coshocton (OH) Daily Age*, April 8, 1912, 1; "The Large Corps of Women with Sells-Floto May Not Be Suffragettes, but Are Capable," *Aberdeen (WA) Herald*, September 8, 1916, 4; "Suffragettes at Tea with Circus Women: Their Feats Prove Them Worthy of the Vote, Declare Their Hostess," *New York Times*, April 8, 1912, 7; *New York Clipper*, May 1, 1915, 14; "Suffragettes in Circus: They Organize as Man-Eating Hyena Grins, Elephant Trumpets," *New York Tribune*, April 1, 1912, 3; "Enlist Suffragettes for a Circus Holiday: Baby Giraffe Named Miss Suffragette at a Votes for Women Rally," *New York Times*, April 1, 1912, 7.

61. *New York Clipper*, July 6, 1912, 17; Adams and Keene, *Women of the American Circus*, 60; "Ringling Bros. Help Wisconsin: Wives Are Members of Suffrage Society—Allow Campaigning on Circus Grounds," *Women's Journal*, July 13, 1912. Although these banners often elicited cheers, audience members were just as quick to applaud the "suffragette clowns" and their mocking re-creation of meetings under the big top.

62. Josephine De Mott Robinson, *The Circus Lady* (New York: Arno Press, 1980), 276–77.

63. "61 Dead, 179 Hurt in Circus Wreck," *New York Times*, June 23, 1918, 6.

64. "Circus Women Interesting," *Star-Gazette* (Elmira, NY), July 7, 1913, 3.

65. "Circus Research," series 4, box 36, folder 3, George Eells Papers, Arizona State University Libraries, Special Collections, Tempe.

66. Adams and Keene, *Women of the American Circus*, 15.

67. "Circus Women: What Life Is Like in a Canvas Home," *Los Angeles Times*, July 25, 1897, 20.

68. "Life of Circus Women: A Credit to Their Calling and an Honor to Their Sex," *Washington Post*, April 27, 1902, 37.

69. "Circus Women and Children Healthy, Happy, 'Homey' Gypsies," *Ogden (UT) Standard*, August 4, 1914, 4.

70. Sharon L. Smith and Stephen T. Fletcher, *Life in a Three-Ring Circus: Posters and Interviews* (Indianapolis: Indiana Historical Society, 2001), 57.

71. "Performer Comes of Circus Family," *Washington Post*, November 8, 1936, PY3; "Life of Circus Women: A Credit to Their Calling and an Honor to Their Sex," *Washington Post*, April 27. 1902, 37.

72. Hugues Le Roux and Jules Garnier, *Acrobats and Mountebanks*, trans. A. P. Morton (London: Chapman and Hall, 1890), 175.

73. *Weekly State Chronicle* (Raleigh, NC), October 11, 1889, 1.

74. Although most scholarship, led by historian Nancy F. Cott, points to 1910 as "the grounding of modern feminism," Susan Glenn examines female stage performers and asserts that their activism beginning in 1880 marks the beginning of feminism. See Nancy F. Cott, *The Grounding of Modern Feminism* (New Haven, CT: Yale University Press, 1987); Susan Glenn, *Female Spectacle: The Theatrical Roots of Modern Feminism* (Cambridge, MA: Harvard University Press, 2000), 4.

75. "Performer Keeps House between Her Circus Acts," *Christian Science Monitor*, April 21, 1952, 10; Lewis Nichols, "Cake and Circuses," *New York Times*, April 21, 1946, 49 (qtd.).

Chapter 4. Animal Motherhood and (Re)Constructed Circus Families

1. These linked histories of oppression between human and nonhuman animal mothers fall into the purview of ecofeminist studies. Nekeisha Alayna Alexis's work on captive breeding, particularly among farmed animals, "highlight[s] the connections between animal liberation and female liberation." See her essay "Beyond Suffering: Resisting Patriarchy and Reproductive Control," in *Anarchism and Animal Liberation: Essays on Complementary Elements of Total Liberation*, ed. Anthony J. Nocella II, Richard J. White, and Erika Cudworth (Jefferson, NC: McFarland, 2015), 109.

2. Victor Rousseau, "Hoop-La! The Circus," *Harper's Weekly* 52 (January 4, 1908): 23; "Barnum & Bailey: Madison Square Garden 3-19-1908" poster (Strobridge Lithographing, 1908), Tibbals Circus Collection, John and Mable Ringling Museum of Art, Sarasota, FL.

3. "Big Animals' Babes in Circus Nursery," *San Francisco Examiner*, September 11, 1908, 4.

4. Charles Andress, *Barnum & Bailey Route Book, 1903, 1904, 1905, 1906, 1907: Five Years in One* (n.p., 1907), 39, Circus Route Books, Milner Library, Illinois State University, Normal.

5. "Here Come the Elephants," *Decatur (IL) Herald*, April 30, 1922, 16.

6. For a larger discussion of public personas of circus animals, particularly genial elephants, see Susan Nance, *Entertaining Elephants: Animal Agency and the Business of the American Circus* (Baltimore, MD: Johns Hopkins University Press, 2013).

7. Howard Y. Bary, "Strange Customs and Weird Beliefs of the Padaung Giraffe-Neck Women," 1933, series 1, box 1, folder 1, American Circus Collection, 1891–1939, Newberry Library, Chicago.

8. See Thom van Dooren, "Extinction," in *Critical Terms for Animal Studies*, ed. Lori Gruen (Chicago: University of Chicago Press, 2018), 169–81; Marcus Baynes-Rock, *Crocodile Undone: The Domestication of Australia's Fauna* (University Park: Pennsylvania State University Press, 2020).

9. Field researchers and animal studies scholars have provided extensive research and analysis around the complex matriarchal social systems among elephants. See Caitlin O'Connell, *Elephant Don: The Politics of a Pachyderm Posse* (Chicago: University of Chicago Press, 2015).

10. This intersects with Lori Marino's argument that self-awareness creates additional emotional trauma for captive mothers. In her discussion of postcolonial milk studies, Marino cites a mother cow, living as a farm animal, who makes a conscious choice to hide one (but only one) of her infants to try to save it from slaughter. See her chapter "Captivity," in Gruen, *Critical Terms for Animal Studies*, 99–111.

11. Anne Innis Dagg, *Giraffe: Biology, Behaviour and Conservation* (Cambridge: Cambridge University Press, 2014).

12. Scholars have analyzed how mass culture reflects larger society in other ways. Janet Davis demonstrated how circus shows acted as an almost real-time reflection of US imperial efforts. Linda Frost widened her scope to understand how American identity was constructed through mass media and culture. See Janet Davis, *The Circus Age: Culture and Society under the American Big Top* (Chapel Hill: University of North Carolina Press, 2002); Linda Frost, *Never One Nation: Freaks, Savages, and Whiteness in U.S. Popular Culture, 1850–1877* (Minneapolis: University of Minnesota Press, 2005).

13. Scientific motherhood signaled a shift away from maternal knowledge systems and toward a more medicalized view of baby rearing. See Rima D. Apple, *Perfect Motherhood: Science and Childrearing in America* (New Brunswick, NJ: Rutgers University Press, 2007); Jodi Vandenberg-Daves, *Modern Motherhood: An American History* (New Brunswick, NJ: Rutgers University Press, 2014).

14. The history of the midwifery industry, and its decline with the rise of the male-dominated obstetrics practice backed by the American Medical Association,

demonstrates part of this displacement. See Jenny M. Luke, *Delivered by Midwives: African American Midwifery in the Twentieth-Century South* (Oxford: University of Mississippi Press, 2018).

15. Peta Tait, *Circus Bodies: Cultural Identity in Aerial Performance* (London: Routledge, 2005), 64.

16. The theoretical framework for this chapter rests on the postcolonial work of Maneesha Deckha, who provides a legal history of animal studies. Deckha meticulously traces how Western animal policies, despite their violence, are labeled as more humane; see, e.g., her book *Animals as Legal Beings: Contesting Anthropocentric Legal Orders* (Toronto: University of Toronto Press, 2021). This work is also predicated on Nekeisha Alayna Alexis's analysis of captive breeding programs; see her essay "Beyond Suffering."

17. "Dailey Bros. Circus Will Attract Circus Fans with Baby 'Butch,'" *Hobby Bandwagon* 3, no. 2 (March 1948).

18. G. A. Bradshaw has examined PTSD among elephants, likening their experiences to those of human children. Bradshaw demonstrates that just as single traumatic events affect behavior in both young humans and animals, "highly invasive" traumatic events that last years and remove the young from a healthy relationship with family figures can be a predictor of abnormal social behavior among both populations. See her *Elephants on the Edge: What Animals Teach Us about Humanity* (New Haven, CT: Yale University Press, 2009).

19. Caitrin Nicol, "Do Elephants Have Souls?," *New Atlantis* 38 (Winter/Spring 2013): 10–70.

20. "Dailey Bros. Circus Will Attract Circus Fans with Baby 'Butch,'" *Hobby Bandwagon* 3, no. 2 (March 1948).

21. "Raymond and Co.'s Menagerie," *Charleston (SC) Mercury*, January 14, 1846, 3; "Animals, Horses, &c. at Auction," 1837, series 75, box 5, folder 15, Somers Historical Society, CT.

22. *History of Animals and Leading Curiosities of the Greatest Combined Shows on Earth* (New York: New York Popular, 1881), 5, Barnum Museum, Bridgeport, CT.

23. *History of Animals and Leading Curiosities*, 5.

24. *History of Animals and Leading Curiosities*, 5, 23.

25. *History of Animals and Leading Curiosities*, 13.

26. "The Crown of Creation: Circus Parade Fulfills the Biblical Prophecy," *Sells-Floto Magazine*, 1934, series 1, box 3, folder 19, American Circus Collection, Newberry Library, Chicago.

27. Al Priddy, *The Way of the Circus: With Man and Animal* (Chicago: Platform World, 1930), 40, series 1, box 1, folder 1, American Circus Collection, Newberry Library, Chicago.

28. "Reporter Joins Russell Bros. Circus for One Day Finds Friendliness, Fascination behind 'Big Top,'" *Journal Times Bulletin* (Racine, WI), July 7, 1935, 14; "Squeezed by Snake," *Evening Times-Republican* (Marshalltown, IA), June 9, 1906, 5; "Unload Circus Train for Show at Fairgrounds," *Mt. Vernon (IL) Register-News*, April 28, 1949, 1.

29. "Circus Secrets and Stories," *Inter Ocean* (Chicago), June 16, 1901, 44.

30. "Life under the White Tops: Making a Circus Zoo, and How Management Keeps in Touch with Wild Animals," *Republic* (Columbus, IN), March 20, 1922, 4.

31. "Life under the White Tops."

32. Nigel Rothfels, *Savages and Beasts: The Birth of the Modern Zoo* (Baltimore, MD: Johns Hopkins University Press, 2002), 53–55; "Circus Secrets and Stories," *Inter Ocean* (Chicago), June 16, 1901, 44; "Long Island City Menagerie Is Jungle Spot Transplanted," *Times Union* (Brooklyn, NY), November 27, 1927, 13 (qtd.).

33. *Billboard*, September 18, 1915, 57; *Billboard*, February 26, 1916, 24.

34. Caitrin Nicol has described family relations among elephants by tracing typical social relations starting at birth; see her article "Do Elephants Have Souls?"

35. Bradshaw, *Elephants on the Edge*, 147–60.

36. "Circus Secrets and Stories," *Inter Ocean* (Chicago), June 16, 1901, 44.

37. Eric Ames, *Carl Hagenbeck's Empires of Entertainments* (Seattle: University of Washington Press, 2008), 155; Peta Tait, *Wild and Dangerous Performances: Animals, Emotions, Circus* (London: Palgrave Macmillan, 2011), 19.

38. Janet Davis, *The Gospel of Kindness: Animal Welfare and the Making of Modern America* (Oxford: Oxford University Press, 2016); Emily Gaarder, *Women and the Animal Rights Movement* (New Brunswick, NJ: Rutgers University Press, 2011); Priddy, *The Way of the Circus*.

39. "Circus Secrets and Stories," *Inter Ocean* (Chicago), June 16, 1901, 44.

40. Cartoon, *White Tops*, July–August 1964, series 1, box 67, folder 12, Dyer Ichabod Reynolds Circus Collection, Ned R. McWherter Library, University of Memphis, TN.

41. *History of Animals and Leading Curiosities*, 4 (qtd.), 12.

42. "A Circus Auction: The Sipe & Dixon Show Closed Out: Fancy Prices for Ponies," *Star Press* (Muncie, IN), November 22, 1902, 2; "Big Southern Circus: Alabama Man Buys Sells & Downs Circus at Auction," *Daily Ardmoreite* (Ardmore, OK), January 26, 1906, 3.

43. "The Coop & Lent Circus," *Bandwagon* 3, no. 3 (May–June 1959): 3–14; *Billboard*, July 14, 1917, 26.

44. Chang Reynolds, "The Bovalapus Brigade," *Bandwagon* 7, no. 6 (November–December 1963): 4–8.

45. "Notes about Women: Circus Women Organize," *Des Moines (IA) Register*, April 5, 1912, 6.

46. "P.T. Barnum's Greatest Show on Earth, the Great London Circus, and Sanger's Royal British Menagerie 7 Monster Shows," handbill, c. 1882–83, P. T. Barnum Digital Collection, Advertisements, Barnum Museum, Bridgeport, CT.

47. "Ten Beautiful Giraffes—from the 22 Foot Giant Giraffe to the Nursing Baby," poster (Strobridge Lithographing, 1882), Bridgeport History Center, Bridgeport Public Library, CT.

48. "Better Than Ever. Circus Delights Its Two Big Audiences," *Boston Globe*, May 31, 1910, 13.

49. "Murray Pennock," *Bandwagon* 6, no. 2 (March–April 1962): 14–17; "Life of a Lion Tamer: Alfred Court—Cat Act," *PIC Magazine*, June 11, 1940, reprinted in *Backyard* 4, no. 66 (April 30, 1999) (qtd.).

50. *Variety*, June 27, 1908, 12.

51. "Breeding Wild Animals: Ringling Brothers Will Establish a Farm near Chicago," *Algona (IA) Republican*, May 19, 1897, 7; "The Ringlings' Animal Farm: Famous Showmen about to Establish Their Vast Enterprise on Three of the Small Islands on the Florida Keys," *Daily Times* (Davenport, IA), August 19, 1899; "Raising Wild Animals: A Two Thousand Acre Menagerie in South Florida," *Dallas Weekly Post*, June 19, 1897, 1.

52. "Raising Wild Animals," *Dallas Weekly Post*.

53. "Long Island City Menagerie Is Jungle Spot Transplanted," *Times Union* (Brooklyn, NY), November 27, 1927, 13.

54. "Missouri Breeding Lions: Lancaster Now Center for American Wild Animal Trade," *Caucasian* (Shreveport, LA), August 2, 1910, 2; "Noah's Ark in His Backyard: A Missourian Makes a Business Out of Buying Second Hand Circuses," *Kansas City Star*, April 18, 1915, 33.

55. Nance, *Entertaining Elephants*, 169.

56. "Noah's Ark in His Backyard," *Kansas City Star*.

57. "Home of Circus Animals Closed," *White Cloud (KS) Tribune*, January 27, 1921, 8.

58. "To Breed Wild Animals: John Robinson Circus Interests Will Do What German Firm Was Forefront in before the War," *Wilkes-Barre (PA) Record*, May 3, 1919, 17; "Wild Animals Are High: U.S. to Become Breeding Center since Kaiser Destroyed Hagenbeck Collection," *Indianapolis Star*, March 17, 1919, 8; "Circuses Hard Hit for Animals," *Daily News-Tribune* (Greenville, OH), December 3, 1920, 4.

59. "The Circus of Circuses," *Lancaster (PA) Intelligencer*, May 13, 1891, 4.

60. *The Circus Annual: A Route Book of Ringling Brothers World's Greatest Shows, Season of 1897* (Buffalo, NY: Courier, 1897), Circus Route Books, Milner Library, Illinois State University, Normal.

61. "Sello Brothers Circus," *White Tops*, August–September 1964, series 1, box 67, folder 12, Dyer Ichabod Reynolds Circus Collection, Ned R. McWherter Library, University of Memphis, TN.

62. "Zoo Nursery at Circus," *St. Louis Globe-Democrat*, May 3, 1909, 14.

63. Bob Sheffield, "Notes from Zoos," *White Tops*, August–September 1938, box 67, folder 16, item 4, Dyer Ichabod Reynolds Circus Collection, Ned R. McWherter Library, University of Memphis, TN.

64. "Cole Bros: Mother and Baby Animals," c. 1900–1910, Tibbals Circus Collection, John and Mable Ringling Museum of Art, Sarasota, FL.

65. "Circus Babies Enjoy Four Freedoms in Captivity," *Statesville (NC) Daily Record*, October 10, 1949, 2.

66. "Circus Cutie Steps Out," *Mount Carmel (PA) Item*, April 17, 1941, 12.

67. Jane Goodall, *Through a Window: My Thirty Years with the Chimpanzees of Gombe* (Boston: Mariner Books, 1990), 45, 88, 229.

68. "Woman's World," *Daily Standard* (Red Bank, NJ), May 5, 1941, 2.

69. "Foster Mom," *Lowell (MA) Sun*, October 10, 1971, 3.

70. "Circus Nursery Has Appeal," *Medford (OR) Mail Tribune*, May 19, 1948, 16; "Why Clyde Beatty Had to Let His Wife Go in the Lion Cage," *Anniston (AL) Star*, May 8, 1937, 3.

71. "Animal Babies Will Delight Circus Throngs," *Clarksdale (MS) Press*, October 29, 1934, 3.

72. "The Circus of Today: The New Woman Invades the Ring," *Statesman Journal* (Salem, OR), April 30, 1896, 7.

73. Priddy, *The Way of the Circus*.

74. W. C. Thompson, *On the Road with a Circus* (New York: New Amsterdam Book 1905), 137–38.

75. "Paterson's Trained Wild Animal Circus," *Mountain View (MO) Standard*, April 21, 1922, 1.

76. "The Circus of Circuses," *Lancaster (PA) Intelligencer*, May 13, 1891, 4.

77. "One of the Great Thrills in Frank Buck's Amazing Sound-Film Record of his Great Adventure *Bring 'Em Back Alive*," *Nebraska State Journal*, September 11, 1932, 18.

78. "Why Clyde Beatty Had to Let His Wife Go in the Lion Cage," *Anniston (AL) Star*, May 8, 1937, 3.

79. "Caging of Animals That Suffer to Stop," *News-Journal* (Mansfield, OH), August 11, 1928, 13; "No More Cages for Animals That Suffer in Captivity," *Daily Notes* (Canonsburg, PA), July 24, 1928, 2.

80. Quoted in "Dr. J.Y. Henderson Has Problems with New Born Wild Animals in Circus," *Kerrville (TX) Mountain Sun*, March 2, 1947, 4.

Chapter 5. Captive, Coerced, and Frontline Sideshow Workers

1. Journalist Beth Macy conducted extensive interviews with Muse family members and community members about the disappearance of the brothers. A distinct local mythology emerged from their abduction that served as a morality tale about outsiders. See her book *Truevine: Two Brothers, a Kidnapping, and a Mother's Quest; A True Story of the Jim Crow South* (New York: Little, Brown, 2016).

2. "Barnes' Big Circus Will Be in This City Today," *Scranton (PA) Republican*, June 26, 1923, 15.

3. "Circus Manager Overcome When His Quarter-Ton Wife Demands a Ride in Airplane," *Montana Standard*, April 13, 1929, 20; "In New York," *Ironwood (MI) Daily Globe*, April 15, 1933, 12; "A Code for Freaks," *Decatur (IL) Daily Review*, August 28, 1933, 16; "Midway Is Ready," *Houston Post*, November 9, 1922, 11; "Eko and Iko from Zanzibar," *Scranton (PA) Republican*, June 23, 1923, 9; "In New York," *Evening Standard* (Uniontown, PA), April 5, 1930, 4.

4. "The Circus," *Time*, April 18, 1932.

5. When Barnum's show came to Baltimore, the newspaper gave a detailed description of the lot and performances in several sections. The arrival of the sideshow was much anticipated. Its recap, however, is indicative of the social status of sideshow workers, as it fell under the heading "Looked at Freaks and Animals." See "Greatest Show Here," *Baltimore Sun*, May 14, 1903, 12.

6. Scholars have examined the wide spectrum of interest in sideshows, particularly in the nineteenth century. Linda Frost argues that viewing sideshow performers as the Other helped cement a sense of inclusion and American identity for the viewer, despite issues of class. See her *Never One Nation: Freaks, Savages, and Whiteness in U.S. Popular Culture, 1850–1877* (Minneapolis: University of Minnesota Press, 2005). See also Benjamin Reiss, *The Showman and the Slave: Race, Death, and Memory in Barnum's America* (Cambridge, MA: Harvard University Press, 2001).

7. *Catalogue or Guide Book of Barnum's American Museum, New York* (New York: n.p., 1863), 113–14.

8. Several historians have examined P.T. Barnum's extensive and successful use of humbug, and even Barnum himself reflected on the marketing ploy several times. The business model that Barnum established was quickly modeled by other big top shows. See James W. Cook, *The Arts of Deception: Playing with Fraud in the Age of Barnum* (Cambridge, MA: Harvard University Press, 2001); Neil Harris, *Humbug: The Art of P. T. Barnum* (Chicago: University of Chicago Press, 1981); Reiss, *The Showman and the Slave*.

9. Louis S. Warren, *Buffalo Bill's America: William Cody and the Wild West Show* (New York: Alfred A. Knopf, 2005), xiv, 404; Jacob Dorman, *The Princess and the Prophet: The Secret History of Magic, Race, and Black Muslims in America* (New York: Beacon Press, 2020).

10. "Mother Rescues Boys from Circus Life," *Pittsburgh Courier*, November 5, 1927, 3; Dorothy Kilgallen, "Under the Big Top," *Wilkes-Barre (PA) Record*, April 18, 1942, 16.

11. "Midway Is Planned for Circus Cotillion," *Brooklyn Daily Eagle*, July 23, 1914, 10.

12. "Men in Barking Business Are Paid Large Salaries," *Elyria (OH) Reporter*, December 18, 1905, 4.

13. C. G. Sturtevant, "Sideshow People," *White Tops*, June–July 1936, series 1, box 23, Raymond Toole-Scott Circus Collection, 1886–1970, University of California–Santa Barbara Library; "Parade Heralds Circus Arrival," *Selma (AL) Times-Journal*, November 9, 1920, 1.

14. Clifford E. Watkins, *Showman: The Life and Music of Perry George Lowery* (Oxford: University of Mississippi Press, 2003); Sakina M. Hughes, "Walking the Tightrope between Racial Stereotypes and Respectability: Images of African American and Native American Artists in the Golden Age of the Circus," *Early Popular Visual Culture* 15, no. 3 (2017): 315–33. Hughes has argued that Black performers like Lowery performed racial uplift, particularly during the nadir (1890–1920).

15. Gregory J. Renoff, *The Big Tent: The Traveling Circus in Georgia, 1820–1930* (Athens: University of Georgia Press, 2008), 114.

16. Renoff, 21, 110; Stuart Thayer, *Traveling Showmen: The American Circus before the Civil War* (Detroit, MI: Astley and Ricketts, 1997), 74–75.

17. Janet Davis, *The Circus Age: Culture and Society under the American Big Top* (Chapel Hill: University of North Carolina Press, 2002), 182.

18. "The Freaks Will Receive," photograph album, Barnum & Bailey foreign tour, 1897–1902, McCaddon Collection of the Barnum and Bailey Circus, Princeton University Library, NJ.

19. *Catalogue or Guide Book of Barnum's American Museum, New York*, 106–15.

20. Davis, *The Circus Age*, 179.

21. Roslyn Poignant, *Professional Savages: Captive Lives and Western Spectacle* (New Haven, CT: Yale University Press, 2004), 59–69; Sadiah Qureshi, *Peoples on Parade: Exhibitions, Empire, and Anthropology in Nineteenth-Century Britain* (Chicago: University of Chicago Press, 2011), 107.

22. For a discussion of American culture and performance on global stages, see Davis, *The Circus Age*.

23. The edited collection *Human Zoos: Science and Spectacle in the Age of Colonial Empires*, ed. Pascal Blancard et al., trans. Teresa Bridgeman (Liverpool: Liverpool University Press, 2008), provides an array of perspectives and narratives on human zoos. See, e.g., Hilke Thode-Arora's essay "Hagenbeck's European Tours: The Development of the Human Zoo," 165–73.

24. Rachel Adams, *Sideshow U.S.A.: Freaks and the American Cultural Imagination* (Chicago: University of Chicago Press, 2001).

25. "An American Circus Manager in Europe after 'Talent,'" *Chicago Daily Tribune*, August 15, 1881, 2.

26. Nigel Rothfels, *Savages and Beasts: The Birth of the Modern Zoo* (Baltimore, MD: Johns Hopkins University Press, 2008), 81–88, 145, 194.

27. Rothfels, 126–27.

28. The Zulu performers have come under the purview of several scholars. See, e.g., Robert Trent Vinson and Robert Edgar, "Zulus Abroad: Cultural Representations and Educational Experiences of Zulus in America, 1880–1945," *Journal of Southern African Studies* 33, no. 1 (2007): 43–62; Qureshi, *Peoples on Parade*.

29. "Zulu Bites Boy," *Baltimore Sun*, August 10, 1892, 2.

30. "He Bit Like a Wild Beast," *Philadelphia Inquirer*, August 10, 1892, 1.

31. "He Bit Like a Wild Beast"; "Zulu Bites Boy," *Baltimore Sun*; "He Bit His Tormentors: John Lucas, Colored, an Alleged Zulu, Held on Charge of Mayhem," *Washington Post*, August 10, 1982, 2; "A Savage Zulu," *Reno Gazette-Journal*, August 9, 1892, 1.

32. Vinson and Edgar, "Zulus Abroad," 48; Zine Magubane, "Ethnographic Showcases as Sites of Knowledge Production and Indigenous Resistance," in *Contesting Knowledge: Museums and Indigenous Perspectives*, ed. Susan Sleeper-Smith (Lincoln: University of Nebraska Press, 2009), 45–47.

33. "Saucer-Lip Ubangi Elopes with Circus Wild Man from Borneo," *Kane*

(PA) Republican, April 30, 1935, 1; Harriet A. Washington, *Medical Apartheid: The Dark History of Experimentation on Black Americans from Colonial Times to the Present* (New York: Harlem Moon, 2006), 90.

34. James W. Shettel, "The Death of Barnum's Cannibal," *Circus Scrap Book*, October 1929, 43.

35. Shettel; "The Prince of Showmen," *Wyandotte (KS) Gazette*, April 18, 1872, 1.

36. The Zulu performers and Fiji cannibals are part of a larger cultural hunger for exotic depictions of Brown and Black people. For an extended discussion of Western stereotyping and exploitative practices, as well as cultural imperialism (a term that has been especially popular in postcolonial studies), see Q. N. Parsons, "Franz or Klikko, the Wild Dancing Bushman: A Case Study in Khoisan Stereotyping," *Botswana Notes and Records* 20 (1989): 71–76; Blanchard et al., *Human Zoos*; Nadja Durbach, *Spectacle of Deformity: Freak Shows and Modern British Culture* (Berkeley: University of California Press, 2009).

37. "The Circus Freak Seen Off Guard as a Human Being," *Daily Arkansas Gazette*, April 13, 1913, 46; Katherine H. Adams and Michael L. Keene, *Women of the American Circus, 1880–1940* (Jefferson, NC: McFarland, 2012), 143.

38. Scholars like Eric D. Lehman have pointed to Tom Thumb as "America's first international celebrity." His popularity and tours with P. T. Barnum around the world attest to this. See Eric Lehman, *Becoming Tom Thumb: Charles Stratton, P. T. Barnum, and the Dawn of American Celebrity* (Bridgeport, CT: Wesleyan University Press, 2013); Lynne Vallone, *Big and Small: A Cultural History of Extraordinary Bodies* (New Haven, CT: Yale University Press, 2017).

39. "The Great Lilliputian Wedding," *Scientific American*, February 21, 1863, reprinted in *Circus Scrap Book*, October 1929, 5.

40. "The Revolt of the Freaks," *Cheshire Observer*, January 21, 1899, 2.

41. "The Uprising of the Freaks," photograph album, Barnum & Bailey foreign tour, 1897–1902, McCaddon Collection of the Barnum and Bailey Circus, Princeton University Library, NJ.

42. "Not Freaks but Prodigies," *Albuquerque Citizen*, February 8, 1907, 2; "Freaks Union," *Pensacola News Journal*, February 13, 1907, 3; "Circus Freaks Are Taking to Warpath," *Post-Crescent* (Appleton, WI), February 8, 1921, 2; "Freaks Fight for the Right to Let You See Them at Fairs," *Sacramento Star*, February 5, 1921, 7.

43. "Annual Roster of the Benevolent Protective Order of the Tigers, Season 1901–2, Touring Continent with Barnum & Bailey," Scrapbook 12: Foreign Tour, 1897–1902, box 28, McCaddon Collection of the Barnum and Bailey Circus, Princeton University Library, NJ.

44. "Girl with Disappearing Head Happy in Sideshow, Refuses to Return Home," *Dunkirk (NY) Evening Observer*, August 5, 1935, 1.

45. G. A. Severence, "Kobelkoff, the Truncate Artist," *Scientific American Supplement*, March 27, 1886, reprinted in *Circus Scrap Book*, January 1931, 23.

46. "Searching World for Human Freaks, Found and Telling of 'Em," *Salisbury*

(NC) Evening Post, August 27, 1921, 6; "Freaks Always Popular," *Sun* (New York), January 3, 1897, 17.

47. Charles Eisenmann and Frank Wendt made careers out of photographing sideshow workers and other circus workers. Their studio portraits included thousands of sideshow performers, with their unique appearance or skills on display. As part of their studio session, sideshow workers typically received copies of their photographs to sell as cards on the circus lot. For a full, digitized archive of Eisenmann and Wendt's work, see the Ronald G. Becker Collection of Charles Eisenmann Photographs, Special Collections Research Center, Syracuse University Libraries, NY.

48. "Bertie: Tattooed by Red Gibbons," postcard, 1928, series 2, box 5, folder 46, American Circus Collection, 1891–1939, Newberry Library, Chicago.

49. While the cards were prized souvenirs for circusgoers who bought them on the lot, they continue to be sought after by circus fans. Jeftichew's cards have sold in more recent history at auction for hundreds of dollars.

50. "Photograph: Fedor Jeftichew (Jo-Jo the Dog Faced Boy)," c. 1880–1904, P. T. Barnum Research Collection, Bridgeport History Center, Bridgeport Public Library, CT.

51. "Fake Freaks, Objectionable Shows Face Ban at Coney," *Brooklyn Daily Eagle*, December 11, 1929, 10; "Fake Freaks," *Buffalo (NY) Commercial*, January 19, 1894, 5.

52. "There's a War in the Sideshow Business," *Times Herald* (Olean, NY), September 25, 1929, 5.

53. "Billy Wells: The Hard-Headed Man," *Circus Scrap Book*, July 1930, 5; "Champion Hard-Headed Man: How a Fall of Fifteen Feet Put Eight-Year-Old Boy in Way of Making Great Money," *Washington Post*, September 11, 1910, 32.

54. "Freaks' Boarding House," *Chicago Tribune*, November 27, 1887, 25.

55. Frank Metzger to Dyer Reynolds, December 16, 1950, series 1, box 1, folder 5, Reynolds Collection, Special Collections, University of Memphis, TN.

56. Rothfels, *Savages and Beasts*, 135.

57. Ronald Butler began advertising the performers, who probably hailed from the Chad area, as Ubangis. His illustrations and descriptions of clowns, Ubangis, Gargantua, and giraffe-necked women proliferate in the circus world. See Tom Parkinson, "Ronald Butler," *Bandwagon* 5, no. 5 (1961): 3–5; Robert Bogdan, *Freak Show: Presenting Human Oddities for Amusement and Profit* (Chicago: University of Chicago Press, 1988), 192–95; Joe Nickell, *Secrets of the Sideshows* (Lexington: University of Kentucky Press, 2005), 189; Bernth Lindfors, *Early African Entertainments Abroad: From the Hottentot Venus to Africa's First Olympians* (Madison: University of Wisconsin Press, 2014), 159.

58. Marcy W. Murray, "Noble Savages and African Natives: Representations of Race in Outdoor Entertainment 1860–1930," *Bandwagon* 58, no. 2 (2014): 18–26; Adams and Keene, *Women of the American Circus, 1880–1940*, 143; Davis, *The Circus Age*, 134.

59. Clifton Crais and Pamela Scully, *Sara Baartman and the Hottentot Venus: A Ghost Story and a Biography* (Princeton, NJ: Princeton University Press, 2009).

60. "Duck-Billed Belles with Circus," *Los Angeles Times*, March 27, 1932, A3; "Fashion Note from Africa Part of Circus," *Chicago Daily Tribune*, July 30, 1930, 14.

61. Frost, *Never One Nation*.

62. "Ubangis in Circus Pleased with City," *New York Times*, April 14, 1930, 44.

63. "What Circus People Eat," *Axtell (KS) Standard*, August 4, 1932, 7; "Ubangis in Circus Pleased with City," *New York Times*, April 14, 1930, 44.

64. Henry Ringling North and Alden Hatch, *The Circus Kings: Our Ringling Family Circus* (Garden City, NY: Doubleday, 1960), 353; "Ubangi Savages from Africa's Darkest Depths," *Reading (PA) Times*, June 4, 1932, 9.

65. "Ringling, Circus King, Sued by Savage Troupers," *Chicago Defender*, May 21, 1932, 5.

66. The educational aspect of nineteenth-century entertainment also extended into the larger tourism industry. People traveled to see things such as psychiatric hospitals and prisons. For a deeper discussion of nineteenth-century tourism, see John F. Sears, *Sacred Places: American Tourist Attractions in the Nineteenth Century* (Amherst: University of Massachusetts Press, 1989).

67. "Ubangi Belle Ran Away with the Wild Man," *Tipton (IN) Daily Tribune*, April 30, 1935, 4.

68. Frank J. Mayer, *Ringling Bros and Barnum & Bailey Combined Circus Route Book for the Season of 1936* (n.p., 1936), 8, Circus Route Books, Milner Library, Illinois State University, Normal.

69. Nickell, *Secrets of the Sideshows*.

70. Gregory Gibson, *Hubert's Freaks: The Rare-Book Dealer, the Times Square Talker, and the Lost Photos of Diane Arbus* (Boston: Mariner Books, 2008).

71. "Chang and Eng: The Siamese Twins," *Philadelphia Medical Times*, 1874, reprinted in *Circus Scrap Book*, July 1930, 41; "Chinese Clerk Human Freak: Autopsy Performed on Body Shows His Vital Organs All Misplaced," *Green Bay (WI) Press-Gazette*, February 25, 1909, 7.

72. "Death Takes Away Famous Missing Link," *Chicago Defender*, May 15, 1926, A1.

73. Kenn Harper, *Give Me My Father's Body: The Life of Minik, the New York Eskimo* (New York: Pocket Square Books, 1986).

74. "Freaks Have Hard Time: 'Sophisticated' Public Snubs Sideshow," *Lincoln (NE) Star*, March 24, 1937, 8.

75. "Exit, the Freaks," *New Castle (PA) Herald*, December 6, 1920, 4; "Highbrows Plan to Banish Sideshows," *Daily Arkansas Gazette*, December 1, 1920, 9.

76. Ed P. Wiley, "Sideshow Freaks and Barkers," *Circus Scrap Book*, April 1931, 25.

Part III. The Circus World from the Outside

1. Gregory J. Renoff, *The Big Tent: The Traveling Circus in Georgia, 1820–1930* (Athens: University of Georgia Press, 2008).

2. Eric Arnesen, *Waterfront Workers of New Orleans: Race, Class, and Politics, 1863–1923* (Urbana: University of Illinois Press, 1994); Dominic A. Pacyga, *Slaughterhouse: Chicago's Union Stock Yard and the World It Made* (Chicago: University of Chicago Press, 2015).

Chapter 6. The Circus as Big Business

1. Fred Dahlinger Jr. and Stuart Thayer, *Badger State Showmen: A History of Wisconsin's Circus Heritage* (Baraboo, WI: Circus World Museum, 1998), 73.

2. Mel Miller, *Ringling Museum of the Circus: The Collection and Its Relation to the History of the Circus* (Sarasota, FL: John and Mable Ringling Museum of Art, 1963), series 1, box 1, folder 3, Kenneth K. Barr Sr. Circus Collection, University of California–Santa Barbara Library; J. G. Nash, "Ringling Show in Sarasota One of the Greatest on Earth," *Chicago Tribune*, October 11, 1987; David Lewis Hammarstrom, *Big Top Boss: John Ringling North and the Circus* (Bloomington: University of Illinois Press, 1992), 25, 29; Tom Ogden, *Two Hundred Years of the American Circus: From Aba-Daba to the Zoppe-Zavatta Troupe* (New York: Facts on File, 1993), 10; "John Ringling—Millionaire," *Fortune Magazine*, reprinted in *Capital Times*, April 16, 1930, 20.

3. "Refuse to Renew Lease," *Oshkosh (WI) Daily Northwestern*, September 4, 1929, 8; Packey Mac Farlane, "Brief Bits of Sports Gossip," *Manitowoc (WI) Herald-Times*, September 12, 1929, 7; A. J. Liebling, *The Sweet Science* (New York: North Point Press, 2004), 165; Sharon L. Smith and Stephen T. Fletcher, *Life in a Three-Ring Circus: Posters and Interviews* (Indianapolis: Indiana Historical Society, 2001), 9.

4. "Ringling to Send Old Show to Big Cities; Others Will Make One-Night-City Stops," *Brooklyn Daily Eagle*, September 22, 1929, 6; Hammarstrom, *Big Top Boss*, 28.

5. "John Ringling—Millionaire," *Fortune Magazine*, reprinted in *Capital Times*, April 16, 1930, 20 (qtd.); "John Ringling Rules as Head Ringmaster of Circus World," *Ogden (UT) Standard Examiner*, September 10, 1929, 5; "Greve's Money Helped Finance Ringling Merger," *Brooklyn Daily Eagle*, September 13, 1929, 1; "Ringling Owns Every Large Circus in the U.S.," *Mount Carmel (PA) Item*, September 10, 1929, 1; "Five Circuses Are Bought by Ringling," *Joplin (MO) Globe*, September 10, 1929, 2; Ogden, *Two Hundred Years of the American Circus*, 8.

6. Henry Ringling North and Alden Hatch, *The Circus Kings: Our Ringling Family Story* (Garden City: Doubleday, 1960), 219; Ogden, *Two Hundred Years of the American Circus*, 8; Smith and Fletcher, *Life in a Three-Ring Circus*, 9.

7. "Mister John Missing," *Ironwood (MI) Daily Globe*, April 15, 1933, 12.

8. Charles H. Day, "An Early Tendency to Monopolize," *Washington Post*, January 27, 1907, 10.

9. Janet Davis, *The Circus Age: Culture and Society under the American Big Top* (Chapel Hill: University of North Carolina Press, 2003), 7.

10. "The Circus King," *Mason City (IA) Globe Gazette*, September 24, 1929, 3; "Circus Merger," *Vidette-Messenger* (Valparaiso, IN), September 12, 1929, 4.

11. Benjamin Reiss, *The Showman and the Slave: Race, Death, and Memory in Barnum's America* (Cambridge, MA: Harvard University Press, 2001). Reiss's book contextualizes Heth's experience and the spectacle created by Barnum against race relations in the North in the early nineteenth century.

12. "A Living Elephant," *Lexington (KY) Reporter*, December 17, 1808, Somers Historical Society Collections, NY; P. T. Barnum, *The Life of P. T. Barnum* (London: Samson Low, 1855), 153, 304–6.

13. Barnum, *The Life of P. T. Barnum*, 112–15; Michael Daly, *Topsy: The Startling Story of the Crooked Tail Elephant, P. T. Barnum, and the American Wizard, Thomas Edison* (New York: Atlantic Monthly Press, 2013).

14. "Elephant Hotel," National Historic Landmark Nomination, April 5, 2005, US Department of the Interior, National Park Service.

15. "Circus Advertisement, 1840," 73.16.334, Dr. Hugh Grant Rowell Collection, Somers Historical Society, NY; "On the Bouwerie," *Literary Digest* 52 (April 15, 1916): 1103.

16. "Beasts and Ballyhoo, The Menagerie Men of Somers," Circus Historical Society Annual Meeting, Nyack, NY, July 15, 2004, Somers Historical Society, http://www.somershistoricalsoc.org/menageries2.html.

17. "Articles of Association of the Zoological Institute," 1835, MSS box 13, item 5, Westchester County Historical Society, Westchester County Archives, Elmwood, NY; "Elephant Hotel," National Historic Landmark Nomination; Marilyn Weigold, "The Beast That Put Somers on the Map," *New York Times*, May 15, 1977; Jo Pitkin, *Cradle of the American Circus: Poems from Somers, New York* (Charleston, SC: History Press, 2012); Stuart Thayer, "The Flatfoot Party and the Zoological Institute," *Bandwagon* 27, no. 3 (May–June 1983): 23–24; Neil Harris, *Humbug: The Art of P. T. Barnum* (Chicago: University of Chicago Press, 1981).

18. Philip A. Loring, "The Most Resilient Show on Earth: The Circus as a Model for Viewing Identity, Change and Chaos," *Ecology and Society* 12, no. 1 (2007): article 9; Pitkin, *Cradle of the American Circus*.

19. Charles H. Day, *Ink from a Circus Press Agent: An Anthology of Circus History from the Pen of Charles H. Day*, ed. William L. Slout (San Bernadino, CA: Borgo Press, 1995), 11, 13, 87; Stuart Thayer, "The Flatfoot Party and the Zoological Institute," *Bandwagon* 27, no. 3 (May–June 1983): 23; Pitkin, *Cradle of the American Circus*; Daly, *Topsy*; Richard Flint, "American Showman and European Dealers: Commerce in Wild Animals in Nineteenth-Century America," in

New Worlds, New Animals: From Menagerie to Zoological Park in the Nineteenth Century, ed. R. J. Hoage and William A. Deiss (Baltimore, MD: Johns Hopkins University Press, 1996), 98.

20. Harris, *Humbug*.

21. Susan Nance, *Entertaining Elephants: Animal Agency and the Business of the American Circus* (Baltimore, MD: Johns Hopkins University Press, 2013), 50.

22. *Omaha (NE) Daily Bee*, March 22, 1896, 12.

23. "Circus Trust Formed," *Pittsburgh Post-Gazette*, April 7, 1899, 2; "Looks Like a Circus Trust: Barnum's, Forepaugh's, and Buffalo Bill's Shows Agree on Non-Conflicting Schedules," *St. Louis Post-Dispatch*, July 13, 1902, 12.

24. *Coshocton (OH) Daily Age*, April 19, 1905, 11.

25. "Circus Trust: Combine to Do Away with Time-Honored Parade," *Mattoon (IL) Daily Journal*, February 5, 1904, 3; *Essex County Herald* (Guildhall, VT), October 24, 1902, 4; "Parade Abolished by the Circus Trust," *Evening Journal* (Wilmington, DE), January 25, 1904, 1; "Chit-Chat," *Great Bend (KS) Weekly Tribune*, September 19, 1902, 5.

26. "What? Cut Out Circus Parades," *News-Journal* (Mansfield, OH), January 27, 1904, 4.

27. "$5,000,000 Circus Merger," *Chillicothe (MO) Morning Constitution*, November 7, 1906, 5; "That Circus Merger," *Scranton (PA) Republican*, December 26, 1908, 1; "Rival to Circus Trust," *Mower County Transcript* (Lansing, MI), December 27, 1905, 4; "'Bet-a-Million Gates' Will Fight Circus Trust," *St. Louis Post-Dispatch*, December 9, 1908, 9.

28. "Brethren of the West—This Statement Is Addressed to You!," box 23, folder 28, McCaddon Collection of the Barnum and Bailey Circus, Princeton University Library, NJ; "Great Wallace Shows," *Sedalia (MO) Weekly Democrat*, July 20, 1899, 11; "Wait for the Great Wallace Shows," *Scranton (PA) Tribune*, May 24, 1900, 6; "Circus Doomed?," *Coshocton (OH) Daily Age*, April 19, 1905, 11; "Opposes the Circus Trust," *Lansing (MI) State Journal*, August 18, 1911, 6; "Defies Circus Trust and Holds onto Old Customs," *Indianapolis Star*, August 3, 1907, 16; "Circus Trust Stops Fights," *Shippensburg (PA) Chronicle*, December 14, 1905, 2 (qtd.).

29. "The Circus Season Is Over," *New York Times*, October 18, 1907, 11.

30. "With the White Tops: News of the Tent Shows," *Show World*, July 6, 1907, 6.

31. "Most Bitter of Circus Wars Is Ended at Last," *Baltimore Sun*, November 3, 1907, 16; "Barnum & Bailey Show Sold to Ringling," *Brooklyn Daily Eagle*, October 23, 1907, 5.

32. "Ringling Kids Backyard Shows Grow into Mammoth Octopus," *Vicksburg (MS) Evening Post*, June 12, 1914, 3.

33. Charles Kitts to George Reynolds, October 18, 1948, MSS 131, box 28, folder 1, Union Strike Papers, Robert L. Parkinson Library and Research Center, Baraboo, WI; Peter Power, "Labor," *Spokane (WA) Press*, May 1, 1909; "The End of a Circus War," *Washington Post*, November 10, 1907, 85; "Ringling Kids

Backyard Shows Grow into Mammoth Octopus," *Vicksburg (MS) Evening Post*, June 12, 1914, 3.

34. Miller, *Ringling Museum of the Circus*.

35. Ogden, *Two Hundred Years of the American Circus*, 7.

36. Smith and Fletcher, *Life in a Three-Ring Circus*, 5.

37. "Injunction Served on a Show Manager," *Democrat and Chronicle* (Rochester, NY), August 25, 1900, 9.

38. Smith and Fletcher, *Life in a Three-Ring Circus*, 5; Ogden, *Two Hundred Years of the American Circus*, 10.

39. Smith and Fletcher, *Life in a Three-Ring Circus*, 5; Ogden, *Two Hundred Years of the American Circus*, 6.

40. "Circus Headquarters at Peru Is Fascinating with Preparations Under Way to End Winter Hibernation within a Few Short Weeks," *Indianapolis Star*, February 26, 1922, 8; "Three Big Circuses at Peru Winter Quarters," *Indianapolis News*, November 8, 1928, 35; Smith and Fletcher, *Life in a Three-Ring Circus*, 5.

41. Smith and Fletcher, *Life in a Three-Ring Circus*, 9.

42. "Largest Circus Constantly Adding Modern Innovations," *Ringling Brothers Barnum & Bailey Circus Magazine and Daily Review*, 1935, 30, Circus and Buffalo Bill Collection, Schwartz Library, Long Island University, Brookville, NY; *Al G. Barnes Ring Clarion* 3, no. 5 (September–October 1939), box 2, folder 5, K. Barr Circus Collection, University of California–Santa Barbara Library; "Five Ring Circus Finally Realized," *Bremen (IN) Enquirer*, July 16, 1925, 6.

43. "Circus Parade Thing of Past," *Journal Times* (Racine, WI), July 25, 1925, 1.

44. *United States v. Kelley* et al., 105 F.2d 912 (2d Cir. 1939); John M. Kelley, "Taxable Value of Circus Goodwill," ed. Fred Pfening, *Bandwagon* 12, no. 1 (1969): 3–11, 14; "Modern Circus Mourns Golden Age of Barnum," *Tribune* (Seymour, IN), August 31, 1936, 5; Ogden, *Two Hundred Years of the American Circus*, 223.

45. *Al G. Barnes Ring Clarion* 3, no. 5 (September–October 1939).

46. "Clowns Gathered from All Parts of the World with Big Circus," *Daily Herald* (Provo, UT), June 18, 1937, 6.

47. *Al G. Barnes Ring Clarion* 3, no. 5 (September–October 1939).

48. "101 Ranch Show Charges Circus Trust Operates," *Manitowoc (WI) Herald-Times*, April 6, 1931, 12; "Circus Monopoly Is Charged by Millers," *Oshkosh (WI) Daily Northwestern*, April 7, 1931, 18; Chang Reynolds, "101 Ranch Wild West Show, 1907–1916," *Bandwagon* 13, no. 1 (January–February 1969): 5; "Suit against Circus Owners Filed in Court: Zack T. Miller of 101 Ranch, Charges Big Circus Monopoly," *Morning Herald* (Hagerstown, MD), April 7, 1931, 1.

49. "Took Boldness, Skill to Keep Early Ringling Circus Alive," *Capital Times* (Madison, WI), July 18, 1956, 11.

50. *Al G. Barnes Ring Clarion* 3, no. 5 (September–October 1939).

51. *Al G. Barnes Ring Clarion*.

52. *Al G. Barnes Ring Clarion*.

53. "The Circus: Across the Continent 25 of Them Are Rolling This Summer,

Doing a 'Straw House' Business," *Life*, July 28, 1941, 47, box 20, folder 5, Heiser-Alban Collection of Circus Historical Materials, Houston Metropolitan Research Center, TX.

54. Frank Metzger to Dyer Reynolds, December 16, 1959, series 1, box 1, folder 5, Dyer Ichabod Reynolds Circus Collection, Ned R. McWherter Library, University of Memphis, TN.

55. "Ringling Barnum Unit Opens Havana Stand," *Billboard*, December 16, 1950, 58.

56. George Teeger, "John Ringling North: The Lowdown on the Big Top," *Confidential*, August 4, 1953, Billy Rose Theatre Division Scrapbooks, New York Public Library for the Performing Arts.

57. North and Hatch, *The Circus Kings*, 281–84; "Ringling Circus Delayed by Striking Teamsters," *Coshocton (OH) Tribune*, June 15, 1938, 10; "Roustabouts End Era, Pull Down Last Big Top," *Alton (IL) Evening Telegraph*, July 15, 1956, 15; "Modern and Mechanized Are New Adjectives to Describe the Circus," *Iowa City Press Citizen*, April 6, 1939, 6; "Circus Died Here," *Daily Courier* (Connellsville, PA), December 24, 1956, 18; "Lights of New York," *Decatur (IL) Daily Review*, May 26, 1956, 6; Fred D. Pfening Jr., "The 1957 Circus Season," *White Tops* 1, no. 6 (December 1957), 18, series 1, box 23, Raymond Toole-Scott Circus Collection, University of California–Santa Barbara Library; "Modernization—the Ringling Way," *Ringling Brothers Barnum & Bailey Daily Review Magazine*, 1949, series 1, box 4, folder 9, K. Barr Circus Collection, University of California–Santa Barbara Library.

58. "Horsepower under the Big Top," *Ringling Brothers Barnum & Bailey Review*, 1946, series 1, box 4, folder 8, K. Barr Circus Collection, University of California–Santa Barbara Library; Ogden, *Two Hundred Years of the American Circus*, 7; Nance, *Entertaining Elephants*, 106.

59. See Bethany Moreton, *To Serve God and Wal-Mart: The Making of Christian Free Enterprise* (Cambridge, MA: Harvard University Press, 2009). Like the circus, Wal-Mart succeeded by promoting cultural values within an economic framework. And despite the global, elitist nature of the company, its success rests on its relevance to its poorer, working-class consumer base.

60. Fletcher Smith, "How to Eliminate the Circus Pass Evil," *Billboard*, January 12, 1929; *Scranton (PA) Republican*, July 9, 1900, 3.

Chapter 7. The Making of the Circus Celebrity

1. "Short Shavings," *Salt Lake Tribune*, February 1, 1931, 65.

2. "Women Who Never Grow Old," *Santa Ana (CA) Register*, February 8, 1931, 8.

3. "Lillian Leitzel Hurt as Trapeze Breaks," *Brooklyn Daily Eagle*, February 15, 1931, 1; "Lillian Leitzel Is Hurt When Trapeze Breaks," *Bristol (VA) Herald Courier*, February 15, 1931, 16.

4. "Garden Fans to Witness Tribute to Lillian Leitzel," *Standard Union* (Brooklyn, NY), February 16, 1931, 1.

5. "The Glint of Spangles," *Kokomo (IN) Tribune*, February 18, 1931, 4 (qtd.); *Ottawa Journal*, February 21, 1931, 19.

6. "Tragic Death of Lillian Leitzel Spurs Relatives to Train Successor," *Bee* (Danville, VA), February 24, 1931, 5.

7. "Mabel Stark Is Clawed by Tiger," *Covina (CA) Argus*, February 12, 1931, 1.

8. "Mabel Stark in Tiger Cage Again, Beating Attack," *Daily News* (Los Angeles), March 5, 1931, 16; "Woman Tiger Trainer Has Many Scars on Her Body," *Garrett (IN) Clipper*, March 18, 1929, 8.

9. "His Leg Fast in Big Lion's Mouth: Audience at Lambertville Circus Got Excited When Savage Animal Attacked Its Trainer," *Philadelphia Inquirer*, May 1, 1903, 3.

10. This chapter intervenes in work examining thrilling entertainments, particularly in the early twentieth century. Most notably, Jacob Smith has examined the history of stunt performance, which shares several parallels to circus work through its strong class association and workers who move between performance stages. See his *The Thrill Makers: Celebrity, Masculinity, and Stunt Performance* (Berkeley: University of California Press, 2012). Other studies have examined the role of women onstage doing dangerous work, especially in vaudeville. See, e.g., M. Alison Kibler, *Rank Ladies: Gender and Cultural Hierarchy in American Vaudeville* (Chapel Hill: University of North Carolina Press, 1999).

11. *Al G. Barnes Wild Animal Circus Magazine and Daily Review*, 1936, 31, box 1, folder 4, Midwest Circus Collection, Newberry Library, Chicago; *Al G. Barnes Magazine and Daily Review*, 1936, box 3, folder 13, K. Barr Circus Collection, University of California–Santa Barbara Library.

12. Lux advertisement, *Al G. Barnes Wild Animal Circus Magazine and Daily Review*, 1936, 31, Midwest Circus Collection, Box 1, Folder 4, Newberry Library, Chicago.

13. Lux advertisement, *Ringling Bros. Barnum & Bailey Magazine and Daily Review*, 1930, box 3, folder 1, K. Barr Circus Collection, University of California–Santa Barbara Library.

14. *Al G. Barnes Wild Animal Circus Magazine and Daily Review*, 1936, box 1, folder 4, Midwest Circus Collection, Newberry Library, Chicago.

15. "Don't Annoy the Animals!," *Ringling Bros Barnum & Bailey Magazine and Daily Review*, 1930, series 1, box 3, folder 1, K. Barr Circus Collection, University of California–Santa Barbara Library.

16. *Ringling Bros. Barnum & Bailey Magazine and Daily Review*, 1936, box 3, folder 4, K. Barr Circus Collection, University of California–Santa Barbara Library.

17. "The Circus Depends on Curity," advertisement, *Ringling Bros. Barnum & Bailey Magazine and Daily Review*, 1949, box 4, folder 9, K. Barr Circus Collection, University of California–Santa Barbara Library.

18. "Three Things You Need for Health and Comfort," *Ringling Bros Barnum & Bailey Magazine and Daily Review*, 1930, series 1, box 3, folder 1, K. Barr Circus Collection, University of California–Santa Barbara Library.

19. Capewell Horse Nail Company, advertisement, *Ringling Bros. Barnum & Bailey Magazine and Daily Review*, 1930, box 3, folder 1, K. Barr Circus Collection, University of California–Santa Barbara Library.

20. Flit advertisement, *Ringling Bros. Barnum & Bailey Magazine and Daily Review*, 1930, box 3, folder 1, K. Barr Circus Collection, University of California–Santa Barbara Library.

21. "Free Tickets to the Circus," *Post-Star* (Glens Falls, NY), June 3, 1918, 8; "Circus Day Bargains," *Norfolk (NE) Daily News*, September 3, 1927, 12; "Circus Day Sales," *Wichita (KS) Eagle*, July 12, 1905, 4.

22. Willard "Tard" Northrop to Dyer Ichabod Reynolds, April 1, 1949, series 1, box 1, folder 2, Dyer Ichabod Reynolds Circus Collection, Ned R. McWherter Library, University of Memphis, TN; "Circus Passenger Cars," *Circus Trains and Modeling*, 1975; Emmett Kelly, "Circus Trains and Modeling," *Circus Trains and Modeling*, 1975; latter two sources in series 1, box 1, folder 20, K. Barr Circus Collection, University of California–Santa Barbara Library.

23. Sharon L. Smith and Stephen T. Fletcher, *Life in a Three-Ring Circus: Posters and Interviews* (Indianapolis: Indiana Historical Society, 2001), 57.

24. Lucia Zora, *Sawdust and Solitude* (Boston: Little, Brown, 1928), 4.

25. Katherine H. Adams and Michael L. Keene, *Women of the American Circus, 1880–1940* (Jefferson, NC: McFarland, 2012), 50, 71.

26. Cartoon, *Lilliput*, c. 1950s; Cartoon, n.d.; both items in series 1, box 27, Raymond Toole-Scott Circus Collection, University of California–Santa Barbara Library.

27. "Not William Hanlon," *Pittsburgh Daily Post*, July 21, 1891, 1.

28. S. L. Kotar and J. E. Gessler, *The Rise of the American Circus, 1716–1899* (Jefferson, NC: McFarland, 2011), 297.

29. "Suggestions and Rules: Employees: Ringling Brothers," n.d., series 1, box 29, Raymond Toole-Scott Circus Collection, University of California–Santa Barbara Library.

30. Al Priddy, *The Way of the Circus: With Man and Animal*, (Chicago: Platform World, 1930), series 1, box 1, folder 1, American Circus Collection, 1891–1939, Newberry Library, Chicago.

31. Susan Nance discusses this phenomenon at length in her analysis of early elephant display in the United States. For these early audience members, see her *Entertaining Elephants: Animal Agency and the Business of the American Circus* (Baltimore, MD: Johns Hopkins University Press, 2013), 22.

32. Smith and Fletcher, *Life in a Three-Ring Circus*, 2.

33. *Al G. Barnes Ring Clarion* 3, no. 5 (September–October 1939), box 2, folder 5, K. Barr Circus Collection, University of California–Santa Barbara Library.

34. "Hagenbeck's Trained Animals," *New York Times*, July 3, 1894, 10;

"Hagenbeck's Arena," in *Art, History, Midway Plaisance, and World's Columbian Exposition*, comp. Frank H. Smith (Chicago: Foster Press, 1893), n.p.; B. Worqenthau, "Carl Hagenbeck Wild Animal Show," *Circus Scrap Book*, January 1929; Nigel Rothfels, *Savages and Beasts: The Birth of the Modern Zoo* (Baltimore, MD: Johns Hopkins University Press, 2008), 186.

35. "Circus Lion Escapes and Causes Panic," *Logansport (IN) Pharos-Tribune*, September 19, 1934, 1.

36. "Five Ring Circus Realized at Last," *Bremen (IN) Enquirer*, July 16, 1925.

37. "Circus Performer Killed," *St. Louis Republic*, February 13, 1902, 9.

38. Linda Simon, *The Greatest Shows on Earth: A History of the Circus* (Chicago: University of Chicago Press, 2014).

39. "The Damsel in the Lion's Den," *Illustrated London News*, July 30, 1870, series 1, box 27, Raymond Toole-Scott Circus Collection, University of California–Santa Barbara Library.

40. "Park Thrillers," *Charlotte (NC) News*, July 15, 1908 (qtd.), 7; "'Dip of Death' Performer Killed," *Pioneer* (Bemidji, MN), September 20, 1906.

41. "Circus Audience Sees Lion Kill Tamer: Rescuers Helpless," *Radar*, 1950; Cartoon, n.d.; both items in series 1, box 27, Raymond Toole-Scott Circus Collection, University of California–Santa Barbara Library.

42. Ed P. Wiley, "Elephants—Good and Bad," *Circus Scrap Book*, January 1931, 14; Frank Bostock, "Training Animal Trainers," *Sunday Magazine*, January 6, 1907, reprinted in *Circus Scrap Book*, July 1931, 6.

43. Joyce Ferguson and Homer Ferguson, interview by Sharon L. Smith, February 23, 2000, in Smith and Fletcher, *Life in a Three-Ring Circus*, 40.

44. "Circus Elephant Wash," box 1845, Herald Examiner Collection, Los Angeles Public Library; Nance, *Entertaining Elephants*, 164, 177; "Hagenbeck, Hamburg," 1889, reprinted in *Circus Scrap Book*, April 1931, 24 (qtd.); "A Chat about Elephants," *New York Dramatic Mirror*, October 19, 1894, reprinted in *Circus Scrap Book*, April 1929, 35.

45. "Wild Beasts and Their Trainers," *New York Times*, January 14, 1894, 20; Ellen Velvin, *Behind the Scenes with Wild Animals* (New York: Moffat, Yard, 1906), 101; Nance, *Entertaining Elephants*, 77.

46. Hartley Davis, "The Business Side of the Circus," *Everybody's Magazine*, July 1919. Top-billing center-ring acts brought in the highest paychecks with circuses. With most shows, top acts were equestrians or animal tamers.

47. Nance, *Entertaining Elephants*, 181.

48. B. Worqenthau, "Carl Hagenbeck Wild Animal Show," *Circus Scrap Book*, January 1929, 33.

49. "Fate of a 12-Year-Old Lion Tamer," *Atlanta Constitution*, December 12, 1911, 13; Nance, *Entertaining Elephants*, 161.

50. "Circus Fight over Trainer to Be Heard," *Edinburg (IN) Daily Courier*, April 26, 1937, 1.

51. Raymond Toole-Scott and the Four Wheelers, contract, April 28, 1938; Fred Rosaire to Raymond Toole-Scott, October 10, 1936; both items in PA

MSS 14, series 1, box 2, Raymond Toole-Scott Circus Collection, University of California–Santa Barbara Library.

52. "Mabel Stark Will Perform in City despite Attack," *San Bernardino County Sun*, September 23, 1935, 3; "Woman Tiger Trainer Has Many Scars on Her Body," *Garrett (IN) Clipper*, March 18, 1929, 8; Janet Davis, *The Circus Age: Culture and Society under the American Big Top* (Chapel Hill: University of North Carolina Press, 2003), 83.

53. "A Notable Circus Change," *Decatur (IL) Herald*, April 5, 1925, 6; "Performing Wild Animals Given Up," *Neosho (MO) Daily News*, March 10, 1925, 2.

54. "Daring Men Call Clyde Beatty a Lunatic," *Ottawa Journal*, July 17, 1937, 18; "Said, Most Thrilling Act in Circus History," *Sandusky (OH) Register*, August 4, 1935, 9; "Cole Bros. Circus One of Largest to Be in Monroe: Clyde Beatty, Famous Animal Trainer to Be Feature of Show," *Ruston (LA) Daily Leader*, October 28, 1936, 4; Peta Tait, *Wild and Dangerous Performances: Animals, Emotions, Circus* (London: Palgrave MacMillan, 2011), 53–54.

55. *Cole Brothers–Clyde Beatty Circus Program*, 1936, 9, series 1, box 3, folder 9, K. Barr Circus Collection, University of California–Santa Barbara Library.

56. "Lioness Rips Trainer," *Washington Post*, May 17, 1910, 12.

57. "Robbins Bros Big 4 Ring Wild Animal Circus," advertisement, *Oklahoma State Register*, August 28, 1924, 8.

58. Harvey V. Deuell, "He Scares the Lions," *Liberty*, July 23, 1927, reprinted in *Circus Scrap Book*, April 1931, 11–12.

59. "Big Bear Attacks Woman," *Detroit Free Press*, December 14, 1907, 6.

60. "Big Bear Attacks Woman."

61. "Leopard Attacks Two Men," *Angola (IN) Herald*, May 22, 1914, 4.

62. "Killed by Elephant," *Roanoke (VA) Times*, April 26, 1901, 5.

63. Elephant executions took several forms. Mary, an Asian elephant in the Sparks World Famous Show who had gained notoriety as a baseball-pitching elephant, was lynched in 1916. More famously, Topsy died via electrocution in 1903. No matter the form of execution, the death became a live or photographed spectacle. See Tom Ogden, *Two Hundred Years of the American Circus: From Aba-Daba to the Zoppe-Zavatta Troupe* (New York: Facts on File, 1993), 135; Nance, *Entertaining Elephants*, 116–17, 193–94.

64. Rothfels, *Savages and Beasts*, 156–57.

65. Nance, *Entertaining Elephants*, 164, 203, 205.

66. "The Crown of Creation: Circus Parade Fulfills the Biblical Prophecy," *Sells-Floto Magazine*, 1917, series 1, box 3, folder 19, American Circus Collection, 1891–1939, Newberry Library, Chicago.

67. "Two Killed, One Near Death When Circus High Wire Performers Fall," *Eureka (CA) Humboldt Standard*, January 31, 1962, 1.

68. "Death and News Coverage," *Bryan–College Station (TX) Eagle*, March 30, 1978, 10.

Chapter 8. Organized Circus Labor and Working-Class Audiences

1. "More Circuses on the Road This Season; Best Year since Late 1920s Predicted," *Corpus Christi (TX) Caller Times*, April 27, 1938, 13.

2. "Circus Goes on despite Strike," *Kane (PA) Republican*, April 13, 1938, 2; "Ringling Brothers Circus Aided by Closed Shop," *Union Labor Record* (Wilmington, NC), July 30, 1937, 3.

3. "Ringling Circus Delayed by Striking Teamsters," *Coshocton (OH) Tribune*, June 15, 1938, 10; *Billboard*, May 14, 1938; "Ringling Show Takes 25% Wage Cut, Avoiding Threatened Shutdown," *Variety*, June 22, 1938, 55; "Circus Leaves Scranton for Winter Home," *Mount Carmel (PA) Item*, June 28, 1938.

4. *White Tops*, July 1938, box 67, folder 16, MS 131, Dyer Ichabod Reynolds Circus Collection, Ned R. McWherter Library, University of Memphis, TN; "Modern and Mechanized Are New Adjectives to Describe the Circus," *Iowa City Press Citizen*, April 6, 1939, 6.

5. "American News," *Sawdust Ring*, Winter 1938–39, series 1, box 19, Toole-Scott Circus Collection, 1886–1970, University of California–Santa Barbara Library.

6. John Ringling North to Joseph Case, May 15, 1940; Leonard Bisco to William Green, May 31, 1940; both letters in box 1, folder 2, Union Strike Papers, Circus World Library, Baraboo, WI.

7. For a discussion of the circus within larger studies of working-class audiences, see Bluford Adams, *E. Pluribus Barnum: The Great Showman and the Making of U.S. Popular Culture* (Minneapolis: University of Minnesota Press, 1997); Richard Butsch, *The Making of American Audiences: From Stage to Television, 1750–1990* (Cambridge: Cambridge University Press, 2000); James W. Cook, *The Arts of Deception: Playing with Fraud in the Age of Barnum* (Cambridge, MA: Harvard University Press, 2001); Janet Davis, *The Circus Age: Culture and Society under the American Big Top* (Chapel Hill: University of North Carolina Press, 2002); John F. Kasson, *Amusing the Million: Coney Island at the Turn of the Century* (New York: Hill and Wang, 1978); Lawrence W. Levine, *Highbrow/Lowbrow: The Emergence of Cultural Hierarchy in America* (Cambridge, MA: Harvard University Press, 1988). For a larger discussion of working-class leisure, see also Kathy Peiss, *Cheap Amusements: Working Women and Leisure in Turn-of-the-Century New York* (Philadelphia: Temple University Press, 1986); Robert C. Allen, *Horrible Prettiness: Burlesque and American Culture* (Chapel Hill: University of North Carolina Press, 1991).

8. Janet Davis provides a detailed history of circusgoers throughout the entire Golden Age. She situates the early history within Marxian cultural studies and shows that the circus was a "unique cultural spectacle," with a diverse audience of men, women, and children at a time when many sites of leisure were gender exclusive. See Davis, *The Circus Age*, 24–34. Newspapers often captured potential walkouts on circus day, as people skipped or left work to attend the circus. "The

Circus Day Strikes," *Indianapolis News*, May 22, 1902, 13; "Penny Shops Close Friday: Shopmen Will Have the Opportunity to Enjoy Circus Holiday," *Altoona (PA) Tribune*, May 3, 1922, 1; "It's Circus Day, Everybody Out," *Charlotte (NC) News*, October 25, 1917, 2.

9. "Circus Day Trains," *Norfolk (NE) Daily News*, September 9, 1907, 4.

10. "Tent City to Be Built This Morning: How the Work Is Done," *Washington Times*, May 10, 1903, 5; Janet Davis also provides extensive analysis of the working men and their "spectacular labor"; see her *The Circus Age*.

11. For a more complete history of other forms of working-class entertainment, see Arthur Wertheim, *Vaudeville Wars: How the Keith-Albee and Orpheum Circuits Controlled the Big-Time and Its Performers* (New York: Palgrave Macmillan, 2006); M. Alison Kibler, *Rank Ladies: Gender and Cultural Hierarchy in American Vaudeville* (Chapel Hill: University of North Carolina Press, 1999); Allen, *Horrible Prettiness*.

12. This concept of democratic amusement derives from Bluford Adams's analysis of P. T. Barnum's cultural influence. Adams demonstrates that Barnum invited audience participation in his various bouts of humbug. See his *E. Pluribus Barnum*. See also Michael Immerso, *Coney Island: The People's Playground* (New Brunswick, NJ: Rutgers University Press, 2002).

13. Susan Nance, *Entertaining Elephants: Animal Agency and the Business of the American Circus* (Baltimore, MD: Johns Hopkins University Press, 2013), 29.

14. For a larger discussion of Barnum's American Museum in the burgeoning New York landscape, see Peter G. Buckley, "Paratheatricals and Popular State Entertainment," in *The Cambridge History of American Theatre*, vol. 1, *Beginnings to 1870*, ed. Don B. Wilmeth and C. W. E. Bigsby (New York: Cambridge University Press, 2006), 468; Les Harrison, *The Temple and the Forum: The American Museum and Cultural Authority in Hawthorne, Melville, Stowe, and Whitman* (Tuscaloosa: University of Alabama Press, 2007), 20; John Springhall, *The Genesis of Mass Culture: Show Business Live in America, 1840 to 1940* (New York: Palgrave Macmillan, 2008), 22.

15. James L. Crouthamel, "The Newspaper Revolution in New York, 1830–1860," *New York History* 45, no. 2 (April 1964): 91–113.

16. *Catalogue or Guide Book of Barnum's American Museum, New York* (New York: n.p., 1863), 106.

17. *Catalogue or Guide Book of Barnum's American Museum, New York*, 4 (qtd.); Springhall, *The Genesis of Mass Culture*, 30.

18. For cornerstone works on minstrelsy as a working-class entertainment, see Robert C. Toll, *Blacking Up: The Minstrel Show in Nineteenth-Century America* (New York: Oxford University Press, 1974); Eric Lott, *Love and Theft: Blackface Minstrelsy and the American Working Class* (New York: Oxford University Press, 1993).

19. *Portland (ME) Temperance Journal*, December 1, 1860, reprinted in *Catalogue or Guide Book of Barnum's American Museum, New York*, 117.

20. Robert C. Allen documents the devolution of burlesque into working-class male entertainment, and M. Alison Kibler makes a convincing argument

for the role of an increasingly feminized vaudeville audience. See Allen *Horrible Prettiness*; Kibler, *Rank Ladies*.

21. Sharon L. Smith and Stephen T. Fletcher, *Life in a Three-Ring Circus: Posters and Interviews* (Indianapolis: Indiana Historical Society, 2001), 2.

22. "Small Boys Out Early to Welcome Circus," *Washington Times*, May 5, 1912, 8.

23. Jimmy Jemail, "The Inquiring Fotographer," *New York News*, April 13, 1954, Billy Rose Theatre Division, New York Public Library for the Performing Arts.

24. "Barking Doggie Starts Circus Elephants on Stampede at Edmonton," *Winnipeg (MB) Tribune*, August 3, 1926, 6.

25. "Elephants' Rush Causes a Panic," *Chicago Daily Tribune*, April 10, 1910, 7; "Plunge of a Scared Horse," *Washington Post*, May 23, 1895, 1; *Gettysburg (PA) Compiler*, August 18, 1891; "A Chance for a Tiger Hunt," *People's Press* (Gettysburg, PA), August 28, 1835, 2. These dangerous interactions between animals and audiences had precedence in early menageries. The Zoological Institute, a menagerie monopoly in the 1830s, made the Bowery in New York its official headquarters. Although the New York area did not have a booming population, it was still more densely populated than most towns that later circuses would visit. When a leopard escaped in the city, the Zoological Institute faced a much more dangerous scenario than circuses would face generally in the same situation.

26. "Leopard Attacks Small Boy at Circus Grounds," *Pawhuska (OK) Journal-Capital*, July 21, 1923, 1; "Leopard Attacks Keeper," *Burr Oak (KS) Herald*, September 12, 1901, 2.

27. "Dog Saves Children from Leopard," *Journal and Tribune* (Knoxville, TN), August 6, 1913, 10; "Circus Worker Subdued Mad Elephant after Wild Chase," *Pantagraph* (Bloomington, IL), January 19, 1929, 13.

28. "Why the Circus Has Abandoned Wild Animal Acts," *Times Signal* (Zanesville, OH), May 3, 1925, 34.

29. "The Animal Man," *Weekly Kansas City Star*, August 16, 1933, 14.

30. "'Haia,' Ringling's Pet Elephant, Went 'Rogue,' and Had to Be Shot," *Holdege (NE) Daily Citizen*, October 18, 1928, 1.

31. "Leopard Attacks Trainer," *San Bernadino County Sun*, September 15, 1917, 10.

32. "Clowns Become Benefactors," *Boston Evening Transcript*, June 21, 1906, 14; "Clowns Delight Little Patients," *Boston Globe*, May 31, 1922, 8.

33. Frank J. Mayer, *Ringling Bros and Barnum & Bailey Combined Circus Route Book for the Season of 1937* (n.p., 1937), 37; Charles Andress, comp. and ed., *Day by Day with Barnum & Bailey Season, 1903–1904* (n.p., 1904), 57; both items in Circus Route Books, Milner Library, Illinois State University, Normal.

34. Gregory J. Renoff, *The Big Tent: The Traveling Circus in Georgia, 1820–1930* (Athens: University of Georgia Press, 2008), 99; see also *The Great Wallace Shows Route Book Season 1897* (Columbus, OH: Nitschke Brothers, 1897), 59, Circus Route Books, Circus World Museum, Baraboo, WI.

35. "Hutchinson, Kansas," *Topeka (KS) Plaindealer*, August 3, 1917, 4.

36. "Washington, Iowa, Notes," *Bystander* (Des Moines, IA), August 24, 1908, 1; "Current Comment," *Maryville (TN) Republican*, August 25, 1898, 5; "Austin, Texas," *New York Age*, October 17, 1912, 4 (qtd.).

37. "Ringling's Circus Attracts 22,000: Big Top Filled at Matinee—Rain Cuts Size of Night Crowd," *York (PA) Daily*, June 11, 1918, 3.

38. *Lima (OH) Times-Democrat*, May 21, 1917, 4.

39. Nance, *Entertaining Elephants*, 46, 86, 99.

40. "Animal Actors: For the Information of the Public," 1925; "English Animal Activism Pamphlet," c. 1925; both items in series 1, box 29, Raymond Toole-Scott Circus Collection, University of California–Santa Barbara Library.

41. Royal Society for the Prevention of Cruelty to Animals, open letter, September 1938, series 1, box 29, Raymond Toole-Scott Circus Collection, University of California–Santa Barbara Library (qtd.); David A. H. Wilson, "Racial Prejudice and the Performing Animals Controversy in Early Twentieth-Century Britain," *Society and Animals* 17 (2009): 151.

42. Nigel Rothfels, *Savages and Beasts: The Birth of the Modern Zoo* (Baltimore, MD: Johns Hopkins University Press, 2008), 49, 58, 148–49. Rothfels notes that Hagenbeck's success rested on his ability to import such a significant number of animals. Claiming that he would pursue any wild animal, "from a white elephant to a flea" (58), Hagenbeck sold more than a thousand lions and three hundred elephants within his first twenty years in business.

43. *Al G. Barnes Ring Clarion* 3, no. 5 (September–October 1939), 5, box 2, folder 5, K. Barr Circus Collection, University of California–Santa Barbara Library.

44. Bertrand Mills to the home secretary, William Joynson Hicks, December 11, 1925, series 1, box 29, Raymond Toole-Scott Circus Collection, University of California–Santa Barbara Library; "Why the Circus Has Abandoned Wild Animal Acts," *Times Signal* (Zanesville, OH), May 3, 1925, 34.

45. "A Notable Circus Change," *Decatur (IL) Herald*, April 5, 1925, 6; "Why the Circus Has Abandoned Wild Animal Acts," *Times Signal* (qtd.).

46. *Report from the Select Committee on Performing Animals: Together with the Proceedings of the Committee and Minutes of Evidence*, Sessions 1921 and 1922 (London: His Majesty's Stationary Office, 1921–22); Royal Society for the Prevention of Cruelty to Animals, open letter, September 1938, series 1, box 29, Raymond Toole-Scott Circus Collection, University of California–Santa Barbara Library; Wilson, "Racial Prejudice and the Performing Animals Controversy," 149.

47. "A Notable Circus Change," *Decatur (IL) Herald*, April 5, 1925, 6 (qtd.); "Performing Wild Animals Given Up," *Neosho (MO) Daily News*, March 10, 1925, 2; "Circus War Centers about Wild Animal Acts This Year," *Times Signal* (Zanesville, OH), May 3, 1925, 3.

48. "Sea Lions and Women Divers: Blowing Bubbles at the Colosseum," *Times* (London), January 11, 1921, 8; "Will You Join the Jack London Club,"

Record-Argus (Greenville, PA), April 9, 1921, 5 (qtd.); Wilson, "Racial Prejudice and the Performing Animals Controversy," 149.

49. Nance, *Entertaining Elephants*, 100; S. L. Kotar and J. E. Gessler, *The Rise of the American Circus, 1716–1899* (Jefferson, NC: McFarland, 2011), 303.

50. "Felix Adler, King of Clowns, Dies," *Oakland (CA) Tribune*, February 2, 1960, 36; Kotar and Gessler, *The Rise of the American Circus*, 297.

51. Katherine H. Adams and Michael L. Keene, *Women of the American Circus, 1880–1940* (Jefferson, NC: McFarland, 2012), 69.

52. Helen L. Sumner and Ella A. Merritt, *Child Labor Legislation in the United States* (Washington, DC: Industrial Series Bureau, 1915), 589; Davis, *The Circus Age*, 139; Kotar and Gessler, *The Rise of the American Circus*, 297, 299.

53. See, e.g., Dinah Craik, *The Unkind Word and Other Stories* (New York: Harper and Brothers, 1870).

54. Lionel Rose, *The Erosion of Childhood: Childhood in Britain, 1860–1914* (New York: Routledge, 1991); Dennis Denisoff, ed., *The Nineteenth-Century Child and Consumer Culture* (New York: Routledge, 2008).

55. Kotar and Gessler, *The Rise of the American Circus*, 299.

56. Alexander Wood Renton and Maxwell Alexander Robertson, eds., *Encyclopaedia of the Laws of England*, vol. 4 (Edinburgh: William Green and Sons, 1907), 261, 340. Historians have looked at European circuses much more deeply than their American counterparts. For an in-depth look at European circuses and government regulation, particularly in relation to child labor, see Dyan Colclough, *Child Labor in the British Victorian Entertainment Industry, 1875–1914* (New York: Palgrave McMillan, 2016), 18; Brenda Assael, *The Circus and Victorian Society* (Charlottesville: University of Virginia Press, 2005), 134–36, 144–47. Assael argues that this sort of regulation actually hurt circus workers as it reduced their potential income.

57. "Children Employees," c. 1901–3, Scrapbook 24: Barnum & Bailey, Information and Address Book, box 40, McCaddon Collection of the Barnum and Bailey Circus, Princeton University Library, NJ.

58. "Freaks Union," *Pensacola (FL) News Journal*, February 13, 1907, 3 (qtd.); "Freaks Form Union," *Vancouver Daily World*, June 6, 1912, 1.

59. "Circus Will Arrive in City Early Tomorrow Morning for Two-Day Stay," *Harrisburg (PA) Telegraph*, May 19, 1917, 12.

60. "Just a Few Looks into the Lives of Big Top Artists and Workers," *Ringling Brothers and Barnum & Bailey Circus Magazine and Daily Review*, 1936, series 1, box 3, folder 4, K Barr Circus Collection, University of California–Santa Barbara Library; "Circus War Ends with Purchase of Big Show," *Evening Star* (Washington, DC), November 24, 1907, 5; "Aftermath of Circus," *Norfolk (NE) Weekly News Journal*, September 13, 1907, 7.

61. Exploration of class consciousness has proliferated in labor history. Sean Wilentz pointed out in 1984 that much of the historiography has centered on the lack of class consciousness in the United States, and has questioned why workers have failed to see themselves as a distinct class pitted against

their employer. But new business history has engaged with labor history to explain class consciousness within the corporate landscape. Moreover, cultural histories have added to this quandary by exploring work culture and identity. Nancy Isenberg's sweeping look at the working class in the United States adds to this conversation by setting the 1920s as a time when class consciousness "sank deep roots" through cultural differences. See Sean Wilentz, "Against Exceptionalism: Class Consciousness and the American Labor Movement, 1790–1920," *International Labor and Working-Class History* 26 (1984): 1–24; Nancy Isenberg, *White Trash: The 400-Year Untold History of Class in America* (New York: Viking, 2016), 205.

62. "Save the Circus," *Sawdust Ring*, Winter 1938, series 1, box 19, Raymond Toole-Scott Circus Collection, University of California–Santa Barbara Library; "Save the Circus!," *Mason City (IA) Globe Gazette*, August 9, 1938, 2.

63. Eleanor Roosevelt, "My Day," August 9, 1938, Eleanor Roosevelt Papers Project, George Washington University, Washington, DC.

64. For a larger discussion of Eleanor Roosevelt and labor union support, see Brigid O'Farrell, *She Was One of Us: Eleanor Roosevelt and the American Worker* (Ithaca, NY: ILR Press, 2010).

65. "Save the Circus!," *Mason City (IA) Globe Gazette*, August 9, 1938, 2; "Sawdust Lovers Organize to Save the Circus in '39," *Call-Leader* (Elwood, IN), August 24, 1938, 8 (qtd.).

66. "Circus Program Is Presented," *Marengo (IL) Republican-News*, December 8, 1938, 8; "Circus Fans Petition President to Save Big Tops from Folding Up," *Zanesville (OH) Signal*, August 21, 1938, 16; "Circus Fans," *Record Argus* (Greenville, PA), February 16, 1939, 10.

67. "Circus Fans in Convention," *Times* (Hammond, IN), July 6, 1939, 10.

68. "Leopard Rises to Stardom by Killing Off Circus Rival," *Brooklyn Daily Eagle*, April 5, 1940, 3; "Clawed by Killer Leopard," *Tipton (IN) Daily Tribune*, April 9, 1940; Ernest Albrecht, *From Barnum & Bailey to Feld: The Creative Evolution of the Greatest Show on Earth* (Jefferson, NC: McFarland, 2014), 129.

69. John Ringling North to Joseph Case, May 15, 1940; Leonard Bisco to William Green; both letters in box 1, folder 2, Union Strike Papers, Circus World Library, Baraboo, WI.

70. *Variety*, July 6, 1907, 8; *Variety*, May 7, 1910, 20.

71. "Modern and Mechanized Are New Adjectives to Describe the Circus," *Iowa City Press Citizen*, April 6, 1939, 6.

72. David Lewis Hammarstrom, *Big Top Boss: John Ringling North and the Circus* (Bloomington: University of Illinois Press, 1992), 70–73; Henry Ringling North and Alden Hatch, *The Circus Kings: Our Ringling Family Circus* (Garden City, NY: Doubleday, 1960), 257.

73. Peta Tait, *Wild and Dangerous Performances: Animals, Emotions, Circus* (London: Palgrave MacMillan, 2011), 170; Tom Ogden, *Two Hundred Years of the American Circus: From Aba-Daba to the Zoppe-Zavatta Troupe* (New York: Facts on File, 1993), 7.

74. "Urge Showman Study Child Labor Laws," *Billboard*, February 14, 1953, 49; "Beers-Barnes in Six States," *Billboard*, November 20, 1942, 38.

75. George Eells, "The Psychology of the Sideshow," c. 1950s, series 4, box 36, folder 8, George Eells Papers, Arizona State University Libraries, Special Collections, Tempe; "Death in the Sawdust Ring," *Leader Magazine*, January 14, 1950, series 1, box 27, Raymond Toole-Scott Circus Collection, University of California–Santa Barbara Library.

76. "Circus Research," c. 1950s, series 4, box 36, folder 2, George Eells Papers, Arizona State University Libraries, Special Collections, Tempe.

Conclusion. Circus Afterlives

1. "W. F. O'Hara Dies; Was Circusman," *Bridgeport (CT) Telegram*, November 28, 1947, 1.

2. "Constitution and Bylaws B.P.O.C.," c. 1900, Miscellaneous Materials: Illustrated Booklets: Barnum & Bailey, etc., box 50, McCaddon Collection of the Barnum and Bailey Circus, Princeton University Library, NJ.

3. "Annual Roster of the Benevolent Protective Order of the Tigers, Season 1901–2, Touring Continent with Barnum & Bailey," Scrapbook 12: Foreign Tour, 1897–1902, box 28, McCaddon Collection of the Barnum and Bailey Circus, Princeton University Library, NJ.

4. Harvey Watkins, *Four Years in Europe: The Barnum & Bailey Greatest Show on Earth in the Old World* (Paris: printed by the author, 1901), 20, 65–66.

5. *Billboard*, January 16, 1904, 9; *New York Clipper*, November 18, 2005, 10.

6. Jake Posey, "With Buffalo Bill in Europe," *Bandwagon*, October 1953, 5.

7. Benevolent Order of the American Tigers, articles of association, September 24, 1903, Record Group no. 006, Records of the Secretary of State Articles of Incorporation, Voluntary Associations without Capital, box 163, vol. 5, pp. 373–74, Connecticut State Library and State Archives, Hartford.

8. "The 'Freaks' Union," *Pine Bluff (AR) Daily Graphic*, February 10, 1907, 11; "Tigers Take in the Women: Circus Benevolent Association Admits Female Performers to Membership in the Order," *Chicago Daily Tribune*, September 14, 1903.

9. "Life of Circus Women: A Credit to Their Calling and an Honor to Their Sex," *Washington Post*, April 27, 1902, 37.

10. "Passing of Circus Freaks," *Cincinnati (OH) Enquirer*, March 14, 1908, 14; "More Freaks in Chicago Than in Any Other City in the World," *Chicago Tribune*, April 12, 1908, 45; "Bequests of Freaks," *Times* (Philadelphia, PA), March 8, 1885, 6.

11. "Showmen Build a Home," *Tampa (FL) Times*, November 25, 1966, 18.

12. "Oddville, U.S.A.," *Daily News* (New York), May 6, 1962, 50.

13. Larry Rohter, "Gibsonton Journal: Carny Performers Build a Haven by Tampa Bay," *New York Times*, January 26, 1992; "Town Shelters a Vanishing Breed," *Seattle Times*, July 20, 1997, A10.

14. "Gibsonton, USA," *Sydney Morning Herald*, January 7, 1995, 79; "Love in the Sideshow," *San Francisco Examiner*, December 28, 1952, 70; "Deformity No Sideshow in Gibsonton," *Pensacola (FL) News Journal*, February 23, 1975, 38.

15. "The Strange People of Gibsonton," *Corpus Christi (TX) Caller*, July 28, 1957, 94; Rohter, "Gibsonton Journal."

16. "Wed. Oct. 21—Animal Sale," *Springfield (MO) Ledger and Press*, October 11, 1959, 62.

17. "Ringling Circus Animals to Zoos," *Express and News* (San Antonio, TX), May 10, 1958, 11. Charles Siebert explores the experience of a single chimpanzee from the Ringling show, Roger, who was one of the first guests in the chimpanzee refuge created for former animal entertainers. See his *The Wauchula Woods Accord: Toward a New Understanding of Animals* (New York: Scribner, 2009).

18. "Horses from the Greatest Show on Earth Put Out to Pasture in Baldwin Park," *Covina (CA) Argus*, July 25, 1954, 3.

19. "Circus Editorial," *Cincinnati (OH) Enquirer*, September 11, 1907, reprinted in *Circus Scrap Book*, October 1929, 3.

20. "Animals Are His Friends," *Circus Report*, no. 49 (December 8, 1975): 11.

21. Tom Ogden, *Two Hundred Years of the American Circus: From Aba-Daba to the Zoppe-Zavatta Troupe* (New York: Facts on File, 1993), 7.

22. "Circus Faces Lawsuit in Leopard Clawing Issue," *Edwardsville (IL) Intelligencer*, August 2, 1958, 1.

23. "Sweden Bans Wild Animals in Circus," *Courier-Journal* (Louisville, KY), November 19, 1959, 8, series 1, box 27, Raymond Toole-Scott Circus Collection, University of California–Santa Barbara Library.

24. *Billboard*, March 16, 1901, 10.

25. "Abilene and Vicinity," *Abilene (KS) Daily Chronicle*, August 25, 1903, 4; "Giraffes Are Scarce," *Daily Herald* (Delphos, OH), August 23, 1899, 2; "Grand Excursion to the Buffalo Hunt," *Winfield (KS) Daily Free Press*, May 4, 1904, 3.

26. "N.C. Law Bans Use of Freaks under Age 18," *Amusement Business*, June 21, 1969, 19, Sideshow Vertical Files, Robert L. Parkinson Library and Research Center, Baraboo, WI.

27. Irwin Kirby, "What, Side Shows Ought to Be Banned?," *Amusement Business*, August 10, 1968, 27–29; "OABA, AGVA, AFM Should Help: Showfolk Join to Protect Side Shows," *Amusement Business*, August 17, 1968, 4; both items in Sideshow Vertical Files, Robert L. Parkinson Library and Research Center, Baraboo, WI.

28. Kirby, "What, Side Shows Ought to Be Banned?"; "No Shame in Exhibiting," *Amusement Business*, August 17, 1968, 36–37, Sideshow Vertical Files, Robert L. Parkinson Library and Research Center, Baraboo, WI.

29. Advertisement, *Billboard*, December 16, 1950, 60.

30. Frank Metzger to Dyer Reynolds, December 16, 1950, series 1, box 1, folder 5, Dyer Ichabod Reynolds Circus Collection, Ned R. McWherter Library, University of Memphis, TN.

31. "Mismanagement Charged in Ringling Lawsuit," *Press-Courier* (Oxnard, CA), September 9, 1957, 13.

32. Fred D. Pfening Jr., "The 1957 Circus Season," *White Tops* 6, no. 30 (November–December 1957), series 1, box 23, Raymond Toole-Scott Circus Collection, University of California–Santa Barbara Library.

33. Pat Kelly, interview by Sharon L. Smith and John Fugate, February 24, 2000, in *Life in a Three-Ring Circus: Posters and Interviews*, by Sharon L. Smith and Stephen T. Fletcher (Indianapolis: Indiana Historical Society, 2001), 64.

34. "A City without a Daub Spot—That's Sandusky—Circus Folks Find," *Sandusky (OH) Register*, August 9, 1962, 9.

35. "In the Back-Yard of the Circus," *Greeley (CO) Daily Tribune*, July 15, 1937, 2.

36. *Altoona (PA) Tribune*, April 20, 1938, 2.

37. "These Days, the Circus Animals Sneak into Town," *New York Times*, February 19, 1995; "Unload Circus Train at Fairgrounds: Elephants, Mechanical Stake Drivers Vie with Tractors, Hammer Gangs," *Mt. Vernon (IL) Register-News*, April 28, 1949, 1; "Circus Scenes Draw Crowds Early Tuesday," *Decatur (IL) Evening Herald*, May 5, 1931, 1.

38. "German Orgs Elect Wacker, Discuss Tax," *Billboard*, December 16, 1950, 59. This body was called the Gesellschaft für musikalische Aufführungs- und mechanische Vervielfältigungsrechte (Society for musical performing and mechanical reproduction rights).

39. Susan Nance, *Entertaining Elephants: Animal Agency and the Business of the American Circus* (Baltimore, MD: Johns Hopkins University Press, 2013), 22–23.

40. "Circus Animals May Be Vanishing Species," *Hartford (CT) Courant*, May 22, 1980, 86.

41. Dolly Langdon, "'Lord of the Rings' Irvin Feld Has Made a Fading Circus the Greatest Show on Earth Again," *People Magazine*, May 12, 1980; "Greatest Show on Earth Sold," *News-Journal* (Mansfield, OH), November 13, 1967, 8; "Feld Family Buys Ringling Brothers," *New York Times*, March 19, 1982.

42. Philip A. Loring, "The Most Resilient Show on Earth: The Circus as a Model for Viewing Identity, Change and Chaos," *Ecology and Society* 12, no. 1 (2007): article 9.

43. "Circus Creates Wonderment, Laughter and Profits," *Times Record* (Troy, NY), November 24, 1973, 16; "Circus World Sold and Closed," *Orlando Sentinel*, May 14, 1986.

44. "Ward Hall: He Is the Carnival," *News-Press* (Fort Myers, FL), April 28, 1975, 3D.

Index

ACC (American Circus Corporation), 128, 136, 138

accidents: injuring audience, 40, 163–64; tent fire, 92; trainwrecks, 2, 15, 92, 212n63; worker injuries, 143, 164, 176, 183

activism, by workers, 7, 12; women's movements, 22, 70, 80–81, 208n12, 212n58; sideshow workers, 109, 170, 180, 208

activism, by audience: animal rights movement, 93, 103, 150, 156–57, 165–77; child labor 168–70, 173; gender roles, 148; worker safety, 145, 151–52, 156

acts, performance: big top, 68, 78, 80, 149–51, 156, 173–74, 231; family, 14–15, 30, 39–40, 44, 63–65, 67, 74, 78, 87, 112, 144, 148–49; mixed animal species, 29, 103, 150, 154, 166

Adler, Felix, 168

advertising: acts, 89, 97; circus day, 10, 28, 182, 190n33; as a job, 30, 132; innovations, 141–42; partnerships, 146; tactics, 95, 119, 138–39, 149, 222n57

AFL (American Federation of Labor), 159–60, 170, 172

Africa: aesthetics in performances, 43, animal trade, 2–3, 38, 91–92, 96;

Zulu performers, 112–13, 220. *See also* Egypt

American Circus Corporation. *See* ACC

American Federation of Labor. *See* AFL

amusement parks, 61, 129, 184

animal actors, 166

animal cultures, 87, 89

animal handlers, 1, 16, 31, 34, 38, 44, 57, 62, 92, 151–53, 164, 166, 170

animal husbandry, 12, 15, 54, 90, 102, 147, 155, 203n32

animal keepers, 43, 47–50, 53–57, 61, 85–86, 156, 179

animal mothers, 22, 85, 87–89, 91, 93, 95, 97, 99, 101–5

animal nurseries, 7, 43, 85–86, 89, 95, 97–98, 102–4

animal, processes of captivity: caged, 3–4, 15, 34–35, 38, 45, 85, 91, 98; capture, 10, 88–93, imported, 47, 90, 92, 96, 131; leased, 94; life compared to noncaptive counterparts, 49, 98, 100, 103; runaway and escape, 140, 155, 163–64; sales and auctions, 10, 94, 132

animal trade business, 3, 15–16, 60, 90, 92, 96, 179

animal trainers, 1, 5, 20–21, 24, 44, 48–49, 53–60, 62, 81, 93, 145–46,

animal trainers (*continued*)
151–53, 155, 158, 164–167, 180, 201n8

Atlantic Ocean, 3, 48–49, 58, 61, 89, 112, 115

attacks, by animals, 29, 59, 144–45, 153–55, 164, 172, 232

Atwell, Harry, 23–25, 123–24

audiences, as democratic amusements, 160–61, 173, 234n212; segregation, 20, 28–29, 41, 110, 125, 165

autopsies: of animals, 29; of people, 120, 204n39

babies: animals, 7–8, 31, 43–44, 46, 85–95, 97–102, 105, 217; human, 63–64, 73, 148, 150, 214n10

Baby Bridgeport, 95

backyard, 3, 37–39, 42–43, 52, 63–64, 67, 77, 79, 85, 87, 100–101

Barnum & Bailey: advertisements, 27, 90, 147, 156; backyard and offseason, 31–32, 56, 76–77, 175; business practices, 130–35, 137; menagerie, 86, 95, 102; performances and workers, 5, 10–11, 14, 16, 30, 35, 37–38, 42–43, 45, 53, 68, 74–75, 80–83, 111, 113–16, 118; profits, 9. *See also* activism, by workers; activism, by audience; Baby Bridgeport; babies: animals; Jumbo the elephant; New Woman; suffrage movement

Barnum's American Museum, 107, 119, 161–62, 168

bears, 4, 154–55

Beatty, Clyde, 103, 137, 151, 153, 179

Benevolent Order of the American Tigers, 56, 115, 175–76

billing crew, 13, 27, 123, 141, 182

birth: animal, 43, 87–88, 92, 95, 97–98, 104; human, 63, 73

Black circus workers, 14, 35, 39–41, 43, 57–60, 106–10, 113, 192, 199, 201, 205, 208. *See also* Lowrey, P. G.; Maccomo, Martini; Muse, Willie and George; Ubangi performers; Thompson, Eph; Africa: Zulu performers

Bostock, Frank, 49, 60–62, 136, 156, 179

breeding programs, 7, 88–90, 94–98, 103–4, 183

Bridgeport, CT, 17, 31, 51, 56, 114, 132, 134, 147, 175, 178

Burials and funerals, 42, 56, 176

burlesque, 52, 161–62

Burmese performers, 77

Butch, the elephant, 89–90

camels, 1–2, 34, 43, 77, 86, 98, 112, 132

carnivals, traveling, 60–61, 174

Chicago, IL, 23–25, 30–31, 95, 101, 117, 150, 152, 176

children: as circusgoers, 2, 19, 123–25, 162–64; as part of the circus world, 17, 42, 53, 63–64, 74, 76, 100; protected by legislation, 53, 152, 169; as workers, 6–7, 38, 78, 106–9, 152, 168–69, 173, 180

chimpanzees, 99–100

circus day, 2, 27–29, 33, 35, 38, 45, 47, 50, 123, 125, 143, 147, 159–60, 165, 185

circus day sales, 230

circus dynasties, 6, 38, 44, 63, 78, 107

circus equipment, 10, 33–34, 50, 94, 133, 139–40, 177, 180

circus mother, 76

circus owner: as business managers, 10, 70, 115, 153, 173; as Gilded Age robber barons, 9, 129; mergers and collaborations, 132, 136, 166, 183; as paternalistic, 11, 32, 163, 176

clowns, 4, 17, 27, 37–38, 43, 77, 79–80, 133, 135, 138, 156, 168, 170, 182

Cody, William "Buffalo Bill," 7, 15, 70, 73, 81, 133, 176

Cole Brothers Circus, 98, 139, 153

colonial business, circus as, 89–91, 96, 111, 113–14

commuter train, circus day, 33, 197n33. *See also* railroads; whistle-stops

company town, circus as, 11, 127

ANDREA RINGER is an assistant professor of history at Tennessee State University.

The University of Illinois Press
is a founding member of the
Association of University Presses.

_____

University of Illinois Press
1325 South Oak Street
Champaign, IL 61820-6903
www.press.uillinois.edu